Dance, Dialogue, and Despair

Judaic Studies Series

Leon J. Weinberger, General Editor

Dance, Dialogue, and Despair
Existentialist Philosophy and
Education for Peace in Israel

H A I M   G O R D O N

The University of Alabama Press

Library of Congress Cataloging in Publication Data

Gordon, Haim
  Dance, dialogue, and despair.

  (Judaic studies series)
  Bibliographical essay: p.
  Includes index.
    1. Jewish-Arab relations—1973–   —Study and
teaching (Higher)—Israel.   2. Existentialism—Study and
teaching (Higher)—Israel.   3. Peace (Philosophy)—
Study and teaching (Higher)—Israel.   I. Title.
II. Series.
DS119.7.G645 1986   956.94'05   85-1113
ISBN 0-8173-0270-0

For Rivca, Nitzan,
Mor, and Neve

Contents

Foreword

T H I S book offers an unusual approach to the Near East problem; an approach which is also relevant to problems arising from the division of mankind into numerous groups, alienated from each other, mistrusting each other, and confronting each other unpeacefully—because of ethnic, cultural, and religious differences. The enmity between Arabs and Jews is merely one such example, certainly a dangerous example for all of mankind since it includes the possibility that military confrontation in that area could extend to become a global conflict. Hence the caution of the superpowers in their dealing with that region, and also their inability to eliminate the causes of strife. Too many conflicting interests are involved, the wounds Jews and Arabs have inflicted upon each other are too deep, and the anxiety of threat when they face each other is too prominent.

The unique approach to the Near East problem presented in this book leads us to the heart of all political problems: the people who live within the states or the social and ethnic groups who are in conflict with each other. Political activity can amend or aggravate the framework within which they live. But real improvement will only be reached when the heart or the center of the problem changes. Such can only occur if persons who until now have faced each other in enmity and alienation learn to live together. Political activity brings a change for the worse—even and up to military engagement—if the framework inculcates separation, and crystallizes this separation instead of mitigating it. When Haim Gordon, in this book, indicates that the situation between Jews and Arabs in Israel in the past five years has gone from worse to terrible—this observation reveals the devastating effects that the influence of political developments can have on the life of individuals.

Yes, the approach of this book is rare. We, as readers, join in the experience of those persons who, armed with goodwill, have transcended their group separation in order to meet and attempt to partake in a message that may help them surpass their dividing barriers. They face each other for the first time as human beings. They learn to listen to each other, to accept each other. In this slow painful development they are supported by the understanding, patience, and continual self-education of their leader, Haim Gordon.

While reading we feel the profound gap between the Jewish and Arab way of life, the depth of their mutual unfamiliarity, the lack of relationships, despite the fact that for decades Jews and Arabs have been living together in the same country. Hence the process of a Buberian meeting between these persons, which we observe as it develops through a period of three years, is so exciting. Much more becomes clear. Many hindrances and setbacks must be expected; again and again new courage, born of the belief of this human mission and the urgent necessity of such efforts, is needed to endure these encounters. Remember, if peace is to be reached, from a situation of mistrust and hatred, in face of threats from both sides, positive relations between persons must be developed. Political activity can create a framework, but it cannot beget much more. Only when hitherto divided persons meet in multiple ways and through multiple interactions can peace between them hope to grow. In this respect Gordon's Buberian Learning Groups were pioneer groups for a better future. The participants in these groups ventured into unexplored territory. Of course, during the process their numbers were decimated. Support from the university was at first half-hearted, in the end, nil. And in their interim conclusion the participants in these groups had no victory to display.

The groups were put together wisely. Arab participants came mainly from the Arab population of Israel, that is, those persons who have been citizens of the state of Israel since its inception. They are used to living together with Jews. They have partaken of the educational level in Israeli schools and the modern Israeli society. It would have been much harder with Arabs from the occupied territories. The fact that despite the goodwill of the participants they face each other with deep alienation bears witness to the neglect of the interior policy of Israel since 1948. These Arabs behaved loyally toward the state of Israel during its clashes with other Arab states and the PLO, despite their understandable sympathy for the other side. They were by and large not a fifth column of Israel's enemies. Despite these facts the Jewish majority and its political leadership have not made every possible effort to help the Arab minority reconcile themselves to their existence in the Jewish State, to win them over to a living together, to reduce the mutual enmity and mistrust. Also the Jewish majority has not passed from disrespect of Arabs to acknowledgment of their language and culture, and to respect of their rights as citizens. Thus, the Israeli Arabs feel themselves as second class citizens. Such has threatening consequences for the inner stability of the state; no less for the moral substance of Israeli society, for its democracy, for its true Judaism. I mean those Jewish values which are contained in the humanity of the Biblical tradition and are endangered by the chauvinism of Jewish fundamentalism. Such true values emerged in Gordon's Buberian Learning Groups, even though most of the participants were alienated from their religious heritage. In the important moments when they, under the guidance of Buber, found in the Bible and the Koran the values which they could call forth to support their efforts, they certainly also encountered the opposing, inhuman parts of their tradition.

Certainly there also has been great neglect among those who saw the urgent necessity of Jewish-Arab communication. In the decades since the establishment of the state of Israel, numerous projects dedicated to talks, meetings in various forms, and temporary living together have been started. In my view these projects were much too sparse, short termed, and above all isolated from each other. Also in Gordon's project one can perceive no connection to similar undertakings elsewhere, no working together, and no exchange of experience. The ignoring or the minimization of Arab problems is an old and faulty tradition within Zionism; Buber struggled against it his entire life. If the young Zionists today do not want to repeat this neglect, they must work in alliance with each other. A network of such projects in all of Israel should be established, so that isolated undertakings should not fizzle out without effect.

It is obvious that political peace efforts and the practice of education for peace complement each other, that they, even though they proceed on different levels, cannot lack each other. The quantitative difference is great: political decisions, agreements, and establishment of rights concern and change lives of millions; education is always work with individuals and the forming of small groups with a changed life style who can then, like radioactive cells, emit rays into their environment. Primarily through them, through their increasingly broad effect, can a deep result be reached in daily thinking, feeling, and doing—a result which cannot be attained through political changes alone. Those who look only to politics with hope, because of its great effects, think all too quantitatively. Such an approach endeavors to change the life of man without changing man himself—and is bound to end in disappointment.

But disappointments were also lying in wait for Gordon's

project. He didn't conceal them. Even if all the participants
had remained in the project, and even if they had all struggled to attain the dialogical life attitude, the political effects
would have been minimal in comparison to the magnitude of
the Near East problems. The report of the results is much less
characterized by Gordon's basic optimism, than by his sober
and self-critical scepticism. He wonders about the changing
of individual participants, primarily concerning the question
whether these changes will prevail in the lives of individuals
and carry into one's everyday environment. Will they confront
the old mechanistic behavior which arises from tradition,
social relations, and negative experiences?

How few become subjects in their life and behavior—and
how necessary today it is to penetrate subjective being.
"Abrahamite cells" is what Dom Helder Kamara, the Arch-
bishop of Recife named those who attempt to become subjects. Gordon's book reports on the attempt to build up such
cells. I have here cited the venerable Brazilian bishop to
remind us that in face of today's tearing apart of mankind,
such cells are necessary everywhere if we wish to survive—no
less between Jews and Arabs living in Israel. Disqualifying
such attempts because of quantitative measuring would be
foolish; there is evidence that such cells can change the
common spirit of great groups, and also of whole societies.
Adverse difficulties also prevail in other parts of the world.
Therefore Gordon's report has exemplary significance for all
similar conflicts in the entire world. Anyone who participates
in similar attempts will be affected by such great scepticism,
because of setbacks and because of the discrepancy between
his doing and the magnitude of the problem. But he will also
be comforted by the experience of realization no matter how
limited such an experience proves to be.

The Lebanon war of 1982, which coincided with Gordon's
closing of his project, seemed to cast doubts on the validity of
this undertaking. But after the closing, a Jewish participant
related the thoughts that arose in him while he was in the
reserves, participating in a bloody battle against forces of the

PLO. The Palestinians he was shooting at, and who were shooting back, were suddenly seen as fellow human beings, human brothers like those Arab participants in Beer Sheva with whom he sat together so long and attempted to reach dialogue. For the first time this follower of the nationalist Likud party saw an Arab enemy as a fellow person, in the manner that Buber described fellow persons. A small change; but for him of great consequences. Such a change should become more prevalent. Therefore, it is worthy to hearken the words of Yaakov Gordon's last partner in dialogue: "Haim, don't give up!"

HELMUT GOLLWITZER

Acknowledgments

E I G H T years ago Gert and Seamour Shavin challenged me to *do* something with Buber's dialogical philosophy, and not only teach it. Thus, in a sense, they "planted the seed," one of whose fruits is this book. Until this fruit ripened, many other people gave me support and trust. I will mention only a few of them here, but I want the others to know that even if they are not mentioned, they have a part in what occurred and in what is written.

The financial support for the Education for Peace Project came mainly from the Hans Seidel Foundation, the Ford Foundation, and from Professor Helmut Gollwitzer's success in raising money in West Germany. Also, Azriel Nitzani helped us gain financial support from the Ministry of Education in Israel. The personal support within Ben-Gurion University of the Negev came primarily from Walter Ackerman and Yair Magen, both of whom frequently "ate gravel" trying to justify my doings. Later, Paul Hare joined them in giving guidance and supportive counseling.

Many people outside Israel supported our endeavors. Our

International Evaluating Committee, headed by John Post, included Michael Wyschogrod, Hazel Barnes, Riffat Hassan, Betty Reardon, and Douglas Sloan, all of whom spent much time at the project or with me, helping me grope my way. The Experiment in International Living supported us from the beginning, and Jack Wallace and Peter de Jong worked very hard to help me in crucial moments; more often than not they succeeded.

Four Egyptians, all of whom are mentioned in the book, were very helpful: Naguib Mahfouz, Enis Mansour, Mohammed Shaalan, Nabil Yunis. Many other Egyptians, all of whom will here remain anonymous, helped us and I wish to express sincere thanks to them.

But the persons who probably ate the most gravel were the staff. Many worked as volunteers, others for a pittance. It was not easy to work with me and I want to thank them for their patience. I can only mention here those who spent two or more years with us: Zvi Gailat, Jan Demarest, Samir Mahagna, Afif Asakla, Yael Weinman, Afif Dagausha, Nazem Zachalka, Rivca Fridman, Sarah Hyam, Diana Dolev, Batya Gelber, Carmela Gur, Rasmi Biyadsi, Cochava Almakawi. To this list I must add two persons from the Gaza Strip, a man and a woman, whose names I will not mention for reasons of their own security.

I wrote this book during a sabbatical spent at the University of South Alabama. I want to thank Bob Perkins, Wes Baldwin, and the staff of the Department of Philosophy for inviting me and helping me along the way. Patti Gaubatz typed the entire manuscript and was most supportive.

I will mention only three of the many friends who helped and encouraged me during these five turbulent years of working for peace in the Mideast: Jan Silverstein, whom I would call from Israel for advice when I was really stuck, and Harold and Myra Shapiro, who supported me spiritually and also supported the Project financially in difficult moments. I am very grateful to them.

Some of the paragraphs or phrases that appear in the book have appeared in my articles in the following journals: *Teachers College Record, Journal of Philosophy of Education, Israel Social Science Research,* and *Educational Theory.* But I must caution the reader that the context in which these paragraphs or phrases appear there is often quite different than in the book.

Finally, my main thanks must go the 204 participants in the Education for Peace Project, many of whose names I fear I have forgotten. It was they who trusted me and allowed me to embark with them on the adventure and the attempt to live a more meaningful life, which is described in the following pages.

Dance, Dialogue, and Despair

1. Introduction:
The Ariadne Thread

To judge a thing that has substance and solid worth is quite easy, to comprehend it is much harder, and to blend judgement and comprehension in a definitive description is the hardest thing of all.
—G. W. F. HEGEL

M A N Y educators for peace seem to be seeking a guiding thread that will help them develop their thoughts and direct their acts in the maze of interlocking conflicts that encompass them. A major tenet of this book is that one can weave such an Ariadne thread from existentialist philosophy. One condition is imperative. Existentialist philosophy can influence education only through the life of the teacher. If the teacher is not willing to expose his own life, his own existence, to the message arising from the text, then he is not teaching existentialist philosophy, but the ideas of persons who were called existentialists. The same is true for education for peace. If the teacher is not involved with his entire being in the teaching process, while he is educating for peace, then he is merely suggesting the idea of peace, not educating for it. Thus, as this book shows, I educated for peace while teaching Buber, and I taught Buber while dancing, and I danced my life while talking about our vicious political situation, and I responded viciously to political attempts to curtail our efforts while attempting to express love, and my sole justification for this mess is that I passionately want peace and dialogue between

1

Jews and Arabs. Or, in other words, I helped initiate this mess, because that was the only way I found myself being faithful to existentialist philosophy.

There is no one way of realizing existentialist philosophy. Once again, the example of dancing is pertinent. Existentialist philosophy is like the music; each person must respond to it personally, through his own harmony. He can best begin to do so by giving himself fully to the music, by floating with it while responding to the movements of his partner. There is no one way of doing disco, but there are dancers who float with the music and dancers who do not. And there are disco dancers whose bodies live the music, and through whom the music assumes a new dimension. These are the dancers whom the teacher of existentialist philosophy should attempt to emulate.

But what is the value of such teaching if, say, the teacher is not concerned with education for peace? As this book will show, teaching existentialism that is true to the intent of the existentialists from Kierkegaard to Sartre is an appeal to the freedom of the reader; it implies a demand that the reader act in accordance with what he learned from the thoughts of the existentialists. Such a manner of teaching existentialist philosophy is character education, it is teaching the student to live freely and responsibly and to work for justice and peace. Furthermore, any other manner of teaching existentialism is false.

"Come on now," someone may ask, "do you mean to say that every philosophy teacher who teaches existentialism as a system of ideas is lying?"

That is exactly what I mean. But let me explain.

Imagine a jazz presentation being discussed merely as a melody; imagine living at the edge of the Grand Canyon, never visiting it, and discussing its great views on the basis of what one sees in postcards; imagine two virgins discussing the pain and the enjoyment of being penetrated by a male's penis; imagine a lecture on the virtue of poetry by a person who never read poetry. These are the kinds of lies that arise when one presents Dostoyevski, or Kafka, or Marcel as systems of ideas. The existentialist dimension is what is missing, the dimension whereby one's own experience testifies to what is being discussed. Of course, as Sartre pointed out, there are moments when one lies in order to tell the truth, but that is because the truth is evasive, or burdening, or despicable. If one's goal is to tell the truth, such moments do not converge to become a method. Teaching existentialist philosophy as a system of ideas which have no relation to one's own existence is methodical; it is the developing of a web of lies.

The educator's problem is not the specific web of lies which a philosophy teacher may weave. The problem is that such webs confront a person wherever he turns, because—as Kafka, Buber, and Sartre pointed out—he himself participates in weaving them. There is only one way of removing such webs: to stop weaving them and to attempt to live truthfully, authentically. Here is where existentialist philosophy can be a boon or a bane. If one teaches existentialist philosophy as a system of ideas, one is adding a web of lies which helps justify one's daily webs. But if one attempts to use it as a guide which can help one reach dialogue, authenticity, creativity, joy, and the ability to rebel against one's existential Hell, one is beginning to confront these webs of lies, to stop weaving them, to cut through them, to live differently.

I was vaguely aware of this relationship between existentialist philosophy and education in 1979, when I embarked on a three-year project entitled Education for Peace in accordance with the Philosophy of Martin Buber at Ben-Gurion University of the Negev in the city of Beer Sheva in Israel. The relationship became clearer as I immersed myself in existentialist philosophy and education for peace. Put briefly, the Education for Peace Project tried to educate Jews and Arabs to establish relations of what Buber calls genuine dialogue between them and to work for peace together. It was evident to me from the outset that, without an Ariadne thread that would help one through the maze of mistrust and conflicts which characterize the Mideast, my efforts would fail. I first believed that Martin Buber's philosophy of dialogue could lead one through the maze; but soon I found that his philosophy ran out of suggestions before my problems ended. My search for new guiding threads led me to existentialism.

When I established the Education for Peace Project I perceived that *existential mistrust* had permeated the relations between many Jews and Arabs living in Israel. Existential mistrust may be defined as a relationship that arises between two persons (or two nations) when one of the persons (or one of the nations) believes that the other person (or nation) denies his right to exist and to realize his potential in that portion of the world to which he is attached. The relationship is expressed by the attitude: If I want to exist, I must not trust you. This mistrust hinders attempts to establish sincere relations between Jews and Arabs and often distorts the mistrusting person's way of life. I soon learned that little had been done to diminish this mistrust. Attempts to bring greater Jewish-Arab understanding had either stressed the casual and the superficial, such as explaining the different norms or customs, or they had been based on joint political or economical endeavors, which have had little effect on personal relations beyond that specific endeavor. In short, before 1979 there had been virtually no long-term attempts to diminish existential mistrust between Jews and Arabs. Here and there short conflict-resolution seminars were held, but these failed to follow up on their stated objectives. Other Jewish-Arab meetings were characterized by apprehension which did not touch upon existential or political problems. If they *did* touch upon such problems, the meeting exploded and the groups stopped meeting.

The uniqueness of the Education for Peace Project was in developing the Buberian Learning Groups as an approach which attempted to educate for peace by working in three interrelated realms. The first realm is the teaching of Buber's dialogical thought and the ways in which a person may attempt to realize that thought in his everyday relations—by learning to trust the Other and to relate dialogically to him. The second realm is the teaching of existentialist writings in a manner which diminishes existential mistrust and encourages the person to assume responsibility for peace in his daily actions. The third realm is the learning of the existential sources of the Jewish-Arab conflict, and the application of all that has been learned to finding ways of resolving specific (albeit minor) aspects of that conflict.

The Buberian Learning Groups that met as part of the Education for Peace Project were comprised of approximately ten Israeli Arabs and ten Jews who met weekly, and were (ideally) led by an Arab and a Jew working together. The two-year educational process, which, during the three years of the Project, encompassed about 200 participants, was intense and included many components. In the group, it included structured lessons, directed readings, small group discussions and exercises. Outside the group, Jewish-Arab pairs met weekly to work on joint assignments; participants met individually once every two months with a group leader to discuss their problems and progress. Weekly lectures on topics related to the conflict and to Arab or Jewish culture, history, education, religion, and other subjects were attended on a voluntary basis. In six-hour workshops, held every six weeks, participants personally addressed issues raised in their readings and discussions. Two- to three-day retreat seminars were held three times every academic year. Once a year all members of the project participated in a dialogue testing field experience in Egypt, the only Arab country to which Israeli Jews and Arabs can travel together.

It is important to emphasize that Buberian dialogue pervades all three realms and the entire educational process. In true dialogue, according to Buber, each participant gives what he or she can, without trying to manipulate the Other or the conversation. At first the student learns Buber's thoughts on dialogue and is personally instructed in how to relate dialogically—in the group, in personal meetings with the leader, in workshops, etc. Later, existentialist writings or problems relating to the Jewish-Arab conflict are discussed in an atmosphere of dialogue. Thus dialogue is both a subject matter of learning and a way of relating within the group. To some extent, dialogue also helps persons assume responsibility for peace.

It will soon become clear that a Buberian Learning Group differs from both a conventional classroom and from a "group dynamics" group. Participants sit in a circle with the leader, who teaches philosophy and literature, but he also brings personal examples to help clarify the text that is being discussed. This sharing of experiences on the part of the leader is a first step to creating an atmosphere of dialogue in the group. The Buberian Learning Group differs from a "group dynamics" group in its ontological assumptions about human relations. One immediate and prominent outcome of this difference is that the discussion does not center around the feelings of the participants: they are told clearly and emphatically that their feelings concern the group only as a component of the existential relations discussed. The leader of a Buberian Learning Group must be well versed in existentialist writings and in Buber's philosophy. He or she must also be able to relate dialogically while working for the realization of a just vision of human relations.

My brief description leaves much to be explained. For instance, Buberian dialogue is often misunderstood as identification with the Other. It is not. Or my style may have given the impression that the Buberian Learning Group approach has, in terms of numbers, achieved great results. It has not, although more than a few Jews and Arabs have been deeply influenced. But before turning to a systematic discussion and description, let us briefly observe one of the meetings of a Buberian Learning Group. The following meeting occurred in 1979, during the first year of the Project. (All names in the discussions that follow are fictitious, except my own.)

A Ben-Gurion University classroom. The walls are bare and whitewashed. The lines of elongated windows are framed by slabs of concrete. The fluorescent lights are on. It is the third week of the fall semester, early in the evening. About twenty students are sitting around the room, on movable chairs, in Jewish-Arab dyads. Each dyad is conversing quietly. I am sitting near one of the dyads, listening. A few students are smoking; all seem relaxed. There are no ashtrays in the room and the floor is littered with cigarette butts and other light trash. I stand up, kick a cigarette butt under a chair, and turn to the participants: "O.K., let's move back into a circle." They quickly comply.

Haim: My impression was that you did not concentrate on answering the question I asked you to discuss, but wavered around it. Let me reiterate the question before we summarize the exercise. We read in Buber's essay "Elements of the Interhuman" that the realm of the interhuman can arise between two persons when one of them relates to the other not as an object but as a partner in a living event. I then asked you to try to explain to your partner in the dyad—each Jew to each Arab and vice versa—what are your difficulties in relating to each other as a partner in a living event. Unfortunately, in the three dyads whose discussion I overheard persons spoke mainly about feelings. Let's see what happened in other dyads. What were your difficulties, Muhammed?

Muhammed (Arab man): My difficulty stems from the fact that I feel that most Jews suspect me.

Haim: Those are not your personal difficulties. Do you accept Jews as a partner in a living event?

Muhammed: Well, no. I am always wondering what this Jewish person thinks about me.

Haim: Explain.

Muhammed: Whenever I talk to a Jewish man, I look at his eyes and try and hear in his words what he thinks about Arabs, about Palestinians.

Dana (Jewish woman): And what happens when you talk to a Jewish woman, Muhammed?

Muhammed: That is even more complex.

Haim: I hope you understand that by such behavior you are making yourself an object and not a partner in a living event. In that case you are responsible for the lack of dialogue and trust between you and the Jews you meet.

Muhammed (angrily): Leave me alone. You don't understand me, and all you want to do is to prove Buber's point. Even *you* probably suspect me.

Kasem (Arab man): Your response is out of order, Muhammed.

Haim: I agree, Kasem. Now listen, Muhammed. Believe me, your anger will not solve much except giving vent to your feelings. I do *not* suspect you. I trust you. I am willing to accept you as a partner in a living event. I want to prove Buber's point because that is the only way I know of that will help us establish trust between us. But I will not identify with your painful feelings or with your suspicions. I reject your suspicions of me and of many other Jews, including those sitting here. And I suggest that you stop taking your feelings so seriously. Let's turn to someone else.

Dana: Something is bothering me in this entire discussion.

Haim: What?

Dana: Why don't you want to identify with Muhammed's feelings or with my feelings or with anyone else's feelings? Why don't you try and check into the psychological reasons for Muhammed's feelings? Only then can you help him overcome those feelings.

Haim: This question is central to what we are doing here, and I'd like to make three points in response. First, we are not a T group. We are not dealing with group therapy. I am trying to show you what you must do to live trustfully, but I am not a therapist who will help you cope with psychological problems. I will say that if you learn to live trustfully, then often some of the problems which are rooted in distorted feelings may evaporate. But even if not, this is not my cup of tea.

Second, dialogue, as Buber taught it, is not identifying with the Other, but rather accepting him as Other while often rejecting his feelings or thoughts. I attempted to relate dialogically to Muhammed.

Muhammed: I didn't feel that you related to me dialogically.

Haim (forcefully): Muhammed, please stop listening to your feelings and try to listen to me, to Haim who is sitting here facing you. Please, listen carefully and try to believe me. I *am* interested in your feelings, but only as part of your entire way of life and not as a main topic for discussion.

The entire situation here reminds me of a short story that Martin Buber was fond of quoting. It appears in his book *For the Sake of Heaven,* which you will read in the second semester. Let me tell you the story as told by the Holy Yehudi:

"When I had begun my wanderings I once encountered a huge wagon full of hay which had been overturned and blocked the way. Beside it stood a peasant, and when he saw me he called me and asked me to help him lift up the wagon. Although we were both husky men, I immediately responded: 'It won't work. I cannot do it.' He got very angry and yelled at me: 'You can, you just don't want to give it a try.' His answer aroused me and I decided to try. We inserted boards under the wagon and with much exertion slowly lifted it until it stood upright. Then we piled the hay on it and the peasant harnessed the oxen. I continued my way with the peasant and asked him: 'How did you know I could lift the wagon with you?' 'I didn't,' he responded. 'But I did know that we cannot decide that we cannot do something until we have tried.' "

Like the overturned hay wagon, we have this problem of existential mistrust between us Jews and Arabs, which many of you may doubt that we can lift together. I believe that we can lift it if you will lend your strength and do not speculate about the problem or indulge in your feelings about it. So let us heave together.

Kasem: You know, Haim, I like that story.

As the above discussion reveals, confronting the Other is central to the educational process in the Buberian Learning

Group. We have found that often dialogue will begin only after such a confronting. Buberian dialogue is not the upgushing of love and empathy which many humanistic psychologists seek to arouse; dialogue is an ontological relation, not a psychological one. Confronting the Other creates an ontological situation with which he must cope and to which he must respond. If we succeed in the Buberian Learning Group, the confronted person will respond dialogically.

Yet what is essentially new about these Buberian Learning Groups? After all, in the 1960s the United States underwent a major revolution in race relations between black and white Americans. At that time there were many instances of black and white college students and adults who participated in dialogue groups in which they confronted each other. Am I not merely rediscovering the wheel?

Of course, there are similarities between the encounters described in this book and the attempts of many white and black Americans in the sixties to encounter each other as fellow citizens and fellow human beings, and not as participants in a racist heritage. When these Americans met and accepted the Other in his or her otherness, they were attempting to realize an aspect of Buber's philosophy, even if they had not read Buber. The radical difference between the approach described in this book and attempts to reach dialogue in the United States and elsewhere stems from my strict adherence to existentialist writings and, especially, to the writings of Martin Buber. These writings allowed me to weave a guiding thread which helped the participants and myself find our way in the maze of existential mistrust that characterizes the Mideast.

Hence this book describes a new method, based on a group of distinct philosophical and literary sources, which can be used to educate for peace. The method relies, of course, on *my* reading of the existentialist texts, but the book also shows that even if my reading may be at times distorted or limited, the texts are a source for developing ways of reaching dialogue in a conflict situation and of assuming responsibility for peace.

Additional characteristics of the Education for Peace Project made it unique. First, the main thrust of the Project was character education, with the main responsibility for this education resting on the leader of the Buberian Learning Group. Interaction, consciousness raising, openness, freedom to learn—all these occurred, but they were stations on the path of self-education of character. Put otherwise, they were a means to the end of educating persons to educate themselves to be dialogical persons. To the best of my knowledge, few encounter groups (if any) in the past three decades put such a stress on character education and self-education. Second, the need to research what was happening concerned me. Until my attempts, no one had taken existentialist philosophy as a basis for educational practice. What are the possibilities and the limits of this philosophy was frequently on my mind. How we conducted research, without allowing the participants to feel that we were using them, emerges in the following pages. I believe that our success in this endeavor testifies to the level of trust attained in the Buberian Learning Group. And third, the situation in Israel is much more complex than the black-white confrontation in the States in the sixties.

Whether one reads Martin Luther King or Stokely Carmichael, or other black and white civil rights leaders who emerged in the sixties, it is evident that they were dealing with a clear-cut issue: racism is abominable; discrimination against blacks is wrong and loathsome. It is unethical and anti-Christian, as King taught; it is a form of colonial exploitation, as Carmichael suggested. In the Mideast, the issues are much more hazy. To partially understand this haziness, one would have to transfer the United States of the sixties into the center of Black Africa and to imagine that, for half a century, the black countries surrounding the States have been trying to annihilate it. Many of the blacks who live in the "United States of Africa," as citizens, covertly support what their "black brothers" across the borders are trying to do to their country. This analogy suggests one small aspect of the complex situation in which the Education for Peace Project was established. Add to that the problem of Jews after the Nazi Holocaust, and the truths and ruses in the Palestinian predicament, and the haziness surrounding the issue becomes a thick fog.

Two additional points need to be mentioned in order to highlight the difference between what happened in the States in the sixties and the Mideast. The participants in the civil rights movement and their adversaries adhered to the Judeo-Christian ethical heritage which is prevalent in the States. There is no joint Judeo-Moslem ethical heritage to which Jews and Arabs in the Mideast can adhere. Worse, I gravely doubt that one can today find prominent ethical expressions of the Moslem heritage, except perhaps here and there in Egyptian literature. And this leads to the second point: The leaders of the civil rights movement came from within the black society, and if they were killed they were killed by whites. The few leaders for peace who have arisen in the Mideast among the Arabs have been killed by Arabs—Sadat and Sartawi are two recent examples. Furthermore, since the killings of Arabs who wished to live peacefully with Jews, initiated by the mufti of Jerusalem in the 1930s, any Arab who is unradical and who does not come out explicitly for the annihilation of Israel is a target for gunmen of the radicals. And this killing of peacemakers arouses no outrage in the Arab world.

So, I was not reinventing the wheel. But what *is* novel about relying on existentialist philosophy to educate for peace?

2. Existentialism and Education

The genuine existentialist must himself "exist." An existentialism that contents itself with theory is a contradiction; existence is not one philosophical theme among others. Here witness is made.

—MARTIN BUBER

L I K E all labels, "existentialism" can be misleading. It seems to be a manner of collecting into one bag a group of philosophers and writers who are concerned about human existence. But the three great existentialists of the nineteenth century—Kierkegaard, Nietzsche, and Dostoyevski—never heard of the label or the concern. Neither did Franz Kafka, who wrote short stories and novels and was definitely not a philosopher. Furthermore, as one reads different existentialists one finds that their approaches seem to contradict each other; Kierkegaard was a believing Protestant who wanted to renew subjective faith in Jesus' message; Nietzsche held that God is dead; Dostoyevski was a believing Russian Orthodox; Kafka was a Jewish nonbeliever, or perhaps an agnostic. Thus, once we abandon the "central concern" of existentialists, we are struck by their disagreeing with each other in many of their basic views.

Our problem has been that we have been trying to view existentialism as a "philosophical theme among others," and not as a witnessing. Woven into the above paragraph are four assumptions that lead to a misconstruing of existentialism.

The assumptions, which are not mutually exclusive, are (1) We can understand existentialism by defining its theme instead of, as Buber suggested, existing its philosophical insights; (2) The results a thinker or writer reaches are what counts, not the process by which he reaches those results; (3) We can disregard the ontology of human relations and be content with "basic views" about an objective reality; (4) The complexity of human relations can be explained philosophically or scientifically (i.e. behaviorism); it is not something to which one essentially only bears witness.

Existentialist philosophers and writers have repeatedly rebelled against these assumptions; one might even say that rebellion against these assumptions is a *sine qua non* of existentialism. I shall briefly review the rebellion against each assumption and its educational significance.

1. Defining the Theme versus to "Exist" the Philosophical Insight

Existentialist philosophy has no central theme. It is a series of attempts to gain insight into what Berdyaev called the riddle of being a person. The philosopher or writer, relying on his own insights and experience, can only be a witness to the manifold expressions of this riddle. Some existentialists testify to what they believe will enhance human existence, but each of them knows that he is testifying, not merely observing. Freedom is a basic component of the riddle of personality, hence, the existentialist who wishes to educate—say Søren Kierkegaard—can only point to a reality which he believes is worthy to attain, that is, becoming a subject. In his writings or in his life, he can forcefully attempt to bring the pupil to the brink of that reality—but further, the pupil is on his own. If the pupil refuses to give himself to that reality, the insights attained within that reality will remain unclear, not fully attainable. In short, Kierkegaard will never be able to fully explain what becoming a subject will mean for each of his readers—the reader must take the plunge and learn it for himself.

Consider the example of dancing mentioned above. In *Thus Spoke Zarathustra* and in other writings, Friedrich Nietzsche suggests that dancing is a way of enhancing human existence. It is our way of countering the "Spirit of Gravity," which is Zarathustra's major enemy. Nietzsche means that by learning often to dance through life a person can counter his taking of himself too seriously, an attitude which limits one's joy and personal development. Now it is not too difficult to perceive how dancing can enhance a person's joy and personal development. While dancing, a person must let the music move him; he must attain harmony with his body and with the music; he cannot be plagued by problems but must let himself go. And in rare moments he will achieve, perhaps, a unity with his partner that will transcend the here and now while living the moment fully. As a witness of an existential phenomenon, Nietzsche is here providing an insight which will only become meaningful if the reader does not discuss the theme of dancing as an expression of human joy, but will himself attempt to dance through some of his life. Following Nietzsche, I would go further and hold that a person who has never danced to music—disco, pop, folk, religious, whatever—a person who has never let a melody flow through his body and move it—that person will never comprehend what Nietzsche means by dancing one's life.

2. *Results versus Process*

Existentialists describe and discuss human existence, which is not only a biological process but also the process of realizing personal freedom. They are often misunderstood because our daily language is very much a language of statements and results; it is not suited to describe the dialectical development of human existence. Their writing is often fascinating because of their ability to capture the process of human existence despite the problems of language. The result of this concern with process is that the basic beliefs by which I characterized each existentialist (i.e. Dostoyevski was Russian Orthodox) are not central to that existentialist's description of human existence. In the case of Dostoyevski, for instance, his religious beliefs hardly emerge when he describes the various processes which lead a person to become a murderer or, in contrast, to succumb to being a victim.

One manner that existentialists have coped with the problem of describing processes of human existence is by writing literature which expresses their ideas. Kierkegaard wrote pieces such as "Diary of a Seducer"; Nietzsche interspersed short stories into his arguments; Buber wrote *Tales of the Hasidim;* Marcel wrote plays; Sartre wrote plays, novels, biographies. Writers such as Dostoyevski, Tolstoy, and Kafka described existential processes without giving philosophical explanations. In short, literary expression is at the heart of existentialist thought.

One hindrance to education for peace is that many persons view themselves as finished products, not as developing processes. They do not grasp that their own mode of existence is contributing to the current situation, and that they can change their way of life significantly—that a Jew *can* learn to trust an Arab. In the Buberian Learning Groups we have found that focusing on human existence as a process may help a person grasp his own life as a developing process. Two ways of encouraging such a focusing emerged in the above-cited group meeting: the telling of a story and the confronting of a student.

Hearing a story often opens new possibilities. Stories are distortions of reality which attempt to capture the flow of events by depicting processes. A listener to a story will lend of his being to the words of the story so as to make the story meaningful. He thus participates in the unfolding of a process, and may, as a result, see his own life as a process. Confronting a person in a Buberian Learning Group is a manner of demanding change. If Muhammed wants to be able to relate as a subject, he must change the way he looks at Jews: he must stop questioning their view of himself as an object. And someone must tell him to change, clearly and succinctly. Often, the person confronted will reject the demands that he change, but even in the process of rejection he will grasp himself as a process.

3. Ontology versus Basic Views

We live in the age of exponentially expanding information, and many persons labor under the illusion that summarizing information can help one cope with the situation at hand. The summary, they believe, will help them formulate a basic view which will guide them through the intricacies of their ignorance. Such a basic view allows them to ignore, and also conceals, ontological relations such as guilt, love, mistrust, which cannot be summarized. No "basic view" or *Weltanschauung* helps a person relate on the ontological level: at that level, only dialogue and self-education are meaningful helpmates. For instance, Buber wrote that a person may be able to cope with guilt by recognizing that he is guilty, by learning to live with that guilt, and by learning to act in a more redeeming manner in other relations, perhaps by trusting or by being more authentic. (Buber is talking about guilt, not about guilt feelings, which may have nothing to do with guilt, as Freud and others have shown.) But instead of discussing the importance of ontology, let us observe a discussion of guilt in one of the Buberian Learning Groups.

The discussion occurred about three months into the Buberian Learning Group process. Participants were studying Buber's essay "Guilt and Guilt Feelings"; the following citation served as the basis of the discussion:

. . . our subject is the relation of the conscience to existential guilt. Its relation to the trespassing of taboos concerns us here only in so far as the guilty man understands this trespassing more strongly or weakly as real existential guilt which arises out of his being and for which he cannot take responsibility without being responsible to his relationship to his own being.

The vulgar conscience that knows admirably well how to torment and harass, but cannot arrive at the ground and abyss of guilt, is incapable, to be sure, of summoning such responsibility. For this summoning a greater conscience is needed, one that has become wholly personal, one that does not shy away from a glance into the depths and that already in admonishing envisages the way that leads across it. But this in no way means that this personal conscience is reserved for some type of "higher" man. This conscience is possessed by every simple man who gathers himself into himself in order to venture the breakthrough out of the entanglement in guilt. And it is a great, not yet sufficiently recognized, task of education to elevate the conscience from its lower common form to conscience-vision and conscience-courage. For it is innate to the conscience of man that it can elevate itself.[1]

In the discussion, participants were asked to examine instances of vulgar and higher conscience in their own lives. Here are some excerpts:

Yafah (Jewish woman): I don't get the difference between a vulgar conscience and a higher conscience. Can you give me an example?

David (Jewish group leader): Buber indicates quite clearly what the difference is, the vulgar conscience torments and harasses while not bringing us face to face with our guilt. We sort of play around with our guilt. The greater conscience encourages a person to face his guilt directly. And conversely, by facing your guilt directly you can develop a greater conscience. One example is the Jewish-Arab relations in Israel. For many of us—Jews and Arabs—the state of the relations frequently torments our conscience; but we do not come face to face with what we have been doing, or not doing, in order to change the situation.

Yafah: You are still not very clear. And you always hit back with the problem of Jewish-Arab relations. I admit that the state of these relations bothers me, at times it even harasses me; but I don't see where some sort of higher conscience will help me here.

Hussein (Arab man): I agree with Yafah. The only thing I feel about Jewish-Arab relations is that my situation as an Arab living in Israel is bad; but I don't feel that my conscience is harassed or that I need a higher conscience.

David: First of all, let me give some literary examples of the difference between a vulgar conscience and a higher conscience. In Tolstoy's "The Death of Ivan Illich," which we discussed recently, the hero Ivan Illich lives with a vulgar conscience until, on his deathbed, at the last moment and as a result of deep suffering, he suddenly recognizes the existence of a higher conscience. In *Anna Karenina,* Anna and Vronsky live according to a vulgar conscience, while Levin is seeking, naively perhaps, what Buber calls a higher conscience. In Kafka's *The Trial* and in Camus' *The Fall* we encounter haranguing monologues of the vulgar conscience, while Dostoyevski's Sonya in *Crime and Punishment* is guided by a higher conscience.

But the problem is not literature but our own life, your own life. For instance, let us speak of the Jewish-Arab problem, even if it sounds overdone. The vulgar conscience can only tell you, if at all, that the situation is bad and it may harass you that you have not done anything to change it. The higher conscience says that if you do not face up to the fact that your own personal way of life is contributing to the bad situation, then you lack what Buber calls conscience-courage and conscience-vision. In short, you are an accomplice to perpetuating the rotten situation.

And what is worse here in Israel is that your unwillingness to see that mistrust and hatred between Jews and Arabs has become a way of life that is ruining you—and it doesn't matter whether you are a Jew or an Arab—is a way of succumbing to your vulgar conscience. Higher conscience means seeing what I have to change in my life today in order to face the problem directly. And many of us are guilty in that we don't dare face ourselves.

What can be done? Here I must agree with Buber, who

indicated that once we accept our own guilt a path opens up. When I saw how much I mistrusted Arabs—I thought them devious and ignorant—I suddenly realized the way I must pursue. Trust, and also some humility, but basically stubborn trust is the only way which leads across our mutual abyss of mistrust and guilt.

Hussein: You know, David, I'm not sure that I know what you mean, but I am beginning to think that I feel what you mean.

David: Please continue.

Hussein: Well, as I said at a recent workshop, I am evading going back to my Arab village up north and am sticking it out here at the university for more years than needed to complete my studies. I then said that I don't want to go back and to face the unmodern reality of the Arab village. But now what struck me, while you were speaking, was that I really don't want to face myself as an Arab who is striving to assert a Palestinian identity and also to be a part of Jewish-Israeli modern society. My not liking the village, my uncomfortableness with older Arabs, is really my refusal to face myself. And then, when I blame Jews or feel uncomfortable with them, it is really because I feel uncomfortable with what Buber calls my Otherness as an Arab. I don't know if I have made myself clear.

4. Complexity of Human Relations

Most existentialists respond with derision toward explanations of human relations on the basis of approaches such as behaviorism, utilitarianism, analytic philosophy, or psychology. How can one take seriously such approaches when all one need do is be a bit authentic with oneself and one will discover the complexity of human relations? Dostoyevski, for instance, repeatedly stressed that he could only describe what happened to the persons who populated his novels— Dmitri Karamazov, Prince Mishkin, Stavrogin, etc.—he could not and did not wish to attempt to explain their behavior. He sensed that any explanation of human relations must some-how efface human freedom and the paradoxical develop-ments in each person's life.

Consider Buber's assertion concerning guilt, which is also evident in the writings of Kafka, Dostoyevski, and Tolstoy: that only when a person recognizes his guilt will he begin to envision a way to transcend that guilt. (Again, one must remember that we are talking here of guilt, not of guilt feelings.) This description of a human response, which many persons have probably experienced in their own life, is simi-lar to a quantum jump; it cannot be explained, it just hap-pens. The same is true of love. Perhaps we can describe aspects of its development, but we cannot explain it.

Education for peace must begin with a recognition of the complexity of human relations and of the wish of many persons, including many prominent politicians, to overlook this complexity and to define human relations in simplistic terms. In educating Jews and Arabs to relate to each other dialogically, we were not only introducing them to a new, complex realm of human relations, we were also threatening many simplistic concepts and relations which had guided them. We soon learned that accepting the complexity of human relations was for many a challenge; for some persons, responding to that challenge opened new vistas of life and profundity.

I hope I have clarified that existentialist philosophy holds both a promise and a threat for education for peace. The promise is that a person who is willing to learn from existen-tialist philosophy how to alter his way of life has in his hands an Ariadne thread which can guide him through the laby-rinth of social and political hostilities in which man is im-mersed. The threat stems from the fact that any Ariadne thread is merely a thread; it can tear under stress. It cannot help a person face the dangers he may encounter while traversing the labyrinth; it will not replace personal courage or readiness to act; it may delude us to believe that we have a remedy at hand, when all one is grasping is a thread.

The analogy of the thread I learned the hard way. When I initiated the Education for Peace Project I believed that Buber's philosophy could guide our activities both within and outside the Project. Today, I admit that I was naive; in many instances it simply didn't work. Within the Buberian Learning Groups, dialogue did not help us reach those persons who were stubbornly resigned to mistrust. And outside the groups, dialogue proved futile in encounters with religious or political fanatics, or mediocre and cowardly bureaucrats, or persons whom Kierkegaard would denote as dreading the good. I learned that existentialist philosophy can indicate where to go next, but it cannot reveal what difficulties you may encounter. It can only hint as to the educational methods you may use to traverse this new terrain. I will clarify all this in subsequent chapters; here I shall discuss two general problems of existentialism and education. I call these problems "the compatibility of different existentialists" and "existentialism and self-education."

Despite their mutual concern with human existence and with the process of personal development, existentialists approach human existence from different, often contrasting, perspectives. For instance, Martin Buber spent much of his life describing the ontology of the dialogical relation, which for Jean-Paul Sartre was a rather insignificant detail of human existence. (Only in his last interview, shortly before his death, did Sartre admit that he may have overlooked something significant when he ignored friendship in his writings.) If so, one may ask: How can the educator intertwine the contrasting approaches developed by various existentialists into an Ariadne thread? I believe that such can be done if the educator develops what Berdyaev would have called an existential awareness. In his autobiography, he describes that awareness:

... the awareness of this supremacy of Truth has put a lasting stamp on my spiritual and intellectual development. This "spiritualism" became the ground and framework of my whole philosophical attitude and probably of my very existence. As I understand it, however, the word spiritualism does not denote any philosophical or mystical, or, indeed, any occult school of thought, but an existential awareness. I came to believe in the primary reality of the spirit at a level which is deeper than, and transcends, the sphere of discursive reasoning, for this latter has a secondary, derivative nature and belongs to the "symbolic" and "reflected" world of externality. I never abandoned this fundamental attitude, not even throughout my Marxist period.[2]

The existential awareness emphasized by Berdyaev is inherent to existentialist writing and allows one to weave together insights of different existentialists, especially when addressing concrete problems. Nay, my experience is that when dealing with a complex educational problem, I have always drawn upon the complementing insights of different existentialists. This finding may seem trivial since no existentialist held that his writings encompassed all of reality, but it struck me again and again in my daily attempts to educate for peace. Many examples of such an intertwining will appear in the sequel, in my descriptions of concrete events. Here I shall present a more general example.

One of the initial goals of the Education for Peace Project was to create an ongoing dialogue with Egyptian counterparts. We soon found this endeavour nearly impossible to achieve: many Egyptians were polite and friendly, they were helpful and nice; they were not partners to dialogue. According to Buber, persons become partners in dialogue when, in a specific conversation, each one gives what he can give, without trying to manipulate the other person or the conversation. When faced with our failure to reach dialogue, some of our participants, both Jews and Arabs, dismissed the Egyptians as antidialogical. Others tried to understand the situation as an outcome of the years of hatred and war. But both the stereotypic and the psychological approaches evade the issue; they do not try to see what is happening to the existing Egyptian.

In my various readings of contemporary Egyptian literature—and I was limited by my being able to read only works translated into Hebrew and English—I perceived that the mistrust which we encountered also prevailed in the relations described by Egyptian authors. Buberian dialogue is almost totally lacking in novels by Mahfouz or short stories by Idris or Ibrahim (in contrast, one often finds such dialogue in novels by Hemingway, Hesse, and other Western writers). Egyptian society, as described by its foremost authors, is ruthless, fatalistic, distrustful, with very few moments of naive communion. Many persons in this society are trapped in a hopeless situation, and they feel superfluous; Sartre would say: they *are* superfluous.

Reading up on Egyptian life taught me that we Israelis did not comprehend the specific manner in which Egyptians did indicate a wish for dialogue; probably because a person who lives in a democratic society, where criticism and verbal conflict are daily occurrences, is basically unaware of the existential situation of a person in a fatalistic, dictator-ruled police state. In such a state, the structure of what Buber calls inter-personal relations has broken down; the person growing up there sees few trustful relations that he can emulate. Borrowing a term from Michael Polanyi, we might say that his "tacit knowledge" does not include the possibility of trustful relations. In his encounter with the Other each person senses that the look of a third person is present; like a vampire, this look sucks the throbbing vitality out of the encounter. In such a situation a person can only begin trusting the Other with his suffering—since suffering is the passive lot of all—but not with his hopes and dreams, his sins and struggles; in short, not with the activities of his being.

Thus many an Egyptian, when he began to trust a member of our group, confided his sufferings, what he had gone through in his life to reach his current situation; he gave himself as a finished product, not as a person who is still in the process of developing and has the freedom to alter his situation. Because such an approach often brings the listener to identify with the person explaining himself, there arises a feeling that dialogue is occurring. But such is *pseudo-*

dialogue—the Egyptian is giving everything but his freedom, which he lacks. Only when a person gives of his current unfinished self, and not of his past self, which has been polished by the rational remaking of one's history—only then is he a partner in dialogue. Such occurred very rarely; I recall dialogues with Naguib Mahfouz, the prominent Egyptian author, and with one of his young friends.

Combining Buber, Sartre, and existentialist descriptions by Egyptian authors, I learned that a person who is constantly faced with the possibility that he will become superfluous evades his current self, with its uncertainties, hopes, and fears. He languishes in habit. He attempts to become his own destiny and thus to overcome his being superfluous; but in the process he is sacrificing his freedom. He thus plays into the hands of the regime, helping it set up a dialectical motor of alienation in his heart. Because he senses that he is superfluous, he fears to participate in dialogue, and his inability to participate in dialogue enhances his awareness of being superfluous. This vicious circle of alienation, this dialectics of antidialogue, emerges again and again in Mahfouz' novels; it is also found in Solzhenitsyn's writings on contemporary Soviet society.

Existentialist philosophy can lead to self-education if the reader reads the writings as indicating areas in his way of life which can be changed, which he should strive to change. I will grant that such self-education can only occur after a level of affluence and of intellectual freedom has been achieved. A Bolivian tin miner who is broken by fatigue each night, or an emaciated mother starving in Cambodia, will have little time or strength for self-education or for existentialist writings. Perhaps this is the reason Sartre called existentialism an ideology and not a philosophy.

I do not believe that one can educate for peace, especially in the Mideast, without each student educating himself to change many of his responses and habits. Existential mistrust, for instance, is not a cognitive attitude that prevails in

Jewish-Arab relations—it is a way of life. Put bluntly, when they meet in public places such as buses, trains, or the cinema, Jews and Arabs "smell out each other." Often an outside observer, say a Swedish tourist, may not be able to perceive how this is done. This habitual response may be justified after decades of hostility, but my point is that for both nations it has become an ingrained habit. And our habits, as Nietzsche indicated, form our reality; one can only change that reality by changing one's habits—that is, by a lengthy and arduous process of self-education.

Existentialist philosophy can lead the person who has the courage and willingness to educate himself along three paths which often merge or cross. First, the writings can serve as a mirror of one's personal existence. Second, they can illuminate hidden, adverse aspects of a person's social reality, and indicate the manner in which he tacitly supports that reality. The third and most difficult path is learning from existentialist philosophy how to change one's way of life and one's social reality. This path may lead to the heights of wisdom or to the fulfillment of a vision.

The two citations from meetings of Buberian Learning Groups given above show how we taught persons to read existentialist writings in a manner which mirrors one's own existence. In its initial stages, such a learning may resemble group dynamics or even therapy. A person learns that he or she is not relating to the Other as a subject, but as an object, and in group or personal discussions one is led to examine oneself and to see where and how such occurs. But as the educational process develops we transcend psychology, basically because we want to give the students a direction for development in which their habits and perspective of reality *must* change. (They must learn to diminish their mistrust!) In short, we must lead them to see adverse aspects of their social reality which they habitually support.

Here is an example of such a discussion, based on a major theme of Dostoyevski's *The Brothers Karamazov*. The discussion occurred during the second year of learning of a Buberian Learning Group and centered around the tacit agreement between Ivan Karamazov and Smerdyakov to kill their father. The leader explained that the treaty between the pseudointellectual and the lackey-type person who makes up the masses has become a common phenomenon in our century. Stalin, Hitler, and Mao initiated terrible manifestations of this treaty; less terrible examples are found today in Judaism and in Islam—Rabbi Cahane and Ayatollah Khomeini. And even Menachem Begin, Yasser Arafat, and Gamal Abdul Nasser often used pseudointellectual rhetoric to appeal to the lackey-type person and to gain his support for unethical deeds. The group leader then asked: Why is there a mutual attraction between Ivans and Smerdyakovs, and how can we work against the treaty they establish between them?

At first the discussion took place in small groups of three or four; the summary involved the entire group. Here are some excerpts from the summary.

Fatma (Arab woman): Our group felt that Ivan was attracted to Smerdyakov because he sensed that Smerdyakov would do what he wished, and Ivan wished his father's death. Smerdyakov was attracted to Ivan because he sensed that Ivan's philosophy would help him justify the murder, which was his revenge on society for having him born and raised in degrading circumstances.

Dina (Jewish woman group leader): What you say is commonly accepted and can be found in many commentaries about Dostoyevski. But I think that something essential is missing. That missing link is what is common in the way of life of Ivan and Smerdyakov and leads to their mutual attraction.

Fatma: Maybe it's the fact that they lie to themselves.

Dina: Yes and no. We all lie to ourselves. It is the specific manner of lying that is unique to both of them and to much of our political and social reality.

Muhammed (Arab man): They both seem to be talking around the subject. They seem to be indicating to each other that they want Fyodor Karamazov killed, but they talk about other topics.

Dina: You are right, Muhammed, and I believe that this point has great relevance for our society, for what is going on here and now. There are certain tacit agreements in our society which do not receive expression, but which allow the lackey-type person to do the immoral wishes of the pseudointellectual. When speaking with each other, these persons evade the major issues and sidetrack to minor issues, but everyone knows what is on the other person's mind. Decisions are made seemingly without anyone making them; by hinting at what is on one's mind, persons receive confirmation of their views and allow the ax to fall.

Let me give a rather neutral example before I show what this has to say about Jewish-Arab relations. In Israel 53 percent of the population are women; but only about 10 percent of the Knesset [parliament] members are women. And since Golda Meir, no minister has been a woman. Now, nobody decided to limit the number of women in the Knesset. Political parties often seek for a larger percentage of women in their lists of representatives. But somewhere along the decision-making line the door was closed and women remained outside the seats of power.

Sima (Jewish woman): Well, what should we do? I know many other places where women in Jewish society are blocked from power, like there is no major woman bank official.

Dina: Let me continue, Sima, and I'll get to the point. Remember we are talking about the treaty between the pseudointellectual and the lackey-type person. What characterizes their relationship is that, while lying to themselves, they allude to their real desires in roundabout language. They do not have the courage to state their desires straightforwardly or to face directly the implications of their desires. Hence they play around with words and insinuations. In short, their treaty is based on their lack of courage to face their desires and to examine them. But such people make decisions which influence our lives.

Just to go back to my example, few men would like to be ruled by a Knesset with, say, 60 percent women; but no politician will dare say this. They let the Other make the decision to bar women from power, seemingly without their knowledge about it.

And the same holds for the second-class status of the Arabs in Israel. Few Jews would say openly: This is what we want. But through hundreds of hints, through thousands of minor deeds, second-class status for Arabs becomes a fact of life. There is no decision to limit the power of Arabs, but wherever the Arab turns his power is limited; and it is always limited by the Other; the person whom the Arab addresses is merely passing on a decision or implementing it; and the person who is limiting the power merely does what he understands certain hints from above or below intend him to do. Thus the Arab is barred from power by a bond of impotency.

For instance, like in a Kafkian novel, an Arab who is denied work as a teacher never knows who made the decision or why the decision was made. Each person will send him to the Other, who will merely explain the workings of the system. If he is stubborn and persistent in his pleas, a message may finally come through that, for reasons of security to the State, he was denied the job. But he can never meet face to face with whoever made that decision. But I know how the decision was made; hints and allusions made by the lackey-type bureaucrat were passed on to the pseudointellectual at the top; this led to an understanding which led to a mutual not-knowing. And the ax fell.

Fatma: What you say reminds me of how Egyptians relate to Palestinians. I learned this on our trip to Egypt last year and now I understand it. Outwardly, they declare that we all are brother Arabs. But the entire bureaucratic machine withholds help from a Palestinian living in Egypt. Nobody decided this. It just happens. . . . I'm beginning to see that you want us to battle this reality by relating straightforwardly.

Dina: That always helps, but right now we want to see the

situation as it is. Such a seeing will help you respond appropriately when the time for a specific response arises.

This excerpt was part of a much longer discussion, which had less exciting moments and a few digressions. And yet, the writings of Dostoyevski and Kafka have helped many of our participants see the underside of what happens in their society. Seeing this underside of society, this decision-making through alienation, is essential for the self-education of any person who wishes to bring about a change for the better.

Examples of how we educate persons to change their way of life and their social reality will be given in subsequent chapters. Here I wish to reiterate that self-education is perhaps the only way one can learn from existentialist philosophy how to exist differently. Hence the role of the Buberian Learning Group is to educate persons to educate themselves—to abandon confining habits of thought and life and to open for themselves new realms of existence.

I have purposely overlooked until now a major question concerning existentialism and education: How does the educator choose what to learn from existentialists about human existence, especially in educating for peace? I believe that much of the answer to this question is personal, but I doubt that one could use existentialist writings, without distorting them, to educate for murder. There are, I believe, two characteristics of existentialist writings which make them extremely valuable for education. First, all existentialists, except perhaps Heidegger, expressed a passionate love for life and for one's fellow man as an individual person. Theirs is not a gushy love; often it is tainted with gloom or irony, as in Kafka or Sartre, but its passion prevails. Without this love, I doubt whether problems of human existence would have so profoundly interested these writers.

Second, almost all existentialists had a delightful sense of humor, which, I admit, may often be camouflaged under their barrage of original ideas. Nietzsche, Kierkegaard, and Dostoyevski set the pace in the past century—for instance, there is great humor in Dostoyevski's *The Idiot,* in Kierkegaard's *Either/Or,* and scattered throughout all of Nietzsche's writings. This humor supported their passionate love of man and also expressed this love. (I would doubt that love could long exist without humor, and vice versa!) Hence any true learning from existentialist writers must be based on a passionate love for life and for one's fellow man and an enjoyment of his sense of humor. I know of no better basis for education for peace.

Every sixth Israeli citizen is an Arab. Arab population growth is more rapid than Jewish growth, and demographers predict that by the end of the century 20 percent of Israeli citizens will be Arabs. There is no doubt that these Arabs have benefited both from the Israeli democracy and the relative affluence of Israeli society, especially when compared with the neighboring Arab countries: Jordan, Syria, Egypt. They have also benefited from the welfare-state laws in Israel, such as full medical insurance, social security, etc. But their power has been limited. They are not represented proportionally in the Israeli Knesset (parliament). A sixth of the Knesset would be 20 members, while fewer than 10 Arabs are Knesset members. In the higher economic, military, security, and governmental posts there are no Arabs at all. In many other areas, such as engineering, their advance has been limited. The explanation for this semiofficial approach has been security, which, due to Israel's international situation and the fact that many Israeli Arabs share sentiments with persons across the borders, has some justification.

Arab education is secularized and in Arabic. The development of the Arab school system since Israel's independence has been astounding. In the 1948/49 school year, only 14 Arabs went to high school; in 1981/82, 22,500 were enrolled. Every Arab boy and girl go to primary school, while around 10 percent went in 1948/49. Yet the education that many Arab pupils receive is inferior to the education Jews receive, both in terms of resources and in quality of teachers.

Jewish and Arab pupils hardly ever meet during the school years. The only places they meet to study together are the Israeli universities; hence a university was a natural background for the Education for Peace Project. Although only 8 percent of the student population at Ben-Gurion University are Arabs, these were persons who had gone through many difficulties in order to reach higher education, including learning to study and to express themselves in a language other than their mother tongue (all instruction at Israeli universities is in Hebrew). Most of them are not members of the Bedouin tribes who reside in the Beer Sheva area, but Arabs from the north of Israel who are farmers and town dwellers. (Many Jewish students at Ben-Gurion University also come from the areas north of the Negev.) They were also persons who had decided to try and live, at least for a few years, in a more modern society, such as the Jews have established in Israel. A strict patriarchal society prevails even today in many Arab communities; many marriages, for instance, are still arranged by the spouses' fathers.

Beer Sheva, where Ben-Gurion University is situated, is a Jewish urban sprawl of drab condominiums, built around an old Arab desert town whose inhabitants fled in the War of Independence. Its 120,000 residents are mainly Jews who emigrated to Israel during the last three decades from countries such as Morocco, Roumania, Argentina, Iraq, and lately Russian Georgians and black Falashic Jews from Ethiopia. In a few small areas of villas and gardens the affluent reside, but outside those areas the desert dust engulfs the city. Parks have been planted, but their green foliage struggles to make an impression against the background of the shimmering sun, the blue skies, and the brownish yellow of the desert. The major encouraging aspect of the city is its openness, to the desert sunset, to the winds, to the ever blue skies.

Around the city reside the Bedouins. Some of them are seminomads, living in black, movable tents with camels and donkeys tethered nearby. Some have acquired land and have begun to build houses. Among the nomadic are the poorest tribes, whose women scavenge Beer Sheva's green garbage bins each morning for leftovers. Few Arabs are residents of the city; I have one such neighbor, a Christian, who tries to play down his being an Arab. But he sends his children to the Bedouin school, where they learn the rudiments of Islam.

The public buildings are examples of what an architect friend called fascist architecture, and among them is the new campus of Ben-Gurion University. Fascist architecture dwarfs the individual and stresses his insignificance as against the grandeur of the concrete structure which encompasses him. It does not feature nooks or spaces where a person can feel nonsuperfluous; everything is built so as to make him succumb to the imposing edifice. In short, fascist architecture worships what Buber called the I-It. Besides being a fascist at heart, the architect of the new campus was a poor artist; he lacked sensitivity to the openness of the desert. He designed the buildings so as to close out that openness, so that any human relationship with what the desert can offer would be stifled.

3. Buber, Dialogue, and Education for Peace

All actual life is encounter. — MARTIN BUBER

P E R H A P S Buber's most important assertion for the educator is that a person develops and realizes his personality primarily through the relationships he develops with other human beings, with nature, and with spiritual beings (i.e. works of art). Thus a person who manipulates, uses, or exploits other persons exists and develops differently from a person who constantly strives to initiate dialogical relations with his fellow man, with nature, and with God. The manipulator views other persons as objects for his use or enjoyment, and he will strive to acquire maximum power over these objects; in the process, he himself learns to act and to respond as an object. He exists in the realm of the I-It. In contrast, the dialogical person will attempt to reach a deep personal relationship with other persons, with nature, and with God; he will repeatedly try to speak the basic word of dialogue, I-Thou. At times, such relationships may bring him pain, but he has learned that such pain often brings with it new knowledge of himself as a subject. Thus a person who cannot or does not ever relate dialogically will not develop the deeper aspects of his personality; he will not realize much of his human potential. His relationships with other persons, with nature, and with God will be superficial, perhaps fanatical; he will be unable to express personal commitment, unable to love, unable to give of himself. Buber also believed that adults who have difficulties in relating dialogically can slowly alter their mode of existence and, by undergoing a difficult educational process, can learn to relate dialogically. But he did not suggest methods, aside from some vague remarks on self-education, that can help persons undergo the process of learning to relate dialogically.

Probably because of the broad appeal of his writings, many of Buber's basic insights have been watered down and misinterpreted. Aspects of human existence that Buber described as ontological have been projected onto the plane of psychology or sociology—a projection that Buber vehemently rejected. Such is especially true of the I-Thou encounter.

In educating for peace, we often had to counter the following three misinterpretations. Many persons mistakenly believe that if one enjoys the beauty of a desert sunset or delights in the flow of a rushing waterfall, one is participating in an I-Thou encounter. But Buber held that enjoying is part of the It world; hence enjoying nature's beauty can be a subtle form of exploitation. For an I-Thou encounter to occur, a person must give and receive; he must be active and passive; he must transcend his thoughts and feelings and be totally present to nature. Usually when a person is enjoying a sunset or delighting in a waterfall, he is primarily receiving; he is being moved by the beauty while absorbing it. Such may be a moment of elation, but it is not an I-Thou encounter.

Buber wanted man to reach, albeit in moments of grace, communion with nature. Reaching such communion requires, as a first step, sincere modesty, which relates not to the surface beauty but to underlying mystery from which this beauty stems. Buber stressed that such a moment of communion may be very rarely realized in a person's life. But educating oneself to be ready for that rare moment is a first step in giving to nature, even as one benefits from it.

I have indicated twice already that dialogue will not occur when a person identifies with the Other, instead of confronting him and relating to him as Other. Thus, as Buber spelled out to Carl Rogers, a relationship in therapy in which the therapist identifies with the patient is not an I-Thou relationship; it is not the basis of dialogue. Neither is empathy, as Buber repeatedly stressed. I am reiterating this point because the problem of identifying with the Other repeatedly surfaced in our Buberian Learning Groups; it often hindered our educational endeavors. We never fully overcame this problem, probably because, as Nietzsche indicated in *The Gay Science*, it is much easier to identify with the Other than to confront him. But we were stubborn. We never abandoned the Buberian principle that dialogue must be built on each Arab developing his personality and life as an Arab and every Jew developing his personality and life as a Jew. Only as whole persons who are not alienated from themselves or from their heritage can they meet in dialogue.

The mistakes concerning an I-Thou relationship, both in creating a work of art and in relating to it, resemble what I described concerning nature. One must attempt to transcend one's feelings and thoughts and be fully present to the work confronting one; perhaps one will encounter the Thou. One point should be added which is significant to all I-Thou encounters. A person cannot withhold any portion of his being and still wish to reach an I-Thou encounter. Such is especially significant when one attempts to create, or when one wishes to relate to a work of art. Withholding oneself, even in order to make a point, will relegate the encounter to the realm of the It. Learning not to withhold oneself is also crucial for religious experience. Great religious leaders, such as the biblical prophets, sensed this intuitively. They dared not withhold any portion of their being in their dialogue with God. Such is also the secret of authentic prayer—learning not to withhold any portion of one's being when turning to God.

Of course, as Buber indicated, when a person does not withhold himself, it involves a sacrifice and a risk. We have found that teaching persons not to withhold themselves is one of the most difficult problems in educating for dialogue and for peace. Consider a discussion which I led in the fall of 1979, after reading the second section of "Elements of the Interhuman," where Buber describes how making an impression hinders dialogue.

Tarek (Arab man): I don't agree with Buber's rejection of making an impression; what's wrong in making a good impression: I know that if I make a good impression I am liked and accepted.

Jeremiah (Jewish man): I feel that especially among Arabs, making an impression seems to be important. Maybe the whole essay "Elements of the Interhuman" is not good for you Arabs.

Tarek: We're not talking now about Jews and Arabs, but about life. I disagree with Buber's rejection of making an impression, as written here in the text. I want to get an academic answer to an academic question. Later we'll talk about Jews and Arabs.

Haim: Buber is against impression making as a way of life because the person who is concerned with making an impression is not giving all of himself to his partner in dialogue. He is giving only one side of his being, which he hopes or suspects his partner will appreciate. In short, one reason Buber criticizes impression making is that it hinders dialogue. But there is another, more positive reason that perhaps does not emerge from the text at first reading. Living dialogically means living fully; not being concerned with making an impression means that I can unite my being in one direction and pursue that direction with all my powers. It means living a more fulfilling life. Buber did not hesitate to mention that such a life involves taking risks; but without such risks, life loses its vigor and meaning.

Tarek: But in many instances making an impression is important.

Haim: Buber would have agreed. He personally loved to have his picture taken, and he knew how to make an impression in those pictures. But we must be aware that we can lose the possibility of dialogue, of an I-Thou encounter, because of our striving to make an impression. Further, if I always suspect that the other person is trying to make an impression, it will be hard for me to trust him. And without trust, life is Hell. Here Buber would have agreed with Sartre, whose play *No Exit* you all probably read or saw.

Jeremiah: Your talking about trust is fine. But how does one develop trust and stop thinking about the impression I am making?

Haim: There is not much that I can say about this that is not in the text. You have to give of yourself freely, without manipulating the other person by trying to make an impression on him or manipulating the conversation by trying to make a point.

Dana: I don't understand why trying to make a point can ruin dialogue or trust. Isn't that what dialogue is all about?

Haim: At times, making a point can encourage dialogue, and at times it can ruin it. What is important is not to try to manipulate the other person or the conversation. Let me tell you a story about how making a point ruined an I-Thou encounter.

Three years ago I was on reserve duty at A-Tur in south Sinai, attached to a U.N. brigade from Finland. We were a small group of eight Israelis, and one night we got to talking about God and religion. I explained Buber's view that we can sense the Godly through an I-Thou encounter; but my buddies did not grasp what I meant. Two days later a platoon of Finns decided to visit Mount Sinai, and four of us accompanied them. After two hours of climbing, near the top of the mountain, they perceived that their time was running out; they decided to double their pace in order to get back to base on time. We parted from them and continued to slowly scale the mountain. Suddenly, toward the top, the whole panorama of south Sinai's rugged mountain range became visible in iron red, deep purple, and dull brown and black. The view was breathtaking; it exhaled holiness. The four of us were wonderstruck. Suddenly I emerged from the encounter and, turning to my companions, said: "You see, this is what Buber would call an I-Thou encounter which bears witness to Godliness." One of my companions, his eyes still taking in the panorama, responded quietly and sadly: "Why did you speak? You've ruined it."

In his essay "Elements of the Interhuman," which was written three decades after *I and Thou*, Buber described and indicated how some of his basic insights on dialogue emerge in a person's daily life. The essay serves as a good introduction to many of Buber's more profound insights expressed elsewhere. What is more, I found that when many a student reads the essay he senses that trying to live dialogically is not beyond his capabilities. The poetic, soul-stirring passages of *I and Thou* often produce a contemplative or dreamy response, while the more mundane descriptions of "Elements of the Interhuman" allow one to relate the text to what is happening in one's own life. In the Buberian Learning Groups, this essay was the cornerstone of our teaching participants how to attempt to enter the realm of dialogue.

One of the significant points of the essay is that Buber distinguishes between an I-Thou encounter and genuine dialogue. While the I-Thou encounter occurs in a moment of grace, in what Berdyaev describes as a moment of eternity, genuine dialogue can be learned. It is the result of an act of will of two persons. Of course I-Thou encounters—if and when they occur—teach us the significance of dialogue. But in this essay Buber also indicated how dialogue can be built up slowly, out of the elements of the realm of the interhuman.

Buber opens the essay by defining the realm of the interhuman as what occurs between persons. A person is not only a member of the various social units which sociologists study. A person is not only a sum of traits, characteristics, behavior, or responses which psychologists discuss. A person is also the creator of the interhuman: the realm of happenings between persons which are mutual or which have the potential of becoming mutual. This realm cannot be reduced either to sociology or to psychology because when a person confronts another person, an additional element is present, which arises between the persons and exists only there. My colleague, Jochanan Bloch, called this element the "dialogical element" of human existence.

One of the basic problems of Jews and Arabs in Israel is that they almost never confront each other as persons and allow the dialogical element to emerge. (Such is, of course, also true in many other areas of hostility: South Africa, Northern Ireland.) The relations which develop between Jews and Arabs are stereotypic. Even the liberal and educated Jew and Arab view the other as a member of a different collective, or as a member of another culture and community with its different set of values, or in terms of traits and behavior—in short, views that are based on the paradigms of the behavioral sciences. But it is precisely the scientific paradigm which teaches us to view the Other as an object, not as a possible partner in dialogue.

In order to allow the dialogical element to emerge and influence the conversation of two persons whose relations have been characterized by existential mistrust, they must meet for a sustained period and learn to relate to each other as persons. This conclusion may seem obvious, yet many attempts to change conflicting relations have assumed that existential attitudes can be altered solely by imparting more balanced information about the conflict and about the history, culture, and behavior of the opposing group. I have found this assumption to be wrong; as Sartre pointed out in *Antisemite and Jew,* a person who is prejudiced will usually use the new information he has acquired to create new arguments that justify his prejudices.

Even for the persons who volunteered to participate in the Education for Peace Project, achieving sustained personal contact was not an easy task. In addition to obvious barriers of fear, avoidance, hostility, ignorance, cultural differences, and political deterrents, Jews and Arabs who chose to meet in a Buberian Learning Group often faced strong resistances from family and friends who sensed that such involvement challenged their ways of living and relating. Moreover, participants in a Buberian Learning Group often learn that they themselves foster prejudices which influence their ways of relating to other persons and to themselves. The mere fact that, despite these and other hindrances during the three years of the Project, over 200 Jews and Arabs met together, for a sustained period on a regular basis, testifies to the strength that persons attain from dialogical relations.

What sort of strength do persons attain from dialogical relations? Buber gives three answers which are paradoxical: they are conditions for the emerging of dialogue, but when dialogue emerges they strengthen the person. First, in dialogue, a person lives according to his being. Second, living dialogically means living fully in the present. Third, in dialogue, a person's potentials unfold. I shall discuss each answer separately.

But first let us recall the fascist architecture of Ben-Gurion University and examine its relation to dialogue. Architecture which dwarfs a person, in which his existence as a particular being is superfluous, does not encourage him to live according to his being. The grand edifice surrounds the person—it does not confront him and demand a response as, for instance, the mosques in Istanbul do—a person's presence and living in the present seem meaningless in the corridors of such grandeur. And finally, the building has no areas which can arouse a person's specific responses, that is, responses in which he finds his unique self unfolding. Fascist buildings, such as our campus, bask in indifference.

Living according to one's being means not being constantly concerned with the impression one wishes to make on another person or persons; it is the sharing with each person whom one encounters that portion of one's being which the specific moment of meeting demands. One's anger may be what one shares at one moment, while one's love may be what a person finds fit to share at another moment. Living according to one's being does not mean sharing one's intimate life with whomever one encounters. I may not want to share my intimate feelings with the person who confronts me. But I must share with him what is relevant to the topic of discussion, without trying to make an impression on him. Even if I share with a person my unwillingness to be intimate with him, I am living according to my being.

The opposite of living in accordance with one's being is living in accordance with the impression one wishes to make on one's fellow man. In this case, a person is projecting a constructed image of himself upon the Other; he himself, his being, is concealed by this image. Politicians are experts at impression making. One rarely—if at all—gets glimpses of their being. Some politicians become so engrossed in projecting an image that their being seems to rot away, leaving them hollow. Of course, one cannot forgo all impression making; being polite is a socially important manner of making an impression. As Buber indicates, what is important is the predominant attitude; and he shows that the impression-making person will slowly but surely evict himself from the realm of dialogue.

Many of the Jews and Arabs in the Education for Peace Project expressed their concern with the impression they were making by taking themselves too seriously. (This point will be broadly discussed in the chapter on Friedrich Nietzsche.) When pressed, they indicated that taking themselves seriously was a manner of asserting, and even justifying, their existence. We disagreed. We repeatedly pointed out that such an attitude hinders dialogue, blocks spontaneity and joy, and interferes with one's personal development. In short, we stressed that being straightforward, as Buber indicated, opens new realms of existence. But we encountered great difficulties. Consider the following excerpt from a personal meeting, early in the learning process, between the Jewish group leader, David, and Dana, a Jewish woman participant.

"But why, David, why should I not take myself seriously?"

"You *should* take yourself seriously, Dana, but in order to do so, you shouldn't."

"What? Now I really don't understand."

"If an element of personal irony does not accompany our taking of ourselves seriously, if we can't laugh at our lacks and failures, we get so engrossed in them that we are stuck. We refuse to develop."

"How about giving me an example, David."

"I'll make a deal with you."

"What deal?"

"I'll tell you a story, and then you give me a personal example."

"Let's try that, but I'm not promising anything."

"Well, there is Buber's story of the famous Hasidic sage who, late in life, said: 'When I was a teenager I decided to perfect the world; when I grew older I decided to perfect only the Jews of our town; later I decided that it was enough if I helped my friends change for the better. Now I am endeavoring to change myself a bit for the better, before my soul is judged by God.' "

"I sense the irony, but I don't have something comparable to tell from my life. . . . Wait, let me think. I'm beginning to sense what you mean. Once I would take every failure to heart, even here at the university when I'd get a low grade. Now I see that I was taking myself too seriously. But what does all this have to do with trusting Arabs?"

"Only this. When I take myself too seriously I can't let go; I'm always worried; and for us Jews, for me at least, I'm sick of being worried. I want to trust my Arab neighbors, but learning to trust an Arab means letting go of many worries and fears. I find it difficult to do so, probably because I take myself too seriously. Hence I often feel that even in our

Buberian Learning Groups we are blind to the possibilities beyond the abyss of mistrust. We have to let go of our fears. Only then will the blind be able to lead the blind."

"I'm glad you feel blind too, David."

Learning to relate dialogically to another person means learning to relate to what Buber calls the "dynamic center" of that person. We cannot contemplate this dynamic center, or analyze it, or observe it; we can only enter an elemental relation in the present with that person and thus relate to the dynamic center. Entering such a relation, as Buber stresses, means abandoning the analytical, reducing, or deriving look between man and man, or, in other words, abandoning what he termed as the modern approach to human relations. Modern social sciences, in their quest to explain personal and social developments, have developed the three methods of examining human relations that Buber described: analyzing, reducing, and deriving. But these methods are essentially historical—they explain the present on the basis of the past or the future. The present, which is the moment in which human freedom emerges, evaporates under their scrutinizing gaze. But one can only relate dialogically—one can only come to know the dynamic center of the person confronting one, by living in the present. Thus living in the present means living one's freedom; it means being surprised by what emerges in one's relationships. Or as Sartre once noted, being free means that I can also surprise myself.

In attempting to teach our students to live in the present, we have eaten gravel, as we say in Hebrew. Countless times, students have asked leaders to analyze a dynamic center, or to reduce living in the present to psychological terms, or to derive the arising of a dialogical relation from previous behavior. We explain that such is impossible, and that one will only learn about such experiences by opening oneself to the world and to other persons, and by trusting. They immediately ask: "How will I know that I am relating to the dynamic center?" We answer: "You *will* know. But you will not be able to formulate the knowledge at the moment of knowing. Later, when you review that moment, you will understand that it fits in with what Buber was describing. But at the moment of relating you are knowing in a different manner than through analyzing; you are knowing in a relating manner—it is the manner which is described in the Bible when it speaks of Adam knowing Eve, or Pharaoh refusing to know Moses' God. In such knowing you are wholly in the present, and no part of your being can attempt to analyze, reduce, or derive what you are living."

Our eating gravel was not only a result of the difficulties of indicating to the students where the experiences that Buber described may be found in one's daily life. It also arose from a basic tension between existentialist writing and education. As Nietzsche and Kierkegaard vehemently and at times humorously explained more than a century ago, persons have begun to believe that if they can formulate an experience, they are living it. But such is merely an engaging in intellectual masturbation, in which one gains satisfaction from the formulating of an experience and forgoes any attempt to live it. Often such formulating is accompanied by harangues of the vulgar conscience (harangues which a person can enjoy, as Kafka showed in *The Trial*), which sap the energies a person could use to realize new experiences. Thus we soon learned that, in certain situations, making a person conscious of his specific problem of trust was a hindrance to the actual developing of trust, because he played with the new ideas and formulations instead of trusting. Again, confrontation helped—but not always.

Through confronting a person and making him present to oneself, one can at times, seemingly, pull him into living the present fully, into giving himself as he is, without thoughts of his past actions or future prospects. But for such to occur, one must live the present fully while confronting the other person. In other words, confrontation is not a tactic which leads to dialogue; it is not a method which results in trust. In training leaders for Buberian Learning Groups, I stressed that one may only confront a person who is playing with his existence when one can make that person fully present to oneself. Or, to be more poetic and still accurate, the act of confrontation must flow from the leader or from any specific person as the natural response to how he sees the existential situation of his partner in dialogue.

But even such an approach does not always help. Some persons are so deeply involved in the harangues of their vulgar conscience and are so accustomed to living outside the present, that unless, perhaps, in a moment of deep personal pain, one will never help them break through into living the present. They will never be able to trust or to love; at every step of a relationship they will find new ways of harassing themselves and the persons whom they encounter. The best literary example of such a person with which I am acquainted is Nastasya Filippovna in Dostoyevski's *The Idiot*.

Buber's emphasis on confrontation and making present is where his way differs from that advocated by many humanistic psychologists and open-educators. Buber holds that making the Other present is developing an ontological relationship with him; it is not being open to, or accepting, the existential failings of the Other. In an ontological relationship, acceptance is secondary to confronting the Other as a whole being and rejecting much that is ruinous to him as a person and to us who encounter him. Thus in the encounter with Muhammed (cited in Chapter 1), I refused to accept him as he is; I refused to be open to understanding his existential mistrust of me. If I accept and try to understand that mistrust while relating to Muhammed, I am allowing it to be a legitimate component of our relationship—and that will probably never allow our relationship to get beyond the realm of understanding and to become ontological. Here Buber is true to the existentialist tradition. Neither Kierkegaard nor Nietzsche wished to develop the kind of superficial openness that, say, Carl Rogers and his colleagues have been advocating. Like Buber, Kierkegaard and Nietzsche confronted their readers and imaginary wards with the profound problems of their human existence and forcefully rejected all that they viewed as basically ruinous to personal development. They had a vision of human existence to which they directed their readers, while many humanistic psychologists and open educators have merely a method.

How does one educate a person to make himself present to the Other? Or, as our participants asked: "What should I do in order to make, say, Kassem or Dana present to me?" Here is one answer: "There are no formulas or recipes; I can only tell you what I try to do. I stop trying to think about what is happening while relating to the Other; I stop trying to sense what I am feeling. I gather all my energies into one beam of relating—somewhat analogous to a laser—and direct that beam to Kassem or Dana as they exist here, here in front of me. At times the beam will illuminate the dynamic center of Kassem or Dana."

And inevitably, the following exchange arises: "Aren't you advocating something like love?" "No. Buber would say that love dwells in the I-Thou relationship, but other relationships dwell there too. He means that I can relate dialogically to the Other without loving him or her; I can make another person present to me without getting emotionally involved. Let me add that here in this Buberian Learning Group I want to try to reach dialogue with each of you, but I will not love you all!"

The third strength that emerges in dialogue is due to a person's unfolding. (I am a bit unhappy with the English translation here—Buber means the sort of personal development in which right dispositions develop.) As Buber explained, in dialogue a person does not wish to impose one's opinions or attitudes on one's partner, but rather, recognizing in oneself a disposition that is right, the person will attempt to arouse that disposition in one's partner and encourage him to develop in that direction. Imposing one's attitudes and opinions on the Other has been broadly developed in advertising and propaganda, while helping the Other develop his right dispositions is prominent in education. The propagandist is merely interested in getting the other person to accept his views or attitudes; the educator wishes to encourage each person to develop his potentials. Buber agrees that his presentation is a bit polarized; in most human relations, imposing and unfolding intermingle. I would add that here is one of the areas where Buber's writings ran out of suggestions before my attempts to educate for peace ran out of problems.

Perhaps the most important problem ignored by Buber in his distinction between imposing and unfolding is the need to use power in the educational process. For instance, in education for peace it would be myopic to ignore the fact that although we are working for dialogue, we are also engaged in a power struggle with persons who have other, often opposing ends. Thus the work of the educator cannot be confined to unfolding what he believes are the potentials of his students. If the educator is not strong enough to survive and, at times, to win power struggles, even while he encourages the unfolding of his pupil's dispositions, his encouragement will seem hollow. In short, I often found that Buber's formulations on imposing and unfolding did not help me with the complexities of educational practice. Buber's lack struck me as particularly poignant when I faced the problem of reaching dialogue with Egyptian counterparts. Here is a broad outline of what happened.

In February 1980 I flew to Egypt with three other staff members to prepare the first trip of the entire Education for Peace Project to Egypt. We also hoped to open avenues of dialogue with Egyptians who were interested in peace. Before our trip, I already knew of two hindrances which we might encounter. First, Arabic is a language of diplomacy and evasion. Speakers in Arabic play with the richness of the language and deliberately choose words and phrases which glitter with ambiguities. This richness of linguistic associations served and encouraged the flowering of Arabic poetry for almost two millennia, but it has often blocked candid exchanges. The specific meaning of the words he is speaking flees from the speaker even while they emerge from his mouth. In *Seven Pillars of Wisdom*, T. E. Lawrence repeatedly mentioned his linguistic alienation from his Arab comrades, with whom he fought and lived for two years. (I have often wondered how such a language influences the innermost thoughts and intimate life of its speakers.)

Second, the Egyptians were proud of their civilization, which had flourished for 4,000 years before the prophet Muhammed united the Arab tribes under the banner of Allah and encouraged them to make history. This civilization was characterized by a pharaonic pyramidal society, which, some writers suggest, persists to this day. It was clear to me that in a rigid, pyramidal society dialogue was not a very common occurrence. Each person was much too concerned with his place in the pyramid to be able to relate to the Other. Buber had not discussed the problems of reaching dialogue in a difficult social or linguistic milieu. He believed in the possibility of a dialogical breakthrough even in the most adverse conditions.

But we reached no breakthrough. Egyptians were nice and polite; they seemed to have buried their hatred of Jews but emphatically refused to commit themselves to any sort of reciprocity. Even the representative from the Experiment in International Living, who arrived from the Netherlands to assist us in finding Egyptian counterparts—even he was soon battering against a wall of polite evasion. In one of our staff discussions, David suggested that I call Enis Mansour. He was once a university professor and now served as Sadat's spokesman and as editor of the influential weekly *October*. He seemed to have received some sort of backing from Sadat to meet with Israelis. I called and told him a bit about the

Education for Peace Project and about my academic interests. He invited us to visit him that evening, at the tall *October* building on the banks of the Nile. When we arrived he was cordial.

"So you are Dr. Haim Gordon, the expert on Buber and dialogue. I am Enis Mansour. And who are these young people?"

"They work with me on education for peace."

"Please sit down. Education for peace in the spirit of dialogue. Wonderful. I hope the German foundations know what they are doing with the money they give you. By the way, you know I wrote a book on existentialism. I discussed Heidegger's *Dasein,* Jaspers' *Existenz,* Nietzsche's Superman, Sartre's Nothingness. It appeared in Arabic a few years back. I don't think I mentioned Buber. But I don't remember. After you write sixty books you don't remember them all."

"Why didn't you mention Buber?"

"Well, let us say that he wasn't in fashion in Egypt. You know, especially since he was a Zionist. But tell me about your project."

I briefly explained the aims of our project in Israel and the importance of reaching dialogue between all Jews and Arabs who were living peacefully together. I explained our failures in Egypt to make any headway with educators or academics. Everybody was nice, but nobody dared to talk about gut problems or to commit himself to meeting Israeli students. We were welcome as long as we behaved like tourists, but if we wished to behave like neighbors, Egyptians became unresponsive. He listened, but it seemed as if he already had the answer ready.

"You Israelis are much too quick for us Egyptians. We Egyptians change slowly. For thirty years we hated each other; we fought five bloody wars and countless skirmishes. Fortunately, President Sadat had the courage to make peace.

Now suddenly you are coming to the Egyptian people and you want immediate friendship. You want dialogue. That is too quick for us. It is a revolution for most Egyptians to have you visit here and to buy something from them at Han El Halili."

"I agree that it is a revolution, but . . ."

"Come, let me show you something. Look out that window. We are here on the eighth floor, so we see the beauty of the Nile and the way it reflects the lights of Cairo."

"It is beautiful."

"Even from here you can see how slowly the Nile flows. So it is also with the Egyptian people. So please don't push us with your beautiful Buberian program on education for peace. Let us continue to be like the Nile which sustains us; let us continue to flow slowly."

Viewing the Nile with Enis Mansour, I felt powerless. He had led me into a dead-end street and was imposing his view of the situation on me. Little did I then sense that he was also showing me a glimmer of an opening. When we returned to Israel and described what we had encountered, quite a few participants in the Project, including staff members, started questioning the wisdom of visiting Egypt and attempting to reach dialogue with people who flowed as slowly as the Nile. Many Arabs added that, for them, going to Egypt was tacitly agreeing with Sadat's Camp David policies, which "short-changed the Palestinians." Citing Buber, they argued that I should not impose my views on them and that we should not impose ourselves on the Egyptians.

I was stubborn as a rock. Using threats, arm twisting, scholarships, and a host of other means, I demanded that each participant go to Egypt. They finally did. But it is important to stress that, on this topic, I imposed myself and my views with almost no regard for either Buber or dialogue. It is difficult for me now to fully explain why. But I would say that here I trusted my gut belief that if only people in the

Mideast would meet, dialogue would emerge. The importance of the trip to Egypt in terms of dialogue will soon be
discussed, but here my point is that, at times, the educator for
peace must be anti-Buberian in order to create situations in
which dialogue may emerge. Or, as Nietzsche held, often only
by imposing ourselves on our students can we teach them
how to live in freedom.

4. Nietzsche: The Conquest of Freedom

May your spirit and your virtue serve the meaning of the earth, my brothers: and may the value of all things be fixed anew by you. To that end you should be fighters! To that end you should be creators!
—From THUS SPOKE ZARATHUSTRA

H O W can one educate for peace on the basis of Nietzsche's philosophy? The question may be perturbing some readers who recall that the Nazis used Nietzsche's writings to justify many of their atrocities. Of course it has now been proved by many scholars, and especially Walter Kaufmann, that the Nazis blatantly distorted Nietzsche's thoughts—but still, education for peace and Nietzsche's philosophy seem to be a rather odd couple. The answer is both simple and complex. I believe that a lasting peace in the Mideast and elsewhere can only be established among people who are free—free from prejudices, from distorted values, from mediocrity, from the rule of the masses, from hatred of oneself, from fanaticism, from a distorted relation to history, from a herd morality—to mention just a few of the manners in which we are enslaved. And I know of no better example of an educator who taught how to live as an unenslaved person than Nietzsche's Zarathustra.

Two comments arise immediately, a scholarly comment which I shall skip over and an educational comment which I need address. The scholarly comment is: Even if it is true that

Nietzsche's Zarathustra educates his disciples to attain human freedom, education for peace does not seem to accord with Nietzsche's entire corpus of writings. My response is that this comment is based on a mistaken scholarly approach to Nietzsche's writings. Without elaborating the mistakes of this approach, I can say that I am not sure that Nietzsche had one specific approach to human existence, and in my educational endeavors I was not concerned about finding or realizing such an approach. I did learn from Zarathustra how to help Jews and Arabs free themselves from some of the hindrances to freedom, to trust, and to dialogue.

The educational comment is: One cannot attain all the educational goals mentioned above, especially with a large number of persons. Freeing persons from prejudices, from self-hatred, from mediocrity, from the rule of the masses, and from other enslavements is an arduous undertaking in which any educator will probably achieve limited success even with a small number of persons. *Thus Spoke Zarathustra* opens with Zarathustra and his message being rejected by the masses in the marketplace. He chooses to be a teacher of the few, but still he encounters difficulties.

My response to this comment accords with what Zarathustra did when he recognized that his message was discarded by the masses. He sought out fellow creators, fellow harvesters, who did not accept the herd morality, and he taught them to live as free, creative persons. He believed they would indicate the possibility of a different way of life to other creative persons. He recognized that such would be a slow, difficult process, he knew that his limited success often imposed a threat upon many, but he persisted in his educational endeavors, slowly picking his way among the many pitfalls that he encountered. I attempted to adopt this approach in educating Jews and Arabs to trust each other. Quite early, I realized that education for peace and dialogue is a lonely, lifelong engagement, with few successes and breakthroughs, and many failures.

Before we examine Zarathustra's educational approach, it

is important to clarify one concept which has often been grossly misinterpreted: the superman. I believe that Martin Heidegger's description of the superman is true to Zarathustra's intent:

Nietzsche does not give the name "superman" to man such as exists until now, only superdimensional. Nor does he mean a type of man who tosses humanity aside and makes sheer caprice the law, titanic rage the rule. Rather, taking the word quite literally, the superman is the individual who surpasses man as he is up to now, for the sole purpose of bringing man till now into his still unattained nature and there to secure him. . . . But where does the call of distress for the superman come from? Why does the prevailing man no longer suffice? Because Nietzsche recognizes the historical moment in which man prepares to assume dominion over the whole earth. Nietzsche is the first thinker who, in view of a world history emerging for the first time, asks the decisive question and thinks through its metaphysical implications. The question is: is man in his nature till now prepared to assume dominion over the whole earth.[3]

Thus, according to Heidegger, Nietzsche's vision of the superman suggested how man must change so as to be able to assume dominion over the earth. We now know that man has the power to destroy human life and to ruin the earth's natural environment. Often he is enslaved by this power; he does not know how to use it to enhance human existence. He has not accepted the educational challenges formulated in *Thus Spoke Zarathustra*—challenges which demand that he become a bridge to the superman by undergoing three *Verwandlungen*. (The German word *Verwandlung* can mean both metamorphosis, a change of one's being, and conversion, a change of one's beliefs.) In short, man is slowly ruining himself as a species and endangering life on earth because he is still living in a manner which does not allow him to cope with the problems that arise from the power he wields. How does Zarathustra suggest that man enhance himself? What must he do to undergo these *Verwandlungen?*

It is important to stress that the three *Verwandlungen* of the spirit are outcomes of self-education. From an educational point of view, *Thus Spoke Zarathustra* is a description of Zarathustra's attempts to encourage and educate his disciples and companions to undergo the process of self-education that will bring about these metamorphoses, these conversions. Throughout the book, he himself continues to undergo the three *Verwandlungen*.

The first *Verwandlung* is the camel—the spirit who ladens itself with burdens so that it can rejoice in its strength. Some of the burdens that Zarathustra lists when he questions the weight-bearing spirit are ". . . to desert our cause when it is celebrating its victory? To climb high mountains in order to tempt the tempter? . . . to wade into the dirty water when it is the water of truth and not disdain cold frogs and hot toads? . . . to love those who despise us and to offer our hand to the ghost when it wants to frighten us?"[4] Such burdens tear off the veil of accepted values which conceals many of the forces which motivate persons; the burdens also help a person overcome his fears, often exaggerated fears, as to the suffering he might incur by rejecting these values. What is more, in the process of such a self-burdening, a person will often discover that he has much more strength than he ever dared to imagine.

The discovery of new sources of personal strength leads to the second *Verwandlung*, the lion— the spirit who "wants to capture freedom and be lord in its own desert." However, in order to capture freedom, the lion must grapple with the great dragon whose golden scales glitter "Thou Shalt" and who proclaims "All values have already been created and all created values—are in me."[5] The lion cannot create new values but he can actively reject historically ingrained values and through the struggle create his own freedom. Hence, the second *Verwandlung* brings with it the courage to seize one's freedom, in the face of what seem to be overwhelming forces, and to live with that freedom by actively denying the validity of those forces. When one has learned to live courageously with one's freedom, one undergoes the third *Verwandlung*—

the spirit becomes a child who can relate to the world innocently and as a new beginning, who can create its own values, its own will, its own world.

Since Nietzsche's metaphorical language may obscure the educational process that he is describing, I shall briefly digress and show that in *The Apology* Socrates discloses that he underwent such *Verwandlungen*. After the oracle in Delphi proclaimed that no one was wiser than Socrates, he attempted to disprove this claim by interrogating wise men, politicians, poets, and craftsmen. To his surprise, he found that he *was* wiser than they, because he knew that he did not know, whereas they were sure that they knew, but did not know. In the process of searching for the truth, he aroused much hatred against him; he found little joy in his wisdom; his discovery was a burden. One might say that he felt as if he had climbed high mountains in order to tempt the tempter, or that he had waded into the dirty waters of truth.

Socrates' willingness to bear the burden of his wisdom endowed him with the power to question the values of his society and to free himself from their power; in Zarathustra's terms, he became a lion. While seeking for the good, the beautiful, the just, he learned to disregard affluence, status, and political power—and once he was free from the dictates of ingrained social values he could create his own values, his own will, his own world; for instance, he could innocently pursue his maxim that an unexamined life is not worth living. True to Zarathustra's description of such a process, there is an element of childish innocence and creativity in Socrates as he is depicted in *The Apology* and other early Platonic dialogues.

Socrates' example reveals that, in a person's development, the various *Verwandlungen* may mingle; he may be free and creative in a specific realm while burdening himself with new challenges where he is still unfree. It also exposes the intolerance of the milieu, which often loads additional burdens upon a person who undergoes such *Verwandlungen*. As

Zarathustra indicates, the freedom to create is not easily acquired.

In the political workshop which was held about three and a half months into the Buberian Learning Group process, we attempted to show participants how they are guided by values and habits of thought which enslave them to the complex situation of conflict in which they find themselves. The rules of the workshop were: There will be no arguments during the discussion. Arguments are allowed during the breaks. Each person will respond personally to four questions: What is your relation to Zionism? What is your relation to the Palestinian National Movement? What should the political leaders in the Mideast do in order to achieve peace? What should *I* do to contribute to the peace process? After a person responds to these questions, two other participants and the leader can ask him to clarify his responses.

Here are some excerpts from one such workshop in which I participated.

Kassem (Arab man, assistant group leader): Your turn, Miryam.
Miryam (Jewish woman): I am a Zionist, but many of the people who speak in the name of Zionism turn me off. They sound schmaltzy and uninspiring; they just keep repeating old clichés. But I *do* think that we Jews have a historical right to the land of Israel and that we should live here. I am ready to recognize the Palestinian National Movement if they recognize me, if they accept me as a neighbor. Right now it still looks like they want to kick me and my fellow Jews out of the Mideast. I don't know too much about what our political leaders should do, except reach some sort of accommodation, where we let the Palestinians set up some sort of autonomy or state and they will recognize our right to exist here. I personally should try to educate myself and my children to tolerance.
Kassem: Any questions to Miryam?

Said (Arab man): Yes, don't you think that we Palestinians also have a historical right to this land?

Miryam: Yes, but still there are sections of the country which I would refuse to give up.

Said: What do you mean by historical rights?

Miryam: Well . . . that the land belonged to my forefathers and therefore I have some right to own it too, but, really, I haven't thought about it all.

Jeremiah (Jewish man): Is being tolerant towards Arabs your only goal in education for peace? Especially in educating your children?

Miryam: Well, no. I'd like them to understand a bit about Arab culture. I'd like them to have Arab friends.

Jeremiah: Is that all?

Miryam: What else should I want?

Jeremiah: Well, you could work for a more democratic system in Israel, in which Arabs would not be second-class citizens.

Miryam: Perhaps, but I'm not sure what that means and what I'd want to do.

Kassem: Don't you think that you are evading the issues, Miryam? You are running in between the raindrops so as not to get wet.

Miryam: You may be right, but that is where I am right now.

Kassem: But there is no reason to remain where you are right now, especially if peace concerns you. People *can* change, as you no doubt know. O.K., Said, your turn now.

Said: If we observe the history of Zionism we can see that it has developed as most national movements do, since the middle of the nineteenth century, into a species of colonialism and racism. This trend is evident in Israel due to three character-istics in which Jewish colonialist and racist policies emerge, first, Jewish work, second—

Kassem: Wait a minute, Said, you are not answering directly; you are giving us a lecture, which by the way reminds me of the usual communist propaganda.

Said (annoyed): Let me continue. The second characteristic is Jewish militarism, third—

Kassem: No, Said, I won't let you continue. Either you answer the question personally and directly or you won't answer at all. This is a workshop, not a political rally.

Said: You won't tell me what to say or how to say it. I'm saying it my way.

Kassem (angrily): Said, let's not argue; either you play it by the rules of the game, or you don't play at all.

Haim: Cool down a minute, Kassem. Said, maybe you did not understand, but according to the rules of the workshop you are only allowed to explain your personal relationship to Zionism and to the Palestinian National Movement. I suggest that we take a break, drink some tea or coffee, and in the meantime you will think about how to formulate your views in personal terms. But before the break, I would like to make two observations about what has been happening here. Quite a few of the Jews have been playing Miryam's game. They have tried to emerge from the workshop as nice people, without committing themselves to any sort of meaningful change in their attitude or values. While quite a few Arabs have been responding with an eye to the other Arabs sitting here. They have not been relating as persons, as subjects.

Jeremiah: What is wrong with being nice? At times this Education for Peace Project seems to me like an attempt to be overoriginal and supercreative, so that being nice is a terrible sin. You enjoy playing the role of the guru too much, Haim.

Haim: Calm down, Jeremiah. Let me be nice to you and explain myself. For me as a Jew, being nice politically means agreeing with values which currently dominate the political and social reality which encompasses us. For instance, Menachem Begin's Zionism is based on expansionist values, exploitationist values, not spiritual values. If we want Zionism to become once again a movement which has some relationship to the Jewish spiritual heritage, we cannot be nice about its degenerating into a justification of exploitation and oppression. We Jews must fight for what we believe Zionism and Judaism are about, say, the search for justice, for a life of spirit, for an authentic and not dogmatic relationship to God.

And fighting against exploitation and oppression means not being nice to whoever does these things; it cannot be done by running through the raindrops and not getting wet. It is done by what Nietzsche's Zarathustra described as "wading into the dirty waters of truth and not being repulsed by obnoxious frogs."

And concerning the fact that each Arab is continually watching how his views are accepted by fellow Arabs, I can only reiterate that it is cowardly never to be able to leave the herd. And if we want to change the political situation of the Arabs in Israel, we need creative, original Arabs—not super-creative, Jeremiah, just creative—who are willing to disregard the morality of the herd and express themselves as persons. Perhaps you Arabs who want a Palestinian state should remember that Theodor Herzl was laughed at and derided as "King of the Jews" when he started advocating a Jewish state. He was not nice, nor was he watching how every single person responded to his proposals. But let's take a break—or I may talk too much.

We did not read *Thus Spoke Zarathustra*, or any of Nietzsche's other writings, in the Buberian Learning Group. (A few of the group leaders had read *Thus Spoke Zarathustra* and other writings by Nietzsche.) But mainly Zarathustra's approach influenced me; it influenced my relations with my students and the manner in which I constructed the educational program. Here the analogy of the thread is important. The student need not be a scholar to be able to weave the insights of various existentialists into a guiding thread. But he must take what the educator offers him and attempt to live it. The educator must be aware of the great gap between, say, Zarathustra's demands and where the student is situated. The student can only cope with this gap, he can only weave the thread, if he has the courage and the readiness to change. That was a major problem.

How can one educate a person to be courageous or to be

ready to undergo major personal changes? There is no one answer. Martin Buber indicated that genuine dialogue is often a courageous act which teaches persons to be courageous in other areas of their life. Such is true. But I believe that Zarathustra's *Verwandlungen* have greater significance. If a person cannot burden himself with personal existential challenges and rejoice in his strength, he will not develop personal courage; he will not be ready to undergo major changes. In educating for peace, I often failed to convince participants to burden themselves so as to learn to be courageous. The situation with Kassem was one example.

One morning, about four months before the Education for Peace Project commenced, government bulldozers started demolishing Arab houses in Lagia, a Bedouin town north of Beer Sheva. This act was in violation of an Israeli supreme court order halting any action against the Arabs while the suit they filed was being examined by the court. When some of the Arab students at Ben-Gurion University heard what was happening, they rushed to the scene and attempted, through peaceful demonstrations, to stop the bulldozers. Many of them were arrested. In the meantime, the supreme court issued a statement to the press that it held Menachem Begin and his government in contempt of court. The government immediately halted the demolition.

Kassem, whom I hired to train as a group leader in the Education for Peace Project, was among the students arrested for illegally demonstrating at Lagia. He sat in jail for forty-eight hours, and was released without any charges being pressed. Within a week, though, he was fired from his job as teacher of Arabic in a Jewish school. He was not told the reason for his being fired, but after a couple of months of seeking work, he was approached by an Israeli plainclothes security officer and told that he had two paths open to him. Either he become an informer for officers of the Israeli security, and they would allow him to go back to teaching, or they would do everything in their power to trail him and to

someday get him convicted. They would also try and block
his being accepted for any job to which he applied. It should
be remembered that Kassem is an Israeli citizen.

Kassem refused to have anything to do with the security
officers. True to their promise, when I sent in a request to
have the university hire Kassem, an administrator of the
university called me, told me that Kassem was not liked by
Israeli security, and suggested that I hire someone else. I
refused, citing my academic freedom to work with whomever
I saw fit.

To get back to education for courage and the burdening of
oneself, here is a conversation that occurred eight months
after the Project commenced.

"Haim, do you have a few moments?"

"Sure, Kassem, sit down. We can talk quietly here in this
part of the library."

"I have a problem."

"I'm listening."

"Ever since I was jailed, I get the feeling that Jews and
perhaps some Arabs are watching everything I do in order to
report it to the authorities. Even when I go downtown and
mingle with the crowds I can't get rid of the feeling."

"So?"

"It makes it difficult for me to trust anyone, and since I'm a
member of the staff, who is supposed to be educating for
trust, I thought you should know."

"Let's assume, Kassem, that your suspicions are true, and
that you are being watched, and someone is reporting on
you. By internalizing this fear you are helping the Israeli
security, who wish to spread mistrust in order to be able to
rule the Arabs successfully. You know I despise this method,
but right now I am powerless to change it. On the other
hand, if you take your being watched as a burden which you
must bear, and decide that you will trust Jews despite that
suspicion, you will be fighting the security with a weapon for

which it has no answer. You also will be teaching yourself to be courageous."

"But it's difficult, Haim, very difficult. My thoughts start mistrusting before I think of what I'm doing."

Five months after this conversation, Kassem resigned from the staff of the Education for Peace Project. He explained that he did not believe that I, or anyone, could educate for dialogue and peace in Israel if we refused to become politically involved in changing the situation of Arabs in Israel. I told him that his explanation was hogwash.

In the five discourses following the presentation of the *Verwandlungen*, Zarathustra attacks the teachers of herd values. He derides the occupiers of the chairs of virtue and the preachers of the afterworld; he ridicules the despisers of the body; he mocks those who define virtues and looks with disdain upon the judges of the pale criminal. In the next discourse, "Of Reading and Writing," Zarathustra mitigates the atmosphere which could hardly prompt his disciples to seek a new direction for personal development. He explains his style and some of his most basic beliefs. His aphorisms are peaks from which one can view human existence; they also help him prevail over his main enemy, the *Geist der Schwere*, the spirit of gravity and ponderousness. A person dominated by the *Geist der Schwere* takes himself too seriously; he accepts himself as a finished product and will rarely endeavor to change his way of life. He will gravely ponder any proposal to alter his existence instead of testing the proposal by attempting to live by it. Zarathustra's aphorisms and apothegms are concise, and often wry expressions which do not let the reader (or listener) take himself too seriously. Each aphorism touches on an aspect of life and leads to another aphorism, much as the dancer's toes nimbly flutter over the floor. Zarathustra, who views himself as a dancer, writes aphorisms to gracefully express his spontaneous response to life. He wishes that his disciples relate to the entire dance and not to a specific step, or apothegm; and he hopes that, by learning to read his aphorisms, his pupils will joyfully join him in rejecting the *Geist der Schwere.*

Zarathustra recognizes that one cannot burden a person with the camel's burdens without showing him that he must also rebel against the herd values which, until now, have guided him. Derision is a wonderful way of rebelling against the preachers of those values. But after the rebellion one must encourage the pupil to live like a dancer. The dancer is enjoying his spontaneous, harmonious, joyful response to the melody; he is also expressing himself creatively. Such harmonious delight, spontaneous joy, and immersing oneself in creativity can counter the horror one often faces when striving to become free. As Zarathustra clearly articulates, becoming free means both facing the horror of pursuing one's calling and celebrating one's ability to face this horror.

Zarathustra's personal concern and love for his pupils help them face the horror of their calling. As in the case of other great teachers—the Hebrew prophets, Jesus, Buddha— Zarathustra's concern also prompts his pupils to respond to the challenge of his vision. This concern is epitomized in the discourse "Of the Tree on the Mountainside." While attempting to ascend to the heights indicated by Zarathustra, a young man discovered repugnant, resistant, and degrading elements in his will, in his being. He complains: "My contempt and my desire increase together: the higher I climb, the more do I despise him who climbs. What do I want in the heights?"[6] Zarathustra affirms the young man, that is, he accepts his entire being and shows him his mistakes. Envy of Zarathustra drew the young man to the heights and not a quest for nobility, and envy leads to the rejection of one's better self and a seeking for self-destruction. To strengthen his disciple, Zarathustra gives of himself; he comradely embraces him when he is weeping and draws him along with him; he guides him by his words, his love, his hope. He is showing the young man that willing alone will not deliver a person from the spirit of revenge; a person must also rely on his love and his hope, and on his ability to create new things, new virtues, and a purer life for himself. Through dialogue, Zarathustra helps the young man purify himself—he helps him identify his mistakes and his sordid passions and learn to draw sustenance from them and, at times, inspiration for acts of creativity. He also points out the pitfalls the young man may yet encounter in his quest for a noble and creative existence.

Many pupils tend toward a superficial interpretation of their teacher's vision. Zarathustra's main success in breaking through his disciples' protective shell of superficiality and complacency stems from his ability to unmask the bearers of traditional values and to describe the deplorable and often disgusting motives which underlie their teachings.

Being exposed to the unmasking of traditional values will not necessarily lead the pupil to seek profundity; he may derive a cynical pleasure from exposing the hidden motives of whomever he meets. Zarathustra counters the possibility that his pupils will not benefit from his unmasking by adjoining to his unmasking discourses other discourses, which instruct them how to live in view of what has been revealed. Profundity for Zarathustra is a way of life, and not only an ability to think. Zarathustra educates for profundity by leading his pupils through a dialectical process of development, whereby the unmasking of bearers of traditional values opens the pupil to the possibility of adopting a new mode of existence; and when he is able, albeit partially, to adopt this new mode of existence, he can unmask other bearers of traditional values. The steps in the dialectical process lead to the *Verwandlungen*, to freedom and creativity.

It is extremely difficult to educate students, especially in a conflict situation, to undergo the dialectical process indicated by Zarathustra. But our group leaders clearly and forcefully attempted to lead the students in that direction. Here is one such example, which shows how works by Buber and Sartre are used in conjunction with Zarathustra's dialectical approach.

I have already mentioned that at the beginning of the second semester, Buber's essay "Guilt and Guilt Feelings" is read. The first meeting is usually dedicated to explaining the difference between guilt and guilt feelings; a person can be guilty without experiencing guilt feelings—Eichmann in his trial in Jerusalem is a well-published example—and conversely, a person can experience guilt feelings without being guilty—psychoanalytical literature abounds in examples of this phenomenon. At the next meeting the students are taught to relate to their guilt.

According to Buber, the act of illuminating one's guilt is the first step in a three-step process of coping with guilt. The second step is the continual accepting of oneself as the person who incurred a specific guilt, even if time has passed since one became guilty. In the third step, the guilty person must endeavor, in his new historical situation, to compensate for the evil he has done by trying to do good—by trying to heal the wounds of the order of being that he unjured—as Buber would have put it.

In her group, Smadar (the Jewish group leader) explained that a person can incur guilt by refusing to see the development of certain historical processes or, when seeing such a development, by refusing to take a stance. A superficial approach to one's heritage is an instance in which many persons incur guilt. Smadar continued: "If we are true with ourselves we will admit that we are living with superficial approaches to both the Jewish and the Arab heritages. We accept the fact that one's relation to one's heritage is expressed in fanatical outbursts, or in uncritical adherence to some unexplainable tenets, or in a schmaltzy feeling. Such an approach does not have an impact on a person's basic relations with other persons or with God." She then requested that each participant note areas of specific guilt in relation to this process. Here are some excerpts.

Dina (Jewish woman): I get what you're saying about our relation to our heritage, but I really don't feel guilty if I have a sort of schmaltzy feeling towards Jewish songs or holidays. You seem to be destroying something positive in me without offering an alternative.

Smadar: An alternative? Yes, you are right; I did not make it clear. The alternative is to make your relation to your heritage a component of your daily life. For instance, you are a teacher, Dina. In your encounters with your pupils your relation to Judaism must be expressed. Not necessarily by outward admonitions or speeches; it must be expressed in your daily acts, in the way you refer to that heritage, mention it, learn from it, live it.

Dina: But I don't know what my relation to Judaism is.

Smadar: Then your coping with establishing a relation should be expressed in your daily encounters.

Dina: That sounds a bit abstract. I'll think about it. But wait, I have another question. What does all this have to do with education for peace and the developing of trust? We seem to have strayed a long way from our goal.

Sausan (Arab woman): I think Dina is right. I don't know where all this is leading us in relation to education for peace. My heritage is not very open towards women and does not attract me in my search for freedom of expression. At times I want to forget about my relation to my heritage. But even if I remember my relation to Islam and cope with it, how will I come closer to reaching peaceful relations with Jews, to developing trust? Where does all this lead?

Smadar: I am not sure that I can make the relationship clear, but let me try. We all know that Jews have incurred guilt towards Arabs, and Arabs towards Jews. We are all guilty. In order to cope with such guilt a person must know where he stands; he must be anchored in a milieu or in his heritage. Most of us here are not anchored in the rigid way of life of Orthodox Judaism or Islam. We are also very uncomfortable in the superficiality of the surrounding milieu which views the Jewish-Arab situation merely in terms of power politics and ignores any profound relationship to one's heritage. So, I believe that we must build a personal spiritual relation to our own heritage and on the basis of that relation cope with the wrong relation between Jews and Arabs. . . . I see by your faces that what I am saying seems abstract . . . let me think a moment . . . well, all I can add is that our situation reminds me of the fantasy Sartre had, which he describes in his autobiography *The Words*. In the fantasy, the teenage Sartre has stolen onto a train to Dijon, without a ticket and broke. The conductor catches him and wants to put him off at the next station. Sartre tries to explain to the conductor that he must reach Dijon; all of France and the entire world rely on his fulfilling his mission in Dijon. Otherwise something terrible will happen. He entreats and explains but the conductor stands firm. As expected, Sartre wakes up without knowing the outcome of his endeavors. My view is that we all lack that ticket to stay on the train leading to our Dijon. And we can only get the ticket—not by explaining our importance—but by relating to our heritage. And without that ticket I am not sure that we will be able to develop the relation of active devotion to the world and to other persons that Buber mentions. Like Sartre, we will be too busy explaining ourselves to have the time or energy to relate to each other.

It would be all too easy for me to suggest that the Education for Peace Project succeeded in educating Jews and Arabs to relate joyfully to each other. Partially, we succeeded. We held the weekend seminars which were part of the program at hotels which had a discotheque, and after the daily program Jews and Arabs danced together. We encouraged humorous exchanges during meetings. We stressed that the erasing of mistrust can bring joy, which it often did. But as I review our endeavors now, it seems that we often failed. The power of the *Geist der Schwere*, the spirit of pondering and heaviness, weighed heavily on many of our doings. We often lacked the perspective to counter this spirit.

Our lack of perspective was best driven home by John Post of Vanderbilt University, the chairman of our International

Evaluating Committee. Upon summarizing his second visit to the Project, John pointed out:

I have spent the past two years engaged in writing a book. The focus of my daily endeavors was that book. My life seemed to accompany the development of the writing. Here in Beer Sheva I encountered the opposite of my way of living during these two years. Here it is your life that is your major concern. Changing yourself while changing the hostile environment is what counts. This is a difficult task, but it is also a way of living fully. You all should be grateful for the opportunity given you to live thus. But I'm not sure that I always sense the joy which should accompany such significant personal development. You all seem to be living next door to your personal development. Only when you move in with yourself, with your personal changes, will you be able to fully express the joy of your accomplishments.

A FIRST WORKSHOP

A living room in Rina's (Jewish woman) family apartment. Modern paintings hang on the wall. A small electric stove is in one corner; a large lamp sheds light in another; soft light comes from above. In the background is a small bookcase with quite a few books. Ten students are sprawled on armchairs, on the sofa, and on the rug, drinking coffee and tea. Some are talking, others sit quietly. David, the Jewish group leader, is sitting in an armchair; he looks at his watch; it is close to 11:00 P.M. He puts down his cup of tea and says loudly: "O.K. The break is over. Let's get back to the workshop." Two students come back from an adjoining room. The other students sit up.

David: Before we begin I have one general criticism. Two hours before the workshop started each of you drew a name of a person sitting here from my hat; you were told to prepare a personal story to tell that person during the workshop; you were also told to prepare a personal question for that specific person. Both the story and the question were supposed to *help* that person, and I am emphasizing the word help. In other words, during the two hours until the workshop started you were supposed to envision the person whose name you drew and to think of giving him or her something of yourself, because both telling a story and asking a question can be an act of giving. This act of giving did not emerge much in the first hour and a half of our workshop.

Hussein (Arab man): I don't understand how asking a question can be an act of giving.

David: If the question relates to the being of the person whom you are addressing and helps that person illuminate some aspects of his or her life, it can be very helpful. Some of my questions during the first part of the workshop were such acts of giving. The same is true of Sahib's question to Ronit. But let's stop talking method and get on with the work.

Tarek, I think it's your turn. Whom did you pick out of my hat?

Tarek (Arab man): Rina.

David: Go ahead.

Tarek: I come from a very poor family. My father has no land and has been working for years as a hired man in a citrus grove. We are many children in the family; I am not the oldest; but my father decided years ago that I would go to the university.

David: Why do you keep looking at me? You are telling the story to Rina. Turn to her.

Tarek (turns to Rina): I never understood that decision, but I complied; he sent me to a Jewish high school in Hadera while my other brothers were sent to pick oranges or to apprentice themselves to a tradesman. In Hadera I at first didn't understand a word of what the teacher was saying; but I stuck it through. At a certain point I started studying because it interested me, but somewhere in the back of my head my father is still pushing me. Now, when I have fulfilled his dream and am studying at the university, I often feel uncomfortable coming home to all that poverty.

Rina: Why did you tell me all this?

Tarek: I thought it might help you understand me, or know me.

Rina: I'm not sure you've succeeded; you told me your history and not a story. Besides your saying that you feel uncomfortable at home, the story fits many Arabs. Where are you in all this?

Tarek: It's my history.

David: I think I know where you are in that story, Tarek.

Tarek: Where?

David: You feel uncomfortable here in this nice affluent house that belongs to Rina and her family; you wanted her to know where you came from and why you feel uncomfortable.

Tarek: There is some truth in what you said.

David: Furthermore, you seemed to be apologizing in advance for being what you are, in order that we should accept you as such. You know that you are bright in academic fields; but you probably have problems elsewhere, so you used an interesting tactic: you apologized for the area in which you are good, so as to lead us to relate to your strength and not to your weakness. Well, my dear Tarek, the tactic didn't work. Tell us a good story.

Tarek: I don't have one right now.

David: Then ask Rina a question.

Tarek (looking in Rina's direction but not at her): Rina, you have three children. What are you going to teach them about Arabs?

Rina: I don't know. I'll tell them what I know and feel, and try to help them evade prejudices. But, damn it, what sort of a silly question is this?

Hussein: It is a silly question, Tarek.

Tarek: Why?

Hussein: Because it has nothing to do with Rina, with this specific Rina sitting here in front of you, with her life as a unique person. You could ask that same question to every Jewish mother of three kids in Israel and get a similar dull answer.

David: Hussein is right, Tarek. Your entire presentation, both the story and the question, has been in what Sartre calls bad faith: you have been acting the Arab student instead of relating as Tarek to Rina. Rina, whom did you pick?

Rina: I picked Fatma. (Arab woman)

David: Go ahead.

Rina (turning to Fatma): Three years ago, on a summer day, I took my three kids to the beach. It was rather windy and the red flag was up, so there were not too many bathers. I am a good swimmer and have passed three life-saver courses, so I was not worried. I lay on the beach, told my kids to play in the shallows, and read a magazine. Suddenly, my eyes went out to the waves, and I thought I saw somebody drowning. I stood up and perceived a woman, about two hundred yards out there, having problems getting back to shore. I yelled to the lifeguard, but there was nobody on the tower. He must have gone to the bathroom or to get a drink. So I turned to my kids, told them not to dare follow me, and jumped into the waves. As I came up for air I heard one of my kids crying.

I screamed back: "Don't you dare follow me," and went on swimming. Now let me tell you the reason I told you this story.

Hussein: Wait a minute. Don't leave us in suspense. Did the woman drown? What happened to your kids?

Rina: Nothing melodramatic. Suddenly a lifeguard on a kayak emerged out of nowhere and headed to the woman. He pulled her onto the kayak. I turned back and found my kids standing on the beach and crying. I comforted them with ice cream.

Fatma: Why did you tell me this story?

Rina: Because as an Arab woman who has come to the university to study, I think you have the problem I had when I decided to jump into the waves. On the one hand, you know that you must study and in the process change your ways of thinking and acting; on the other hand, you are afraid of abandoning what you left behind. This problem is expressed in some of your responses in this group. You seem to know very well what needs to be done to relate dialogically to Jews, but you keep looking over your shoulder to see what you left behind. I can only tell you, jump into the waves.

Fatma: You are right. I'm working on it. But it's hard.

But there is a danger in such a telling of stories. Sartre pointed out this danger in his first novel, *Nausea*. Every story is a rupture in the flow of events and decisions which preceded and follow the event described. Thus Rina's story is intelligible in terms of her background—the life-saving courses she took in high school, her educating her children to take care of themselves, and her love of the sea—especially the waves.

Fatma, in contrast, bought her first bathing suit when she came to the university; every act of independence on her part meets with criticism from her family and from the conservative Arab students whose eyes constantly follow her. Sartre would say, these eyes, this staring look, continually cause a hemorrhage in Fatma's freedom. Thus Rina's story is meaningful for Fatma; but it also describes an impossibility of her possibilities. The impossibility can only become a possibility slowly, on the basis of minor changes in the everyday, or perhaps, by leaping into a new mode of existence.

But that is the secret of dialogue, which I believe Sartre overlooked. Dialogue is often a breakthrough in which one person's seemingly natural history meets and merges with another person's impossibility. It somewhat resembles what occurs at Khartoum in mid-Sudan: the forceful Blue Nile, rich from the rains on the Ethiopian plateau, rushes into the placid White Nile and feeds it with six-sevenths of their mutual volume of water; from that point on they slowly flow together.

Two hours later; same workshop.

David: Jeremiah, I believe you are last. Whom did you pick out of the hat?

Jeremiah (Jewish man): Muhammed.

David: Oh, yeah; he's the last one left. Go ahead.

Jeremiah: I really don't know too much about Muhammed.

David: Please, without introductions; it's late. Just tell your story.

Jeremiah (looking at Muhammed): My story is very short. Three days ago a person who was my friend came to borrow a book and I refused to give it to him. My reason was that on previous occasions he had not returned my book on time. He left in anger. The reason I'm telling you this, Muhammed, is that I felt that I was partially overcoming the problem of making a favorable impression, which I believe is also your problem. And my question is: Is making an impression your problem, and if so, what are you doing about it?

Muhammed (Arab man): It is one of my problems. But I learned nothing about dealing with it from your story or question. I really have no response.

David: Jeremiah, there is something a bit too short and sweet about that story.

Dana (Jewish woman): I agree; you sort of skimmed over your own feelings and responses.

Jeremiah: Well, we were told here that our feelings were not of interest, that doing is what counts.

Hussein: Jeremiah, you seem to be always getting the wrong message. Your feelings are important, but we don't want you to indulge in them.

David: Jeremiah, you remind me of Buber's story about a novice who once came to a famous rabbi and said: "Rabbi, what should I do? The evil urge is running after me." The rabbi looked him over and then answered: "My dear young fellow, you have not yet reached the stage where the evil urge runs after you. At present, you are still running after it."

Jeremiah (his voice quavering): Whatever I do you all tell me that I'm barking up the wrong tree. I'm sick of this workshop and of education for peace.

David: Easy, easy. You may be sick of us, but we are not sick of you. We still want you and like you. Let's go back to your story. What you wanted to say was important, but you skipped the act of giving yourself through the story. That is the reason we responded a bit vehemently. When you tell of yourself and give only the results, without the problem involved in reaching that result, you miss out in the act of giving. Basically because you are giving of yourself as a finished product and not as a process; in other words, you first alienate yourself from your life, which is a process, and then give us that alienated object, that being of alienation. But we want you, the live process, and not the alienated being which did something. Try and give us a bit of the problematics of your story.

Jeremiah (looking at the floor): It's hard for me right now, David, but I think I know what you mean.

5. Kafka:
The Rationalizing Self

Blessed is he who may do a deed! The deed is like a bed of balsam to rest the soul which is a wound, a blight, an ulcer, and a flame!
— HUGO VON HOFFMANNSTHAL

J O S E P H K., the hero of Kafka's *The Trial*, makes two fatal mistakes. First, he accepts the acts of the bureaucracy which arrests him and charges him with being guilty as legitimate— even though there are no outward expressions of these charges until the night of his execution. Second, he refuses to recognize his existential guilt. Buber dealt broadly with the second mistake in his essay "Guilt and Guilt Feelings." He suggested that if Joseph K. had accepted his existential guilt the doors of the hall of justice would have opened before him and he would have been able to cope with his guilt and to change his mode of existence. He explained that this point was brought out in Joseph K.'s meeting with the priest at the end of the book. Buber totally ignored the first fatal mistake made by Joseph K., a mistake which repeatedly emerged in our attempts to educate for peace.

One would have expected Buber to see how powerful the bureaucracy in many contemporary societies has become and that we must repeatedly question the legitimacy of its actions. The Nazis, relying on their bureaucratic efficiency, succeeded in killing six million of his Jewish brethren, many of whom diligently fulfilled the insidious commands of minor bureaucrats. Stalin recognized that bureaucracies have learned to "justify" themselves and any atrocities which they perform. The Gulag, with its millions of dead and many more ruined lives, is a macabre monument to how bureaucrats relentlessly fulfilled his evil intentions. Buber's discussion of dialogue and guilt, and in general his writings on society, do not suggest how one can cope with bureaucracies which help propagate injustice, hatred, and distrust.

Joseph K. is fascinated with the bureaucratic establishment that is organizing his trial. He is intrigued by its irrational rationality, by the method of its madness. (It is interesting that Alexander Solzhenitsyn, who was charged and convicted by Stalin's henchmen, spent years studying the workings of the Gulag. But unlike Joseph K., he wished to unmask this Golem and its Satanic creator. The result: his three-volume *The Gulag Archipelago.*) Instead of dealing with the exigencies of his existence, Joseph K. examines the bureaucracy's reliability, argues with its representatives about their vocation, learns in great detail that its manner of functioning is incomprehensible, discovers its corruption, and gossips about various cases. He does not dare reject the legitimacy of the bureaucracy, even though (and perhaps because) it is dealing with his life. Kafka shows that Joseph K.'s response strengthens the bureaucracy as a viable determinant of his existence. He also hints that there are only two ways of limiting a powerful bureaucracy's hold on one's life: the first is to forcefully question its legitimacy; the second is to learn methods of deceit by which one learns to bypass its determinations.

As Kafka indicates, the outward rationality of a bureaucracy appeals to us, especially since we sense that behind this rationality lurk deep, irrational drives which we often dare not comprehend. If a bureaucracy were merely rational it would bore us—but the blending of rationality and irrationality lures us into the net of a specific bureaucracy, as Joseph K. was lured into the intricate web of the court administration, whereby one begins to accept its goals and methods as legitimate in determining one's reality. Living within the bureaucratic net, a person makes no ethical choices; everything for him is merely a matter of paper work, of learning how best to facilitate a seemingly complex process. He does not care much about the outcome of this process; he merely wants it to move forward with the least annoyance.

Action research, such as the Education for Peace Project, defies any bureaucratic net. It is not the typical research whose budget, variables, and hypotheses can be planned ahead in great detail. The research must respond to, and change in accordance with its development. (Thus in our Project we soon learned that dialogue was not enough and we must suggest where to go after dialogue has been achieved.) Put otherwise, the minute a person who is engaged in action research, say in education, is more concerned with his research model or with pleasing the bureaucracy handling his grant, than with being sensitive to the process he is studying, he has greatly diminished his force as educator and researcher. In action research the researcher must live within the process even while studying it—his approach is more akin to the anthropological model than to the statistical model of the social sciences. But unlike the anthropologist, he is not studying a specific culture but rather a process which he initiated, must direct, and often change.

In our case, we were educating Jews and Arabs to relate dialogically to each other within a milieu of conflict that was supported by a powerful bureaucracy, which feared the moral development for which we were working. The manner in which these bureaucrats responded to my endeavors was not by confronting the moral issues but rather by bringing up administrative difficulties. When I questioned the legitimacy of administrative dictates, I was told that *I* was making difficulties and, even worse, making enemies of people who were favorably disposed toward peace.—And in general, always fighting for one's principles was not prudent—I should take it easy, take more advice, and believe less in Buber's philosophy; I should stop making a fetish of my originality and of Buber's dialogue; after all this was real life here.—Of course, professing Buberian dialogue between Jews and Arabs was a nice way to get money out of those Germans, but in the real world, I should already know, that dialogue just doesn't work. It soon became evident that, for the Education for Peace Project to survive as an attempt to realize Buber's philosophy, I had to employ means which were antidialogical. I had to become a political animal, with all the deviousness and deceit that such an existence entails. That was dangerous. If I became too much of a politician I would not be able to educate for dialogue. As Buber noted, trying to live dialogically means traversing a narrow ridge. Consider the following telephone conversation which occurred about a month after the Project began.

"Hello."

"Haim, this is Meir."

"Good morning; how are things at the administrative end of the university?"

"Fine. Listen, I understand that you want to hire another Arab for your staff, and in general, you want to have an equal number of Jews and Arabs participating in the Project."

"True."

"Well, someone here expressed the thought that Arabs should be represented in the Project in accordance with their percentage in the student body, you know, about eight percent."

"Whose stupid idea is that? We want to reach dialogue which means working in Jewish-Arab dyads."

"You know, Haim, I'm just passing on information. So don't ask names. I can say that it was brought up by two of your professional colleagues, from the academic side of the fence. They asked why the Arabs should benefit percentage-wise in such large numbers from the subsidized trip to Egypt. Even though the money comes from Hans Seidel

Foundation in Germany it is university money now, and they are not sure that 50 percent of the beneficiaries should be Arabs."

"I don't even want to respond. The question stinks of prejudice."

"Look out, Haim. Remember, you still do not have tenure. You may be pissing into the wind."

Kafka vividly showed that, through his ability to rationalize, contemporary man has found ways of justifying his distorted existence and the most terrible social developments. What is more, these rationalizations are traps, which do not allow a person to relate fully to the reality which he encounters. Of course Nietzsche and Dostoyevski warned of this development before Kafka was born; but the lengthy, insipid harangues in Kafka's stories and books showed the devastating powers of the rationalizing self which blocks spontaneity, love, dialogue, and the ability to grow through *Verwandlungen*. Thus if Nietzsche, Berdyaev, Buber, and Marcel showed what can occur to a person who has transcended his rationalizing self through dialogue, creativity, love, or personal growth, Kafka showed what happens to those persons who remain stuck within their rationalizations. Kafka described the illness, the other existentialists described the cure.

Why do persons rationalize? Kafka showed that both Nietzsche and Dostoyevski gave valid answers. A person's rationalizations, Nietzsche stressed, give him the feeling of power over at least one realm, his mind. When a person feels that he cannot cope with other adverse environments or, like Joseph K., he is afraid to ask himself what a specific environment is showing him about his life, he will begin to rationalize his weakness away, or try to show that his weakness is really a strength, through some feat of rational trickery. In such a situation, as Dostoyevski showed, one's rationalizations may begin to justify criminal actions—for instance, Raskolnikov in *Crime and Punishment*. Thus, when in a climate of conflict such as exists in Israel, one attempts to educate persons for dialogue and responsibility for peace, one must teach persons to go beyond the rationalizing self. Such is not simple. Much as an experienced piano player's fingers lead themselves over the piano keys, our mind leads itself through rationalizations which allow us to continue to justify our deeds.

In his parables, Kafka gave some very good hints as to how one can be less rationalizing. If a person tries to relate his life to such a parable, in addition to learning from it, he may be able to view his life in its entirety, as a process which transcends rationalizations. Of course, like Joseph K., a person can attempt to rationalize the parable away. Here nothing helps except, perhaps, telling the person that he is missing out on something essential to his life which might open a door to a new mode of existence.

In our second workshop we used two of Kafka's parables to help students transcend their rationalizing self. The students read Kafka's story "The Great Wall of China" and each one was asked, during the workshop, to explain how two parables which appear in the story express one's own life. Here is the first parable:

Consider rather the river in spring. It rises until it grows mightier and nourishes more richly the soil on long stretches of its banks, still maintaining its own course until it reaches the sea, where it is all the more welcome because it is a worthier ally. Thus far may you urge your meditations on the decrees of the high command. But after the river overflows its banks, loses outline and shape, slows down the speed of its current, tries to ignore its destiny by forming little seas in the interior of the land, damages the fields, and yet cannot maintain itself for long in its new expanse, but must run back between its banks again, must even dry up wretchedly in the hot season that follows. Thus far you may not urge your meditations on the decrees of the high command.[7]

The second parable describes a messenger who has been sent by the Emperor to you, a humble subject. On his deathbed, he has sent you a special personal message, and has whispered it into the ear of the messenger. But when the messenger turns from the Emperor's deathbed and tries to reach you, he is unable to traverse the vast distance and the many obstacles which he encounters. First he must go through the chambers of the innermost palace; then, if he ever gets through them, he must attempt to get through the chambers of the outer palace, which are filled with persons; then the packed courtyards; then the big capital, which can hardly be traversed in a lifetime. He will never be able to reach your door and to hammer on it in order to deliver the message. But you, the humble subject, sit at your window and fantasize about the possibility of his appearing.

During the workshop we focus on each participant for about thirty minutes. Here is an excerpt from one such workshop which I led.

Dana (Jewish woman): I seem to be both happy and unhappy about both parables. On the one hand, they seem to justify my complacency, my merely comprehending the rotten situation between Jews and Arabs in Israel; why struggle to bring about change if the messenger will never reach you? Why try to overflow your banks if whenever you overflow your sources will merely dry up? But these parables are so good at justifying what I am doing that they make me a bit suspicious. Should I explain my suspicions?

Haim: Go ahead.

Dana: Maybe there is something very important about life that I am losing by being complacent; maybe by flowing in accordance with my destiny I am just like the person who sits by the window and fantasizes while life passes me by; even though I am married and have two sons that thought slowly began to perturb me. Perhaps I am saying that I will always find justifications in my mind so as not to change my path, but I may be losing out on the real show of what life is all about. Haim, do you understand what I mean?

Haim: Yeah. Without being too poetical I would say that you are at the stage where you are viewing your life as a melodrama and suddenly sense that there is also a tragic sense to human existence.

Dana: Now I don't understand you.

Haim: There is something tragic in being a messenger. You try to bring an important message to persons and you may never reach them. Often, I wonder at night, even after a good workshop, have I reached these people with Buber's message or am I merely in one of the innumerable chambers of the innermost palace, and the real person I am trying to reach is sitting far away, fantasizing that I will reach him. I could also say the same about the river parable—is my overflowing and seeking out a new direction, against the decrees of the high command, is that overflowing not really an exercise in futility, where my sources of nourishment will soon dry up in the hot sun? Then I understand that the struggle is no less important at this stage than the actual reaching. Perhaps because the struggle for something better is what makes human existence more noble. Don't misunderstand me, though, I do want to reach you, I don't want to dry up, but I must be less concerned with actual results and more concerned with the process, with the struggle. Now you, Dana, sense there is that struggle out there and feel that perhaps you should try to overflow, perhaps that will give a new meaning to your life which has become rather mediocre. Have I explained myself?

Dana: Yes, but what should I do?

Haim: Let go, especially of your thinking. Just do what needs to be done and don't worry about the results. It is just like trust. At a certain moment in this Project you have to begin to trust your leader and Arabs who are participating here with you and not think about trust anymore. But let's stop here. Dany, you're next.

Dany (Jewish man): The only one I can relate to in both parables is the messenger who keeps trying to bring the message but is stuck in the middle of the way.

Haim: Why? Why can't you relate to other aspects of the parables?

Dany: Because I can't find anything that appeals to me in them. You seem to be trying to push me into a way of looking at my life that accords with your philosophy.

Haim: I don't think you are right, but . . .

Dany (interrupting): Let me finish. I think that one of the short-comings of this entire workshop is that everyone here agrees with you about the parables, but later they say that it is all bullshit. And besides . . .

Haim (raising his voice): Shut up a minute, Dany. Look, we are not discussing the workshop or the course. Do you want to explain why you feel you are the messenger and why you cannot relate to other aspects of the parables? Yes or no?

Dany: Not now, after you shut me up.

Haim: O.K. then; let us go on to someone else. Fatma, your turn.

Fatma (Arab woman): I want to say something. Dany, I don't agree with all your generalizations. I, for one, have often been angry at what occurred in this Project, or in a specific meeting, but I never said it was bullshit. Really, it's about time you learned to speak for yourself and about yourself. Now to me. I am not quite sure how the parable about the river relates to my own life. Perhaps through the fact that I always attempt to flow slowly and evenly.

Haim: What do you mean by that?

Fatma: Just what I said. That I try to keep my life even and unsurging. I don't want it to expand beyond its accepted borders.

Haim: Give us an example.

Fatma: Well . . . like my studies. I always choose the courses which do not demand too much of me.

Haim: Your example is superficial—and besides, why did you choose this course? I don't think we've been flowing easily here.

Fatma (smiling): If you know everything, why don't you tell me about myself and the parable?

Haim: You are again evading responsibility. Why don't you at least try to understand how your life is flowing? I accept your assertion that you do not extend beyond fixed borders; but I would have mentioned the fact that as an Arab woman you begrudgingly accept your degraded second-class status in Arab society. Here and there you try to acquire some freedom which does not fit in with the decrees of the high command, but in general you accept your destiny. I suspect that you fear any overflowing in this direction, perhaps because you fear being misjudged and alone, perhaps because you fear your passions.

Fatma: You may be right, but what confuses me about this entire exercise is that you give an analysis but do not suggest a solution. You leave me aground with some new insight about myself but no way to change my existential situation as you call it.

Haim: I agree that I don't give solutions. But I believe that many of the solutions are there if we are willing to undergo the difficult process of self-education, and if we are willing to suffer the pain involved in changing the encompassing milieu. You see, Fatma, you are now acting like the person in the second parable who is sitting by the window and waiting for the messenger from the Emperor to arrive. Well, as Kafka suggests, he will never arrive, and waiting for him is just a fantasy. And in general, our impotence to change our life exists because we allow it to exist. You fear you have much to lose by challenging your position as an Arab-woman, so you stay put.

Fatma (quietly): You know why I remained in this course even though it doesn't flow easily. Because I learned that when I hate what you are saying, I feel that you really love me, and that I have what to learn from you.

Haim: Thanks, Fatma. I do love you now . . . Let's all take a break.

In Kafka's writings, the sexual relations of the hero are often a manner of relief from the distorted situation in which he finds himself. Trapped by a bureaucracy which dictates and determines one's mode of existence, Joseph K. in *The Trial* and K. in *The Castle* develop sexual intimacies at the spur of the moment and cling to these relations as if they were a last possibility of expressing themselves as individual human beings. Their promiscuity seems to be sanctioned and perhaps even encouraged by those who spread the bureaucratic net which traps them. But as Kafka shows, this expression of desires is an illusion of freedom which demotes intimacies to relationships of lust, not expressions of freedom. Sexual intercourse can contribute to a person's quest for freedom; it cannot lead that quest. Thus, a person enslaved to his rationalizing self or to the rationalizing milieu surrounding him lives his sexual life differently than a person who is engaged in seeking to express his freedom.

Put differently, Kafka describes contemporary man as careening between rationalism and lust. Most hours of the day he is confined to and guided by the rational system in which he finds himself; he responds by continual rationalizing. He lives as an abstraction, a shadowy number, a case. He suspects that he may become less of a shadow if he indulges in the expression of desires. But in the random expression of sexual desires no basic relationship to another person is established, and Kafka's heroes remain shadowy beings. They return to their abstract existence bewildered and unsatisfied, seemingly chained to a dialectic of alienation.

In each contemporary heritage, a different dialectic of careening between abstraction and lust has been developed. The Jew, as described by hosts of contemporary writers in Israel, Europe, and the United States—Agnon, Brenner, Bialik, Zweig, Roth, Bellow, Singer, to mention a few—this Jew thrives personally in the realm of abstractions, be it in art, science, or business, while hiding his lusts from himself behind humor or behind a "holier than you" attitude. He fears these lusts. Modern social norms, with their greater freedom of physical expression, have allowed this Jew to be less afraid of his lusts, but, like Joseph K., he is still careening from his seeming comfort in the corridors of rationalization to what he believes to be his lower being.

This careening is very much in accordance with a strong stream of male chauvinism that characterizes contemporary Judaism and life in Israel. The two types of heroes whom many Jews admire are either those men who succeed in the realm of abstractions or those who have freely expressed their lusts. An army general, who blends his lust for power with a spattering of abstract knowledge, fits the bill perfectly. The man in the street often feels that he must attempt to emulate him and prove his worth by such careening in his own life. To give just one prominent example, Moshe Dayan was admired and emulated by many because of his ability to careen with *chutzpah* between the realm of political, military, and tactical abstractions and a very adventurous sexual life, interspersed with a constant lust for power. (One should perhaps add that in the last interview before his death, Dayan admitted that, in his eventful life, he had never—but never!—experienced friendship.)

Women are not heroes for the Jew in Israel. Hence many women who attempt to attain equality with men wish to excel in the areas in which men attain glory. They thus condemn themselves to a Kafkian dialectic similar to that of Jewish men. It may already be clear that I shall hold that only through dialogue and personal responsibility can a person attempt to break through the dialectic of careening which Kafka described. Such is only partially my intention. But first let us describe the Arab dialectic of abstraction and lust.

As T. E. Lawrence repeatedly stressed, the Arabs believe in abstractions. But these are narrow and confined abstractions, with almost no imagery, without a hint of skepticism, without systems of philosophy or complex mythologies. Such confined abstractions constrict the person, even while opening to him a direct avenue to his Maker, or to a promised redemption. Often, personal life is regarded as secondary, or even as superfluous, when compared with the glory emanating from these abstractions; hence the spendthriftness of many Arab regimes with the lives of their adherents. Lawrence also showed that certain lusts are sanctioned and encouraged in the narrow confines of these abstractions, bringing birth to fanatic outbursts, to a ruthlessness in one's quest for power, to avarice, to a ballooning sense of honor. Egyptian authors have shown that alongside the sanctioned lusts flourish the unsanctioned ones: homosexuality, prostitution, drug orgies.

This Arab manner of careening has one characteristic mistake, which Egyptian authors such as Mahfouz and Idris expressed but which T. E. Lawrence seemed to ignore. The Arab believes that by throwing himself, once and for all, into a new adventure or a new experience, he will find himself renewed, he will attain personal freedom. But such is an illusion. All he will have attained, as Joseph K. repeatedly learned, is himself, with one new mundane experience. As Mahfouz and Idris show, an Arab's fascination with words, with abstract expressions can conceal the poverty of his attainments; but not for very long. Reality catches up with the person, revealing to him his alienation, his lack of dialogue and love, the meaninglessness of his life. He may respond by once again throwing himself into an experience in which an abstract idea sanctions lusts, but by this dialectic he will never transcend his enslaved situation.

In their careening, both the Jew and the Arab refuse to cope with life in its complexities and to relate personally to the profound spirit of their heritage. Thriving in an abstract milieu or believing in an abstract idea often helps a person evade facing up to daily exigencies, daily responsibilities. Furthermore, finding one's personal path between abstraction and lust is an arduous task, with little immediate satisfaction. As Zarathustra pointed out, one must begin with taking upon oneself the burdens of the camel.

During its first year the Education for Peace Project was often criticized by nonparticipants as either playing around with abstract notions or as being a meeting place for Jewish-Arab promiscuity. It would be simple to reject these criticisms as projections of the criticizer's own problems and fears. Such fears and problems exist. But during this year we learned that dialogue is not only wrongly perceived by external critics; often some of the participants in the dialogical encounter will translate their experience into terms with which their bodies and minds are better acquainted, say, a meeting of ideas, or physical and personal attraction. We learned that for persons in a conflict situation dialogue can be a meaningful beginning; but dialogue will influence these persons' lives only when it is followed by the assuming of personal responsibility.

Buber vaguely recognized this problem. He held that the dialogical response is the basis of responsibility toward one's partner in dialogue. Such may be true, but it confines personal responsibility to the realm of the interhuman. Buber did not discuss the assuming of responsibility in society; he ignored social struggle and conflict, and the reification and alienation of man through the dialectics of economic relations. In short, he ignored major forces of history. He seemed to believe that assuming responsibility in the realm of the interhuman will guide one's interaction in the social and economic realms. Such is not the case. Even after reaching dialogue, persons will often choose to evade assuming responsibility for bringing about change in their society. This tendency to evade responsibility emerged forcefully on the first visit of participants of the Education for Peace Project to Egypt.

The first-year trip to Egypt lacked a structured program. In accordance with my guidelines, participants divided themselves into groups of four or five, with at least two Arabs in each group. Before the trip, each group decided on an aspect of Egyptian society that it would observe, i.e. the role of the women, culture, religion, secondary education. (The aspects were defined rather broadly; now I recognize that they were too broad and lacked focus.) Each day, the groups were free to pursue their interests, as long as they did not split up; they were required to submit a written report of their activities at the end of each day. But after four days in Egypt, the program had broken down and in all the groups' dialogue and understanding between Jews and Arabs seemed to have been buried.

Although there were some logistical reasons for this breakdown, it stemmed mainly from an identity crisis which the

Israeli Arabs were undergoing. Here is an excerpt from the workshop held in order to try to mend relations.

Mustafa (Arab man): Haim, you defined the topic of this workshop as "What have I done wrong in our small group?" Well, I'm not sure I did anything wrong. Let me explain. I came here to Cairo, despite some peer pressure not to come, because I wanted to see this center of Arab culture and to be part of the peace project. The first day it was just wonderful to walk around here and see what a big Arab city is all about, you know, millions of people speaking Arabic, movies in Arabic, books in Arabic, nightclubs in Arabic, many Arabic newspapers—for the first time in my life I felt sort of fully at home. What is more, after being a second-class citizen in Israel all of my life, I suddenly recognized that here I have to lead the Jews; I am responsible for them.

Josepha (Jewish woman): I'm not sure you acted responsibly. You were not always ready to translate what was happening.

Mustafa: Let me continue. Now the Jews in the group did not sense my elation; they just wanted me to help them enjoy Egypt, by using me as a translator, as a sort of tourist guide who doesn't get paid.

Josepha: That is an ugly statement, Mustafa.

Haim: Josepha, let him go on.

Mustafa: Josepha, stop being a bitch; you know I *did* try to translate. I'm just telling how I felt, at times. But on the second and third days things got worse, not because of this translation problem, but because I began to learn that these Egyptians, those whom I met at least, know nothing about Israeli Arabs, and don't give a damn about the Palestinian cause.

Jeremiah (Jewish man): I sensed that you were especially angry yesterday, after that merchant called you a Jew. First you laughed, then you got real mad.

Mustafa: Right. Here I am talking to this fat Egyptian for three quarters of an hour in a sidewalk cafe, explaining to him at length that we Israeli Arabs are part of the Palestinian nation, even though we live in Israel and are Israeli citizens; and then when we get up to go he says to me: "For a Jew, you sure speak good Arabic."

Hussein (Arab man): Something like that happened to me, too. This cab driver asked me: If I live in Israel, and talk to the Jews in their language, and study at their university in Hebrew, and have Jewish women friends, why do I say that I am an Arab?

Haim: Let Mustafa continue.

Mustafa: Well, suddenly I felt that the Jews are much more accepted by the Egyptians than we Israeli Arabs, who are supposedly their brothers in origin and faith. At times they acted obnoxiously. Once, when I identified myself as a Palestinian, a young Egyptian in a store said: "Who are the Palestinians? Those who sit in camps and live off the dole, or those who frequent plush hotels in Paris and Vienna and send off press releases?"

Haim: That made you angry?

Mustafa: That, and the nagging of the Jews that I translate for them, turned me off. I didn't want to talk to anybody.

Josepha: Why didn't you tell us your problem? We might have helped you.

Haim: Perhaps you were too aggressive, Josepha, and didn't sense that there is a problem here.

Josepha: Perhaps, but you are good at being smart after the event, Haim.

Haim (laughing): Yeah, but that is better than not being smart at all. Getting back to Mustafa, I believe that the problem goes much deeper, and until you face up to it you will not be able to cope with the Egyptian response. The Palestinian nation with which you, Mustafa, say you are affiliated is very much of an abstraction in which you believe. Even as an abstraction it did not exist, say, seventy years ago. Before the First World War the entire area south of Damascus, almost up to Mecca and Medina, was called Greater Syria. Palestine was a small region of Greater Syria. Arabs who lived there called themselves either Syrians or Arabs. The concept Palestinian did not exist. Today the Palestinian Liberation Organization is fighting for an abstraction which it calls the Palestinian nation. But this nation in which you fervently believe has no unique culture; furthermore, it has no territory, no history, no tradition, no unique customs. Yasser Arafat and George Habash and their movements are primarily negative responses to Israel's existence. Under their leadership, the Palestinian nation has made no positive impact on the Arab world in terms of culture or spirit. Sartre would say that today you Palestinians define yourselves as a negation—a negation of Israel, a negation of Greater Syria, a negation of Jordan. The Egyptian response you are now encountering in the streets of Cairo is a negation of that negation, because the Egyptians accept Israel. Your only way to bring about some sort of change is by trying to make your identity as a Palestinian accord with positive doing; I mean that you must work to develop positive Palestinian values in culture, art, society, religion, and other fields.

Mustafa: Haim, at times your philosophizing is out of place, and this is one of those times.

Hussein: I didn't like what you said, too, Haim.

After the breakdown of dialogical relations in Egypt, there was a seeming return to business as usual. During the four weeks until the end of the year, some personal relations were mended. But there were some additional crises, which seemed to be a foreboding. We held summary workshops. The results seemed encouraging, even if problematic.

Forty-four persons had been accepted into the Buberian Learning Groups at the beginning of the year. During the year, ten persons—six Arabs and four Jews—left the groups. Four were asked to leave because they did not fulfill requirements. Two Arab students were expelled from the university on discipline charges connected with political involvement. Four dropped out. Our results relate to the thirty-four persons who completed the year.

In the summary workshops, twenty-four participants asserted they had significantly advanced in learning to relate
dialogically and trustfully, in accordance with a scale of
development which I had formulated (see section entitled
"Initial Research Problems"). Those who had advanced the
least were persons who, before joining the group, had been
conscious of the need to change, but who had difficulty
mustering the courage to effect that change. Doing is much
more difficult than becoming aware of what needs to be done,
and few participants had made significant strides beyond
becoming aware of the need for trust and dialogue and
attempting to achieve it within the Buberian Learning Group.
Five persons, all of them Arabs, made no progress. They did
not understand Buber's basic concepts, and neither private
lessons nor weekly personal meetings helped them acquire
the Buberian conceptual framework. Five other persons felt
that they had not progressed significantly because of personal reasons—for example, a prolonged illness and marital
problems.

The twenty-four participants who asserted that they had
advanced declared that they now trusted some group members from the other ethnic community, and that they had
related dialogically to a few of them. They often mentioned
that work in subgroups and dyads had encouraged dialogue.
But ten of these persons, most of them Arabs, pointed out
that such experiences had only slightly diminished their
existential mistrust of persons who belong to the other ethnic
group. One Jewish participant explained: "I can reach dialogue with Muhammed, but when that happens he is no
longer an Arab. I erase his Arab being. What is more, all other
Arabs I continue to mistrust." On the other hand, at least
eleven persons asserted that their personal development had
significantly diminished their existential mistrust of any person belonging to the opposing ethnic group. The remaining
three persons were ambivalent in their answers.

Accompanying these successes there was a general mood
of letdown. It came to the fore in a day-long staff meeting

chaired by Dina. For about three hours, Kassem tried to convince us all that the Education for Peace Project must become a political entity. He failed, and resigned from the staff six weeks later. More important was a dialogue between David and Dina. It arose when David responded to one of the questions we had put to ourselves as a theme of the meeting: What have you learned from this year of work in the Project?

David: Perhaps I should first describe how I feel the encompassing milieu. I read Kafka's books before joining the staff; they seemed weird to me, describing something that happened out there to somebody not doing important things with his life. Well, I was wrong. Ever since my first trip to Egypt the realization has been growing on me that we are operating in a Kafkian world that refuses to acknowledge itself as Kafkian and sees our rejecting its manifestations as a sin or crime.

Dina: Kafkian is a big word. Can you break it down to something more concrete?

David: It is a problem to break it down. Because if you take every detail in itself, it could be something that occurred by chance. Perhaps what I mean can be described best by what happened in Egypt, but I also want to talk about Israel. In Egypt we soon learned that our travel agent was lying to us; he was charging us above regular prices and not keeping any of the promises he made: like we paid for an air-conditioned bus and got one without air conditioning. Now it can happen that a travel agent cheats you. But add to the fact that our phone conversations were listened to by the operators at the hotel and that the secret police were constantly keeping an eye on us. That can happen also. Add to that that all our attempts to talk straightforwardly to Egyptians were frustrated. For instance, the Egyptian woman from the Experiment in International Living who spoke to us as a friend on the first trip was reportedly out of town whenever we phoned her house or office. But we checked, and she was in town. The same was true about some professors we met on the first trip. Add to that the Egyptians talking about lofty ideals—our travel agent was a specialist in that—while disregarding the filth in the offices, the streets, the stores. Add to that the politeness which hides complicity and mistrust, the elevators that perpetually don't work, the smiles in order to evade responsibility, and the sensuousness of the entire atmosphere, the constant pinching of our girls in the streets, the sexual lust in the gaze of every Egyptian man—If all that isn't Kafka, what is?

Dina: What you are saying is that we have a tendency to break down our lived experience into factors with which we can deal rationally. But such a breaking down does not let us see the Kafkian society within which we exist. We deal with specific details and therefore do not see our situation in its entirety.

David: To tell you the truth, I'm not sure I meant that, but now that you say it I agree that you are very right. O.K., now what does all this have to do with us? Since we are much more at home in Israel, and are supposedly better acquainted with how things work here, we tend to ignore the entire Kafkian milieu encompassing us. But let me start enumerating things and you will see that even though it is different, it is still the same. We never—but I mean *never*—get a straightforward answer from the representative of the Hans Seidel Foundation who is giving us money; he is smooth and slippery as a snake, seemingly nice but always hiding the truth from us. Add to that that the way the budget is run by the finance office of the university is a farce; their inefficiency and mistakes are so sad that it would be a joke, if it didn't give us so many problems. Add to that the fact that Israeli security planted someone in our Buberian Learning Groups to report to them on our doings, and that even though Haim told it to university officials, they smiled with complicity. What can be more Kafkian than the fact that we are teaching a mole or two to relate dialogically in the spirit of Martin Buber? Add to that the remarks we constantly hear. Believe it or not, one professor came up to me and said: "I understand that your project went to Egypt so that some Jewish women could get into bed with Arab men." I told him I know of enough Jews and Arabs who do it in Beer Sheva, Tel Aviv, and Jerusalem, without having to go to Egypt for the experience. But he smiled "knowingly." In short, we are in a no less Kafkian atmosphere, even though we may be at two levels of subtlety or supposed sophistication above the Egyptians.

Dina: But what have you learned from all this, beyond the descriptive level? That we were naive?

David: Of course we were naive, but maybe that was good. It gave us a sort of youthful power. As for me, I learned two things. First, if we want to educate for peace we are going to have to live and operate in this Kafkian milieu; that means we should think about finding ways of dealing with it. As we all learned, as Haim learned, even in talking with the university administration dialogue is useless. Buber seems to have never coped with incompetent bureaucrats, with devious bigots. The second point is that we have been limited in our vision. This came to me in one of our discussions on vision in one of the groups. Like Joseph K., many of our visions end at the bureaucrat's desk. We must go beyond that desk and dream even the most crazy dreams about peace in the Mideast. In the movie *The Trial* Orson Welles said that Kafka's stories resemble terrible nightmares; we need to counter those nightmares with some crazily wonderful dreams of peace.

6. Kierkegaard:
The Becoming of a Subject

The true ethical enthusiasm consists in willing to the utmost limits of one's powers, but at the same time being so uplifted in divine jest as never to think about the accomplishment.

—SØREN KIERKEGAARD

N I E T Z S C H E and Kierkegaard would probably have been very unhappy with the wealth of scholarship which has arisen since their deaths to elaborate upon and to suggest new exegeses of their writings. They wanted their writings to influence the lives of persons who are struggling to attain and to express their freedom; they wanted to influence their readers to live differently, not only to think differently. They both sensed that their contemporaries lived with a distorted relationship to their passions and that this distortion enslaved the person to the mediocrity which encompassed him. At this point their paths part: Nietzsche wished the person to formulate new values and to live as a free, creative being. Kierkegaard wished the person to become a subject who could relate with all his passion to God.

Kierkegaard repeatedly emphasized that only a person who strives to be a subject can rebel against an oppressing objective reality. He personally rebelled against the Lutheran state church of Denmark, against bourgeois mentality, and against Hegelian dialectics, yet his insights are valid for any rebellion against an objective reality. Put briefly, only a person who strives to be a subject can find in himself the power to counter the pervading and insidious forces of objectivity which encompass him and attempt to dissolve each person's being in an acidic bath of mediocre superficialities. Kierkegaard did not suggest how to educate persons to undertake the quest of becoming a subject. He *did* describe existential situations along the path of becoming a subject, moments which Buber pretty much ignored. Buber seemed to believe that dialogue is the key to becoming a subject. The making present of the Other with his otherness builds a person as a subject, with his own otherness. Such may be true, but it is not the entire truth. A person also becomes a subject through creativity, through facing dread, undergoing despair, having faith, falling in love.

Furthermore, Buber did not recognize the importance of a person's struggling against an objective reality within the I-It realm. In such a struggle, a person can hopefully bring about a change for the better and develop as a subject. Socrates is a well-known example of a person who developed as a subject while struggling with passion, irony, and faith against an indifferent objective reality. Buber's ignoring of struggle as central to human development is reflected in his inability to write great literature, except in the form of Hasidic anecdote. The characters in his chronicle *For the Sake of Heaven* (Buber's only book-length literary attempt) lack depth. They resemble ghostly figures with no earthly passions, no need to struggle.

In educating for peace, we soon learned that many persons prefer to bask in the delights of dialogue within the Buberian Learning Group rather than to struggle for peace outside the group, in Israeli society. But in-group dialogue turns stale if it is not followed by attempts to counter the milieu of enmity between Jews and Arabs outside the group. In other words, the Buberian Learning Group could only continue to educate for peace if it encouraged its participants to develop in two areas beyond dialogue: first, to become subjective; second, to attempt to change history. In the first area, much of our work was based on Kierkegaard, Dostoyevski, and Nietzsche; in the second area it was based on Mahfouz and Sartre.

Kierkegaard indicated that one can become a subject either through a leap of faith or through an arduous process of self-education in which one learns to will the ethical to the utmost. Most persons play with their lives, or attempt to seduce their way through life's various stations and exigencies. As Kierkegaard shows in "Diary of a Seducer," such a person is never fully involved in his doing—his doing is play-acting. If he succeeds, he is aesthetically enjoying himself and consciously enjoying his enjoyment. If he fails, he seeks solace in fatalism. Yet how does one educate a person to transcend such seducing or such fatalism? One approach the educator can use is historical awareness. Consider these excerpts from a personal meeting between Dina and Yafa, a Jewish woman participant who was considering leaving the Project at the beginning of the second year.

Dina: I see your point, Yafa, but I think you are wrong in judging the Education for Peace Project in terms of what you are getting out of it.

Yafa: Why not? I really don't feel that you or other participants have made me sense that I belong to what is happening. I read at home, I come to the group meetings, I listen, at times I learn a bit about Buber or Dostoyevski, or Kierkegaard, but all this sort of passes by me. I am not involved. But what did you mean by not judging in terms of what I get out of it? How else should I judge?

Dina: When you evaluate something by what you get out of it, you really are sitting on the fence, always thinking of the possibility that you will not get involved. Like in a friendship; either you are friends with someone or you stop being friends, but you cannot sit on the fence and always think, "What am I getting out of this relationship?" and still be friends. If you do that you are really seducing your friend, because you are not giving what there is to give to the friendship; you are play-acting friendship in order to enjoy what is happening. It is similar in working for peace. Either you are fully with us or you are part of the majority who doesn't care. Furthermore, Yafa, in your approach you are missing out on historical involvement and awareness. It reminds me of the ancient Egyptian statues.

Yafa: Now you have me all mixed up.

Dina: Well, what did you feel when you saw the ancient Egyptian statues on our visit to the Cairo museum? Think of Ramses II or Akhenaten.

Yafa: I felt I was viewing good art.

Dina: Don't give me general answers. What did *you,* Yafa, feel?

Yafa: Let me think. Well, there was some awe, but not much more. What are you driving at, Dina? Don't play riddles with me.

Dina: I am saying that the Egyptian Pharaohs were sculptured so as to be constantly beyond us mortals. They wanted to be beyond any involvement in the life of the persons they ruled. Hence, you cannot develop an I-Thou relationship with a sculpture of Ramses II or Akhenaten, because the sculpture is beyond history. And when one lives beyond history, one cannot relate to others as a subject and one does not develop oneself as a subject. This is one of the important contributions of monotheistic faith—that even God is involved in history and by His involvement He helps us become subjects. But you are acting as if you are beyond history, Yafa, that is why you don't get involved, that is why you don't develop as a subject.

Yafa: What you really are saying is that I am stuck. On the fence, but stuck. What should I do?

Dina: I wish I could formulate what getting unstuck means. I myself often feel stuck. Perhaps Buber's Hasidic anecdote about Yaakov Yitzchak, who later became the Holy Yehudi, has relevance. The Seer of Lublin, who was the most important Hasidic Zaddik of his age, asked Yaakov Yitzchak when he finally arrived at his court; "You are now close to thirty-five years old. Why didn't you come to me sooner?" Yaakov Yitzchak responded: "Until a few days ago many people told

me that I should go to visit you. But last Monday my friend
Rabbi David said to me suddenly: 'Pack up. We are going to
visit the Seer of Lublin!' So I had no choice but to pack up and
come."

Perhaps you and I, Yafa, should say to each other ever so
often: Pack up and come with me to do something for peace
and dialogue.

Getting unstuck was one of the basic problems the Education for Peace Project faced at the beginning of its second
year. One reason was our naive outlook concerning our
action research, especially in a realm where ethical decisions
with political overtones often had to be made. Israeli society
is basically divided into the either/or that Kierkegaard described in his book by that name. Either you live in the realm
of senses, the aesthetic realm according to Kierkegaard, and
wish to satisfy your senses by seducing, victimizing, refining
your pleasures—even the melancholy pleasures, as Kierkegaard brilliantly showed—so as to greaten your sensuous
enjoyment in life. Or you live in the quiet, rather boring
ethical realm, where you guard your "beautiful soul," as we
say in Hebrew, and priggishly follow the dictates of the high
command. But as Kierkegaard indicated and as we intuitively
sensed, ethical responsibility begins when one transcends
both realms, when as a subject a person is passionately
interested in educating for peace and constantly seeks ways
to realize these passions.

Put otherwise, our development, like a person's growth,
was dialectical; we had constantly to transcend the current
situation if we did not want to remain stuck. Thus two things
were occurring simultaneously. On the one hand, we were
following our intuitions as subjects while rebelling against
the objective reality of bigotry, fatalism, and ethical priggery
which confined us. On the other hand, we constantly battled
with that objective reality on its own terms. Some of the most
ludicrous and aggravating instances of such a dialectic had to
do with the Steering Committee of the Education for Peace

Project, which the rector of the university set up so as to ensure himself that no "adverse political outcomes" would arise from my doings. In the meetings of that committee, topics such as research, educational aims and goals of the Project, and programming were discussed. But they were always discussed, seemingly, after the decision had been made. I did not come to the committee with a problem and ask for suggestions how to solve it. I came to get a stamp of approval for my doings. My colleagues soon understood this and refused to be my rubber stamp; but they also refused to immerse themselves in existentialism. The result was that the meetings were a battleground between manipulators—often aggravating the participants. Today, in hindsight, the meetings seem to be a comical and often ridiculous component of my endeavors. I now know that in manipulating my colleagues so as to be free to follow my ethical passions, I was right. If I had acted otherwise, we would have remained stuck. The dictates of the university high command, the priggery of the objective reality, would have obliterated my ethical intuitions, ruined me as a subject, and effaced my power to educate for peace.

Ultimately, a person must choose whether he will attempt to get by somehow in a Kafkian world or endeavor to develop as an ethical being in accordance with Kierkegaard's teachings. There is no third choice. Following Kierkegaard means constant battle with the dictates of the high command; it means relying on one's personal faith in oneself. It means suffering failure and scorn such as Kierkegaard himself experienced, but it also means developing personally as a subject. Yet how does a person know that in following his ethical passions he will do the good? As Kierkegaard stresses—he doesn't! Choosing to act as an ethical person is a risk; and if there were no risk the act would not be ethical. In acting religiously, the risk is even greater. Even reading about the patriarch Abraham, Kierkegaard's knight of faith, sacrificing his son to God arouses fear and trembling.

Choosing to become a subject does not ensure a person that he will fully extract himself from the Kafkian swamp. This cold, muddy area of alienation and rationalization will continually attempt to suck a person into its adhesive reality. As Kierkegaard noted, becoming subjective is a lifelong task in which a person seeks out paths to develop personality, paths along which his ethical passion can attain some fulfillment. This passion will not lead him astray if, following Kierkegaard, he will be on constant alert not to deceive himself or, at least, to deceive himself as little as possible. Such an approach was adopted by Sahib, an Arab man from Gaza who joined the Education for Peace Project at the beginning of the second year.

The Arabs in the Gaza Strip have been living in a trap since 1967. They are governed by Israeli military rule; they identify themselves as Palestinians, but are aware of the weakness of the PLO; they know that, in most instances, other Arab nations wish merely to exploit the Palestinians' plight in order to attain political clout in their own inter-Arab or international maneuvering. Some Palestinians respond to this situation by joining terrorist groups, some work with the Israelis, some emigrate, and many sink into apathy. All feel bottled up in a hopeless situation.

Sahib was one of the Arabs who joined the special Buberian Learning Group we set up at the beginning of the second year for participants from the Gaza Strip. In this group the Arabs read contemporary Arab literature in Arabic while the Jews read the same texts in their Hebrew translation. Thus we were educating for peace and Buberian dialogue on the basis of contemporary Arabic literature. Sahib was among the most educated among the Gaza Arabs, having studied toward a master's degree in Moslem theology and philology in Cairo. His relationship to his knowledge was subjective; it was part of his being. Consider the following conversation between

David, who helped me lead this group, and Sahib, which took place about two months after the group was established.

David: You often make me feel uncomfortable, Sahib.

Sahib: In what sense?

David: There is something overpathetic, too beautiful in the words you choose to describe your life. For instance, you were complaining about the Israeli military rule in Gaza. You said that the Israeli military men with whom you worked, as superintendent of elementary education in the Gaza Strip and Sinai, were incompetent. But I did not feel any bitterness in your saying it. I know that if I had as responsible a job as you and believed in the importance of education as you do, I would be peeved at having to listen to a lot of military dummies who know nothing about education. But you seem to view your present life from the point of view of history, so as not to get involved too deeply with your feelings.

Sahib: Perhaps. But there is also an aspect of my way of doing things that you don't seem to perceive.

David: Which aspect?

Sahib: That my viewing my situation from the point of view of history allows me to direct my powers in a specific direction. Take my relation to the Israeli military men who are my bosses and who know very little about education. These Jews were chosen to be part of the military rule in Gaza because they know Arabic and they grew up in Arabic countries like Iraq or Morocco. Supposedly, they know how to relate to our mentality. But they relate in the wrong manner—by trying to manipulate us solely so as to make the Israeli military presence a fact of our life. I recognize all this and see its significance. But by rejecting it outwardly, I will gain nothing; even by rejecting it inwardly I will gain nothing. The best way of rejecting it is by my doing good deeds for our Arabs without sacrificing my integrity.

David: See what I mean by your using pathetic words? What do you mean by "doing good deeds without sacrificing your integrity"?

Sahib: I believe that I have taught my Israeli military bosses three things. First, they cannot buy me. If I disagree with a policy decision, I will say so clearly. Thus quite a few times when they wanted to close a school because of political trouble in the school, I said no, and I took upon myself to make the school run quietly. Second, I tell our teachers and students that our main power now is knowledge. If we ever want to create a different situation in Gaza, we must make sure that we read and know. Ignorant people will not be independent. Never. Thus I have taught the Israelis that even under their restrictions I can take my job in all seriousness and do it for the good of my people. Slowly but surely, some of them have begun to respect that. And third, if I disagree with what one of the teachers does and he does not listen to my counsel, I will not hesitate to censure him. I am critical of him because we are in such a messy situation and we need him to do his best.

David: You are very courageous, Sahib. Let me ask you one more thing. How do you know that you are right?

Sahib: I don't know I'm right, I just try to be right. I often read the Koran and get guidance from it. Not in terms of religious tenets. But after I've read a Sura I ask myself what does this mean for me? What should I do to be better tomorrow? You see, I believe that our Prophet [Muhammed] required primarily that we live better, as persons with other persons. Only then is it meaningful to pray to Allah. It's a pity, David, that so many people choose to be bad.

Kierkegaard recognized and repeatedly emphasized that becoming a subject is only possible if a person takes upon himself the task of self-education. Such self-education must not only relate to the changing of one's personal way of life but also to a transcendental goal. But one can only relate to such a goal, at least in the Western monotheistic tradition, by relating to the social reality within which one finds oneself, criticizing it concretely and coping with its mendacities— much as Kierkegaard criticized the Lutheran state church of

Denmark and pointed out its manner of propagating self-deception among its adherents. Put differently, Kierkegaard believed that a person's self-education should resemble the personal development of his hero, Socrates. For Socrates, self-education was an attempt to become better while rebelling against the seductive and mendacious reality that encompassed him.

During the second year of participating in a Buberian Learning Group, we tried to teach the participants to take upon themselves the task of self-education as understood by Kierkegaard. In many instances we failed. But before discussing these failures, I would like to bring a rather complex example of one of our better discussions. It occurred after second-year participants read at home André Gide's *The Immoralist*; in class, they received a lecture on Kierkegaard's description of the aesthetic realm and its dangers for a moral way of life. Some participants had read sections of Kierkegaard's *Either/Or*. The questions put to the participants were: What is immoral about Michel, the hero of *The Immoralist*? What can I learn from his behavior about my life here in Israel? The questions were first discussed in small groups. Here are some excerpts from the final discussion:

Yaakov (Jewish man): **Our group felt that Michel was very egocentric. The way he set up his entire life was so as to satisfy his personal wishes, whims, and desires. That is the source of his immorality.**

Haim: **It is true that Michel is egocentric, but that is just another way of saying that he is immoral; it is an aspect of his being an immoralist. Words like "egocentric," which merely label the person, do not help us understand existential processes; they even, at times, cloud the perception of the specific process that is described. Thus you still have to explain the process that led to his egocentricism and immoral behavior. Further, you have to explain that immoral behavior. But let me give you a hint: When did the process commence?**

Yaakov: After his sickness.

Haim: What happened?

Yaakov: He began to pamper his body.

Sausan (Arab woman): I would say he fell in love with his body.

Haim: I think Sausan is right. That is where his immorality begins: in his falling in love with one aspect of his being, in his pampering that aspect and, hence, in his inability to relate fully to other persons. Even in his love with Marceline, his wife, he was more in love with his own love than with Marceline as a person. She passes through the novel and his life like a shadow, with almost no influence on Michel's life and development. What can we learn from all this about our life here in Israel? About our own immoralism?

Yaakov: Well, that we shouldn't fall in love with one aspect of our being.

Haim: Don't sell me back what I just sold you; be concrete. Give me an example.

Ilana (Jewish woman): I think I know, although our group did not discuss it. For instance, the Jewish admiration and love for the Israel Defense Force is becoming a sort of a fetish, and it is leading to immoral deeds. But wait, let me be more specific, because I know that is what you all will ask me. Well, like Michel, who develops a theory about history to justify his falling in love with his body and with his health, we are also developing a new view of history to justify our constant military buildup. Even though there already is peace with Egypt, we keep saying that the Arabs really do not want peace, that they are not to be trusted, that military strength is what matters in the world. You know, as I am speaking, I see that it really fits in with Michel's development. Yes, even if the army steals a bit from the country, like Michel steals from himself, we tend to overlook it.

Haim: Great! You know, when the current army chief of staff was chosen, people in the army told me that he would be a good man because he was honest. He would not use his position to exploit the nation, like other generals have been accused of doing. They wanted someone morally respectable representing the country's succumbing to the immorality you described.

Hussam (Arab man, assistant group leader): I can also give an example from our way of life. Our love for and admiration of honor can lead to immoral deeds, and even an immoral way of life. You all remember the Bedouin member of parliament who was murdered by the sons of a Druze member of parliament, all over a matter of honor. Everything Ilana said about the Jews' relationship to the Israeli Defense Force has its parallel in the Arab relationship to honor.

Haim: I would like to add a few reflections that tie our discussion to Kierkegaard and to what you can do in your own lives. As André Gide shows, and Kierkegaard holds, such immoral behavior becomes a way of life with no way out: Immoral behavior leads to a justifying rationalization of that behavior in our consciousness, which leads again to new, similar behavior. I believe that there are only two ways to get out of such vicious circles: One is to leap out of them, and the other is slow self-education while working against the general trend. Kierkegaard discusses both possibilities in *Either/Or,* not very convincingly in my view, but each possibility is there.

Examples of a leap are when someone like Sakharov suddenly comes out for peace and against the proliferation of atomic bombs, which he helped develop. He abandons his entire set of former commitments, which he views as immoral, and leaps into an entire new set of commitments that are moral. With self-education, it is much more difficult to give an example, because we are dealing here with a process in which each of you must daily demand of yourselves a change, while also attempting to change the encompassing milieu. When each of you strives to develop trustful and responsible relations with persons of the other nation, there is a process of self-education. But the entire process should resemble an ever receding mountaintop toward which you continually climb. Such climbing is what develops you as a subject.

Ilana: Something here is bothering me. As long as you ask us, you demand specific answers. Now, give me a specific example of self-education.

Haim: You are right, but there is a problem here, since self-education is a process. Consider a husband who slowly begins to recognize his wife as a separate, independent person, and then to accept her as such, and finally to love her as a separate human being; he has probably undergone a long, difficult process of self-education. In political and social life, the process can be no less painful and difficult. We must work for change even while changing ourselves. Thus the husband I mentioned, or his wife, or both together, during the process could work together for changing the social status of women.

Ilana: You are still not specific. Give me an example from Jewish-Arab relations, an example that concerns our group.

Haim: It is interesting that we often do not see or appreciate our own good actions. Quite a few persons sitting here, Jews and Arabs together, have tried to spread our ideas among workers, among youth, in various other settings. They have often failed, and I hope they have learned from such failures. The working for this goal, the developing of educational methods while educating yourself, is the direction I am indicating.

Some of our failures in encouraging participants to educate themselves were a result of our overemphasizing the importance of dialogue. Relating as a Thou is a breakthrough in the I-It world, which can teach a person much about himself, about other persons, about spirit, about God. Experiencing this breakthrough is crucial for a person who wishes to develop as a subject. But after the dialogical encounter, as Buber knew, one must passionately educate oneself so that relating subjectively will become central to one's being. Such is what Buber meant when he quoted the Hasidim as saying:

One must direct one's evil urges to loving God.

During the first year and a half of the Project, I believed that dialogical encounters can be the major steps along the path to subjectivity, to the assuming of personal responsibility. Later I learned that the self-education of a person as a subject requires much more; it requires coping with some of the existential situations that Kierkegaard discussed, such as dread of the good, despair, the fear of standing alone; it also requires overcoming the little hindrances and hangups which impede self-development. Such became clear in a conversation with our group leader, Dina.

Dina: I agree that we failed to teach this group to assume responsibility for peace, and I've been thinking about it. There is something problematic in your entire approach, Haim. You demand things which seem simple, and even your way of demanding is simple—you say: Go out and do it. But for many a person even doing the simple thing seems very complex; he does not see the simplicity of the act but concentrates on the complexity surrounding the act. By saying to him that it is simple you encourage the person, but then he is left alone to try and work out the complexities.

Haim: I'm not sure I understand your criticism. I do know, though, that if a person tries to work out all the complexities surrounding an act, he may never do the act. Give me an example.

Dina: Think a minute about Fatma. In one of our meetings, in which we discussed becoming a subject and giving some freedom to one's passions, she decided to do something which is simple but not acceptable in her *hamula* and Arab village: to kiss her father. What is simpler than a daughter kissing her father? But when she was surrounded by the complexities of life in her home, she suddenly got scared; it took her three weeks to muster the courage for this simple act.

Haim: Perhaps if I had not emphasized that becoming a subject begins with the most simple acts, Fatma would have done nothing.

Dina: I have already said that, on the one hand, I think it is wonderful that you encourage persons to take on the simple challenges. Before your encouragement, for twenty-three years Fatma never dared to kiss her father. But your myopia as to the complexities accompanying simple acts can also lead a person to despair if he fails to take upon himself the challenges that you describe as simple.

Haim: I see what you mean. But I also tell participants in our groups that Kierkegaard held that becoming a subject is a lifelong task, that Buber suggested that in undertaking this task we should start from what seems to be least difficult, so that we struggle from a position of strength. I often mention the burdens of the camel that Zarathustra describes; I give examples of my own personal difficulties in becoming a subject—what else can I do?

Dina: Perhaps you can tell people how to jump over the little hindrances that interfere with their becoming subjective.

Haim: I disagree. Persons learn that they have the power to change their situation by working against the little hindrances, the seemingly small hangups. If I discuss these little hindrances too much, I inflate their importance and they become big hindrances—which they definitely *are not.* In this day and age, when Hollywood movies are shown daily on TV in every Arab home in Fatma's village, it is not that difficult to kiss your father. I don't want to be stubborn, but there is also a laziness in most of us that prompts us to deal with the big, political, worldwide, objective problems and not to cope with our daily hindrances. All I have been saying again and again, quoting Nietzsche and Kierkegaard, is that if we wish to become subjective we must educate ourselves to allow our passions to lead us to deeds, not only to emotions.

Dina: I agree with what you are saying, but what about the complexities?

Haim: That is the point. Your so-called complexities of daily life are our internalizations of the mediocre objective reality that Kierkegaard detested. Becoming subjective means transcending these complexities.

Dina: Haim, you still do not see my point.

Haim: Go ahead.

Dina: For many people who join our Buberian Learning Groups the ideas we present on dialogue and on becoming a subject are so simple that they feel threatened. One's mind, one's body, one's personal history, seems to be saying—if all this is so simple, why in the world haven't I lived like that? Then when they fail to fulfill a simple challenge, they blame us for not seeing or warning them of the complexities; they may sink back into apathy or even express anger about what we taught them.

Haim: —So what else is new—that is what educating for peace is all about!

Dina: O.K., Haim. But at least tell them that you recognize the complexities. Really, do me a favor.

Kierkegaard continually questioned the legitimacy, the validity, and the morality of the objective (Kafkian) reality which encompassed him, which seemed to swallow up his personal significance. He also continually questioned himself as a person seeking to fulfill the task of becoming subjective. Such continual questioning can encourage the process of self-education which Kierkegaard believed all persons should undertake. Yet neither Kierkegaard nor Buber, nor any other existentialist, ever suggested how to educate persons to ask self-educating questions. Why? —Because they all understood that such questions arise naturally when a person strives to be authentic and is seeking to fulfill a vision. But there is a vicious circle here: One can only strive to be authentic and seek to fulfill a vision by the continual asking of such questions.

Here is where the importance of confronting cannot be

overemphasized. There is no striving to be authentic and no seeking to fulfill a vision of a better human existence without the constant confronting of oneself with questions. In such confronting, the regular classroom procedure must change. The teacher or group leader must ask questions to which there are no specific or correct answers; he must learn to ask questions which demand that his pupil examine his way of life and strive to change it for the better. I will give an example of such a question shortly, but first it is important to note that the academic world, and especially many pedantic cowards in the humanities and social sciences, detests anything that exudes an odor of vision. For them educating for a vision is not academic; it reeks of guruism, of Khomeinism, of the Jonestown suicide-massacre in Guyana. —In academia, objectivity must rule. At best, vision is one's personal business. —For instance, the movement called humanistic psychology has succumbed to this approach. These so-called humanists profess no vision of a better human existence; in their lives as psychologists they do not seek justice, or friendship, or peace in the world. They seek to develop techniques which can be discussed and measured objectively, and while working with these techniques they remain detached, even while becoming emotionally involved. In short, most of them are inauthentic.

As most existentialists note, there is no way of developing as a subject without relating to a vision. Simply because in order to educate oneself one needs a direction. Kierkegaard, Buber, and Berdyaev believe that one must direct oneself by relating to God, Sartre would probably suggest that we direct ourselves away from the social Hell that man has created, and Zarathustra directs us to the superman. In short, a vision gives the direction for self-education; and if one continually questions oneself in light of that vision and direction, and strives to change in accordance with these questions, one is educating oneself in the direction of that vision. These simple truths are ignored by the heroes of objectivity in the academic establishment—today, much as in the time of Kierkegaard's bitter rejection of the Hegelian establishment. But today the inauthenticity of the academics has a unique flavor. The Hegelians, at least, admitted that they embraced the vision of history developed by their spiritual mentor. Today, the pseudowarriors of objectivity refuse to admit that their rejection of any vision allows them to concur with the pseudovision of the establishment which sustains them.

Consider the Jewish-Arab relations in Israel. Any person who merely studies these relations objectively—there are no few studies on perceptions, attitudes, expectations, stereotypes—is already accepting the Jewish-Arab conflict as given, as an inert reality. He will agree that any attempt to change that given situation requires the realization of some sort of vision of justice and peaceful, humane relations, but that is not his cup of tea. In short, he is not at all concerned with the developing of Jewish and Arab subjects; and therefore, in a roundabout manner, he is helping to perpetuate an oppressive objective reality which merely co-opts his findings. As Kierkegaard repeatedly stressed, the attitude underlying the attainment of objective scientific knowledge often strives to diminish the significance and the power of the subject.

Kierkegaard knew that, by questioning a person, one can endow him with the power and the possibility of developing as a subject. But only if one questions the person as a whole person, and not as a complex problem which one wishes to analyze or to explain. Put differently, the questions a psychotherapist poses are meant to help the patient adjust to the encompassing reality. The questions that Kierkegaard asked were meant to help the subject develop as a person, often in defiance of the values and mood of the encompassing reality. Hence he questions innocently—much as in many early Platonic dialogues Socrates questions innocently. He makes no attempt to elicit a sophisticated or clever answer. He questions so that the person will answer innocently, with the answer that arises from his existence, from his way of life. Here, also, is where our attempts to educate for peace differed from prevalent group-therapy approaches. We did not want

participants to adjust; we wanted them to defy the encompassing reality of conflict while developing as subjects. In
short, we tried to question innocently and to direct the
question to the whole person whom we confronted.

The "Death Game," which will be described in the chapter
on Sartre, is an example of a two-day exercise in which
innocent questioning can encourage personal development.
Here I shall cite a rather concise exercise which is based on
the following story. A student once asked a Zen master to
teach him to attain enlightenment. The master agreed: "Live
with me and learn my skills; perhaps you will attain enlightenment." Years passed. The student excelled in learning the
skills of his master. He did not attain enlightenment. At the
end of every year the student would ask: "Why after all this
time and all this learning have I not attained enlightenment?"
The master would respond: "You are not ready." At the end of
the twelfth year the student approached the teacher while he
was cutting onions with a machete. In response to the
question the master seized the pupil's hand and chopped off
the thumb. The pupil screamed and grasped his crippled
hand. And suddenly he was enlightened.

We explained the story thus: It is often those capabilities
which help a person grasp the world of objects and manipulate it for one's needs that hinder that person's development
as a subject. Hence, if a person wishes to develop as a subject
he must often cut himself off from such capabilities. Participants were then divided into small groups of three or four
and each one described which of his capabilities, he believed,
hindered his development as a subject. Here are some excerpts from the general discussion that followed.

Dana (Jewish woman): I want to ask you a question, Haim, before I
report what we discussed. Why do you ask us these sorts of
questions? Can't you just tell each one of us what needs to be
done, without our undergoing all this questioning and discussing?
Haim: Does the questioning bore you?

Dana: No, not really, but it is repetitive. Since I joined a Buberian Learning Group, about a year and a half ago, I have been questioning myself. At first it was interesting, but now I seem to be treading in one place. Each Thursday I know that I'll come to the group and will have to question my life here in Israel, as a Jew, as a woman, as a mother, as a friend, as a subject. Why can't I, at times, leave what seems well enough alone? I don't believe I will reach enlightenment, like the student in the story, and I'm not even sure that I care.

Haim: One of my teachers once told me: A good personal question, with which you live and develop daily, can lead you to heaven; no questioning of yourself is a form of spiritual death—and there is no third choice between these two possibilities. I believe that you are right; there is something repetitive and tiring about our constant demand that you question your life. But isn't that the only way to begin to change things in one's life?

Dana: I agree. But at times I just want to lie back and flow down the river of time. Do you understand what I mean?

Haim: Sure. It can be great. But the floating will also get repetitive if you don't come back to the asking of questions. Now let's hear what happened in your discussion.

Dana: All three of us felt that in cutting ourselves off from one of our capabilities we would weaken ourselves and diminish our power to cope with the hatred and mistrust which surround us. The whole idea of enlightenment was also foreign to us. Perhaps Shlomo should give his example.

Shlomo (Jewish man): I feel that I am very good at organizing my life. I have everything set up so that things will flow smoothly, without arousing too many ripples. Why should I cut myself away from this capability? Let me give an example that has nothing to do with education for peace. When I go on a trip, everything is set up so that I will have minimum distractions, even when I go to Tel Aviv or Jerusalem. Why should I invite back these distractions? What enlightenment will it bring me?

Hussam (Arab man, assistant group leader): There is a basic point here that Shlomo and Dana seem to be missing. Both of you seem to think that the goal of cutting yourself off from a personal capability is to reach enlightenment. No. The goal is to become a subject. Now, Shlomo, I've said this to you before: Being subjective is being able to surprise yourself. From what you describe, you will never surprise yourself; you will never discover in yourself new capabilities and new fears. Primarily because you are afraid of being afraid.

Shlomo: What is wrong with not wanting to be afraid?

Hussam: None of us wants to be afraid. No, your problem with your overorganizing, as I see it, is that you are afraid of meeting yourself as a person with fears; so, through the organizing of your life, you do everything you can to evade such a meeting with yourself down the road of your life. But being a subject is living with fear, coping with it, overcoming it, and then living with it again the next day.

Shlomo: You still have not convinced me that I should want to meet myself as a person with fears. And you have not told me what I will learn by cutting myself away from my well-organized life.

Haim: It is hard to say what anyone will learn from such a cutting away. Perhaps I can answer you by pointing out what is the difference between self-fulfillment and the realizing of a vision. All of us here are concerned with the realizing of some sort of vision of peaceful relations between Jews and Arabs. We also wish to live self-fulfilling lives. Both your approach and Dana's approach see self-fulfillment as your major goal. Dana is asking: Why so many questions? I am living a quite self-fulfilling life. You are asking: Why cripple myself with giving up my organizing skills, when I am satisfied with how they help me cope with this rotten reality?

Shlomo: Exactly. Why give up the security and the control I have over my future?

Haim: That is your mistake. You grasp lack of security and lack of control as a weakness. Often it is just the opposite. A person who takes upon himself the task of becoming a subject is strong because he no longer needs to be in control in order to survive. He knows that he will take the risk and endeavor to face directly and forcefully any difficulties he encounters. The most terrifying example of such a risk that Kierkegaard mentions is Abraham going to sacrifice Isaac. Abraham was not in control and he took the risk. We have much smaller risks to take. But here is where true self-fulfillment meets with the realization of a vision. The realization of a vision gives us the direction of development, but it also teaches us to be subjective while, say, fighting for justice.

Dana: Haim, please explain more. All this is not too clear.

Haim: We already mentioned a couple of times that Kierkegaard said that one must relate to God with infinite passion. What struck me about both your response and Shlomo's response was the lack of passion. A vision of justice or of peaceful relations between Jews and Arabs here in Israel will never be realized if we do not embrace it passionately. We must not only sit back and criticize, but go out there and do, passionately. And when a person can express his passions in the search for justice—say in fighting the Kafkian establishment in Israel or the Arab tendency to fanaticism, both of which perpetuate the conflict—he is also developing as a person; he is fulfilling himself.

Dana: You seem to have gone off on a new tangent. What does all this have to do with my not wanting to ask myself questions?

Haim: Perhaps you haven't asked those questions with passion. Because when you *do* ask a question with all your heart you are already beginning to change, and you are already seeking to make things different. But instead, it seems that you both are playing a game of hide-and-seek with yourselves. And in this game you do not have to seek beyond your accepted capabilities.

Shlomo: But who says that if I start seeking beyond my so-called accepted capabilities, I will find something worthy?

Haim: Nobody. But if you don't seek you surely will not find. In one of Buber's Hasidic stories, Rabbi Pinchas' grandson was

playing hide-and-seek with some of his friends. He hid himself and waited for them to find him, but after a while they
got tired of the search and ran away to play elsewhere. The
boy burst into tears and ran to his grandfather, who took him
on his lap to comfort him. But when he told his grandfather
what had happened, Rabbi Pinchas also started crying.—
"Why are you crying, grandfather?" the boy asked.—"Because God says the same thing: I hid for a while and now no
one wants to search for me!"

POLITICAL RHETORIC

The Education for Peace Project developed on the background of political rhetoric, which proved to be an important component of the situation in which Jews and Arabs in Israel find themselves. We learned that, as T. E. Lawrence repeatedly showed, in Arab society political rhetoric is an art, a way of life, and a trap. It is an art because Arabs play with the multiple shades of meaning that abound in Arabic, creating sentences pregnant with expressive and associative ambiguities. It is a way of life which ensures the Arab of continual support of the surrounding milieu, since it allows each person to interpret the rhetoric in accordance with his own wishes. And it is a trap because the Arab—like Nasser before the Six-Day War—is frequently unable to emerge from the flood of rhetoric which he initiated, and which suddenly has begun to engulf him and to drag him into situations that he never envisioned. It is also a trap because the person for whom rhetoric becomes a way of life will begin to believe that words and not daily deeds are ways of changing reality. Doing will then mean frenzied actions or fanatic outbursts.

Many Jews in Israel seem to be less attracted to political rhetoric. Three immediate reasons come to mind. First, Hebrew is a straightforward and concise language. Any reader of the Bible in Hebrew will sense the brevity, the straightforwardness, the unwillingness to allow ambiguities to arise. Second, Judaism is a religion of the daily deed, the Mitzvah. From early life the Jew learns that the deed is what counts and not the rhetoric surrounding the deed. And third, the building of Israel was mainly a result of hard day-to-day Jewish pioneering work, which succeeded in cultivating and modernizing an undeveloped and rather abandoned land that in 1900 was part swamp, part bog, and part desert. It seems that many a Jew is willing to accept political rhetoric when it leads to deeds or summarizes them: without deeds, rhetoric sounds hollow.

The above generalizations may be an oversimplification. Menachem Begin has used rhetoric to lead Jews to accept immoral deeds or political failures. Think of the Lebanon debacle. Yet I still believe that the generalizations do describe basic existential differences. For instance, during the past years two movements arose in Israel which, with minimal rhetoric, attempted to change the political scene. One is the ultrarightist Gush Emunim movement and the other is the Peace Now movement. Both movements scored a few political victories; but they did not rely on political rhetoric to precede or to accompany these victories. Compare this approach to the decisive significance of political rhetoric in the history of the PLO, or in the lives of Quadaffi, Nasser, or Sadat—and the difference between the Jewish and the Arab relation to rhetoric will emerge.

One additional point should be added: Arab rhetoric is generally much more radical than Jewish rhetoric. I shall exemplify this point with two citations. Consider articles 20 and 22 of The Palestinian National Covenant.

ARTICLE 20

The Balfour Declaration, the Mandate for Palestine, and everything that has been based on them, are deemed null and void. Claims of historical or religious ties of Jews with Palestine are incompatible with the facts of history and the true conception of what constitutes statehood. Judaism being a divine religion is not an independent nationality. Nor do Jews constitute a single nation with an identity of its own: they are citizens of the states to which they belong.

ARTICLE 22

Zionism is a political movement organically associated with international imperialism and antagonistic to all action for liberation and to progressive movements in the world. It is racist and fanatic in its nature, aggressive, expansionist, and colonialist in its aims, and fascist in its methods. Israel is the instrument of the Zionist movement, and a geographical base for world imperialism placed strategically in the midst of the Arab homeland to combat the hopes of the Arab nation for liberation, unity and progress.

Compare these articles to the following excerpt from the statement submitted by David Ben-Gurion to the Anglo-American Committee that examined the situation in Palestine in 1946.

Now, Sir, for one minute or two I want to say a few words to the Arabs who are here and to those who are not here. What I want to say to them is this: The conflict between us today is the most tragic, for it is in a way a family conflict. But it will not last long. We shall carry out the work of our regeneration even if the obstacles in our path increase, for it is a matter of life and death to us. We are returning to our country as of right. It is your wish that this land, too, should be Arab. Perhaps it is a natural desire. Many of you prefer a poor Arab country to a prosperous Jewish country. That does you honor, but we are not strangers to this land. It always has been and remains forever a historic homeland. History has decreed that we should return to our country and reestablish here the Jewish state, and the Jewish state will be established. Many of you know it as well as we do.

In the name of the Jewish people, I say to you: Even though you are still opposing us, we want you to know that you have not throughout the entire world a more loyal and useful friend than the Jewish people. We will build our country on the foundation of Jewish justice, brotherhood and peace. The closer and more quickly we draw together, the better it will be both for us and for you. The Jewish people and the Arab people need each other in the fashioning of their future as free peoples in this part of the world.

We are convinced, with the arrival of the Jewish state on the one hand and independent Arab unity on the other, we shall be able to cooperate closely in a spirit of mutual aid, in a true covenant of brothers and equals.

7. Dostoyevski:
The Quest for Love and Joy in Life

Love is a teacher; but one must know how to acquire it, for it is hard to acquire, it is dearly bought, it is won slowly by long labor. For we must love not only occasionally, for a moment, but forever. Everyone can love occasionally, even the wicked can. —FYODOR DOSTOYEVSKI

QUITE often Dostoyevski has been branded as morbid, as continually depicting the destructive tendencies of persons on the verge of abnormality—Stavrogin in *The Possessed,* Rogozhyn and Nastasya in *The Idiot,* Ivan Karamazov in *The Brothers Karamazov.* Such a branding is unfortunate because some of Dostoyevski's characters express a profound joy in life, in one's ability to love, to live courageously, to create, to educate, to break out of the social conventions which chain a person to mediocrity. Dostoyevski shows that this joy, which may be accompanied by intense suffering, can thrive, despite the degradations which a suffering person may undergo; furthermore, he believes, joy in life has a redeeming power.

Like love, joy in life can open aspects of being which previously seemed to have been concealed; hence such joy often accompanies creativity, or dialogue, or any authentic giving of oneself. Through his characters, Dostoyevski shows (as Nietzsche and Kierkegaard discussed at length) that the problem facing each person is his being rooted in a mediocre existence which hinders any breaking through of love, creativity, or authentic giving of oneself. In such an existence one

125

is taught always to be careful, to make sure that one never confronts and is never confronted, always to adhere to what one's superiors suggest, to acknowledge the wisdom of social conventions, and never to hurt another person's feelings, unless, of course, his status is inferior. In short, it is by seemingly good deeds that the morality of mediocrity quells any outburst of love or of joy or of creativity.

All this is not new. —Socrates was killed because he confronted his peers and rejected their mediocre morality. — What *is* new is that Dostoyevski describes how persons less talented than Socrates can strive to live authentically, even in a situation riddled by conflict. Dimitri and Alyosha Karamazov are not intellectual geniuses, yet they seek to live authentically, joyfully, lovingly. In many of their attempts to attain love and joy they fail, but as a result of these attempts they do succeed in somewhat freeing themselves from the confinements of mediocrity. The same is true of Sonya Marmeladov in *Crime and Punishment* and of Prince Myshkin in the first part of *The Idiot*. Such a seeking is often not an outcome of a conscious decision to reject mediocrity. Raskolnikov and Ivan Karamazov, who ponderously deliberated, and finally decided to become "nonmediocre," failed. Dostoyevski indicates that one succeeds only if one begins with a recognition of one's weaknesses and a profound wish to give of oneself through love, or through the struggle for justice or beauty or truth, or through the lessening of other persons' suffering. In short, Dostoyevski shows that the salt of the earth—Dimitris, Alyoshas, Sonyas in any society—can respond to their existential situation in a manner analogous to Socrates responding to his calling.

Thus the reading of Dostoyevski can teach many a person how to respond in the specific existential situation in which he finds himself. Such a reading differs ontologically from reading so as to discuss ideas. In reading so as to respond existentially the reader is involving his entire freedom in the reading process, he is giving himself fully. (Nietzsche would say—he is dancing through the story.) Reading so as to discuss ideas is much less demanding—ideas are out there in the realm of intellectual indifference, they can be totally divorced from the reader's person. For instance, I cannot learn much from Dimitri Karamazov's love for Grushenka without having loved, without having suffered for my passions. Of course, I can discuss Dimitri's love in the manner in which I discuss a used car or Leibnitz' monads; but I will learn nothing from such a discussion about my own love. Only if I question my own love while reading about Dimitri's quest for love will I be learning to acquire love as a teacher. And contrarily, as Ivan Karamazov painfully learned, when one lives in the realm of ideas, one retains the frustration and perspectives of adolescence. Like Ivan, one plays with one's life so as not to mature and to have to accept full responsibility for one's existence.

Reading so as to respond existentially is also an antidote to the eroding power of rhetoric. Often, rhetoric leads persons into the trap that Hegel developed in philosophy, and against which all existentialists rebelled—that one's being can and should be swallowed up by an all-encompassing ideal. In trying to educate second-year participants to read *The Brothers Karamazov* and to respond existentially, we encountered difficulties. Here is one such instance.

Muhammad (Arab man): There is something inauthentic about your entire approach, Dina. You are trying to show us how not to be led by rhetoric, but you yourself are using rhetoric in order to convince us not to be rhetorical.

Dina (Jewish woman group leader): I agree that I use rhetoric, but only if my wishing to convince you is more important to me than relating to you as a person do I become rhetorical. I don't mean to be saying that I am never rhetorical; often I am. Yet I do try to accept you and other members of this group as more important than my winning the argument.

Jeremiah (Jewish man): I don't understand what all this has to do with Ivan Karamazov's rebellion and his wishing to kill his father. Ivan wasn't rhetorical. He hardly spoke to anyone.

Dina: That is a point you missed, Jeremiah. Ivan *was* rhetorical, but he himself was both the speaker and the listener. Such a path can be creative and dangerous. It can lead to eloquence, to poetry, and to madness; Ivan followed this path to the bitter end. Interestingly, his eloquence and poetry always seemed to be more important to him than his own person. In that respect he resembles some of the political leaders who surround us. I often get the impression that many Jewish and Arab leaders have allowed their rhetorical abilities to become more important to them than their personal existence. Their rhetoric has become a *Golem* which they created but which is now out of their control, like Ivan's poems at the end of the book that come back to haunt him. But let us get back to Ivan's rebellion. Why did it lead to the killing of his father? And what does all this teach us about assuming responsibility in a specific historical situation?

Muhammad: Ivan was rebelling against society and history. And I really don't see what his rebellion has to do with me. I don't want to rebel against society and history; I would like some basic things to change, but otherwise I don't want to rebel.

Jeremiah: I'm not the rebellious type of person either.

Ilana (Jewish woman, laughing): Don't worry, Jeremiah. You never fooled us on that point.

Dina: Let me first explain why Ivan's rebelling leads to his father's murder. Seemingly, all Ivan wants to do is to return his entrance ticket, the ticket that allowed him to enter into the world. Now one of the persons who brought him into the world was his father, and when you return the ticket you are no longer obligated toward your father. You can agree to his being killed by his lackey. All this is simple. But the problem is much more complex when we understand that what Ivan really refuses to accept is human history. I agree that human history has moments—many moments—of atrocities. Ivan describes some of these atrocities eloquently. But rejecting human history is also rejecting your responsibility for the here and now.

Muhammad: Now you really have convinced me not to rebel.

Ilana: Muhammad, you seem to be wanting to find things in Dina's words that will justify your current existence. You are overlooking, perhaps deliberately, that there is a way of rebelling that does not reject history but rather affirms it. Think of the rebellion of the Zionist pioneers against Orthodox Judaism.

Dina: Ilana is right, Muhammad. There are two ways of not assuming responsibility for the here and now. One way is by rebelling against history, like Ivan; the other way is by floating down the river of time without really being concerned with what happens. You reject Ivan's extreme approach and thus justify your wanting to take it easy and float your life away. But there is a third approach, which requires rebelling against the atrocities that surround us and going out and doing something so as to change what is happening. That is what Ilana means by rebelling against history while affirming it.

Muhammad: There is something bookish about what you are saying. What in the world can I do tomorrow that would be rebellion, that would be a changing of history while affirming it?

Dina: At least you are beginning to ask meaningful questions. The problem is that most people, like Ivan Karamazov, think that there is *one* thing to do—*one* panacea—and if we do that, we assume responsibility. Well I have news for you both, Muhammad and Jeremiah: There are no panaceas! There are only tiny daily acts along the way which help us change history. For instance, very few of you Arabs are knowledgeable about Arab history, or about the Moslem religion, but you will not take the time to develop your knowledge. Instead you sit for hours in the student café and bullshit each other. We have stressed here again and again that knowledge is a way of assuming responsibility for history. But more important, Muhammad, I don't think that most of you Arabs are willing to work for changes—slow but meaningful changes— in Arab society. Even changes that you agree here need to be made. For instance, talking about the role of the Arab woman has become a cliché in this project; but hardly any Arab male I have met, including you, Muhammad, has worked on himself to become less of a male chauvinist pig.

In short, Jeremiah and Muhammad, you both are ready to demand changes but not to change by yourselves, while demanding and bringing about other minor changes. You are like Ivan, who not only rejects history, he also rejects the small deeds that can bring about change. He refuses to understand that if he slowly changes himself, he will also be changing the persons who interact with him.

Muhammad: You probably are right. But, to be honest with you, I doubt if I'll get out and do much tomorrow. How about giving me an example of how Jews reject history.

Jeremiah: I also feel that you are right, Dina. But something in your approach makes me feel impotent, if you know what I mean.

Ilana: I'm not sure that, at times, feeling impotent is all that bad, Jeremiah. But I want to give an example of how Jews do not rebel against history while affirming it, and not preach to you. Take the whole problem of Zionism. As a movement, Zionism is dying, because it is no longer built on day-to-day deeds that change people for the better while changing history. It is now a great fund-raising and political organization which is so general in its goals that it has nothing personal to say to anyone, except for the career Zionists who make a living by raising contributions or issuing political statements. I'll tell you another thing; since I joined this Project, and I'm thirty-two years old, this is the first time I feel myself doing something Zionistic, because I'm trying to change my own personal history of rotten relations with Arabs while also influencing the developments around me.

One of the major problems with which we struggled while educating for peace was that many participants play-acted their lives. Perhaps the best literary example of a person who play-acts his life is Hamlet; but *The Brothers Karamazov* also abounds in such play-actors who do not accept full responsibility for their daily deeds—that is, Fyodor Karamazov, Ivan Karamazov, Madam Hohlakov, her daughter Lise, Katrina, and Dimitri until his conversion. Dostoyevski shows that persons can only overcome such play-acting through suffering and active love. Thus Madam Hohlakov and Ivan Karamazov, who are admonished early in the book by Father Zosima for their play-acting and who evade suffering and active love, continue to play-act; but Dimitri, Grushenka, Katrina, and the schoolboys whom Alyosha educates—all of whom undergo deep suffering and express active love—stop their play-acting and begin to live more fully.

Dostoyevski explains that play-acting is born of fear and falsehood, especially lying to oneself (bad faith, which Sartre explained eighty years later, can also be included in the source of play-acting). Pain and passion can help a person break through the clouds of fear, falsehood, and bad faith that obscure his path, but few persons are willing to experience pain and passion fully. Such unwillingness underlies Muhammad's final remark in the above discussion, when he tells Dina that her thoughts make him feel impotent and, therefore, he will not do anything tomorrow. What is worse, Jeremiah's rhetoric and falsehood, coupled with his embracing his impotency, allow others to engage in evil deeds. As Dostoyevski shows in *The Idiot* and *The Possessed*, those persons who admit their social and personal impotency, and demand that we identify with their sad situations, allow persons with fanatic and extreme views to flourish. Thus agreeing to be socially impotent supports those persons who are willing to commit crimes in the name of some far-fetched ideal or base passion. And no one is responsible for Muhammad's or Prince Myshkin's impotence except Muhammad or Prince Myshkin.

In many instances, personal impotence and play-acting one's life are two sides of the same coin. When questioned about their impotence, many persons explain that they remain in such a situation because they do not wish to suffer, and they believe that any nonconventional doing will cause other persons to suffer too. Thus impotence becomes the play-acting of unwillingness to inflict suffering. Dostoyevski showed this approach when he prefaced Ivan Karamazov's bitter rejection of human suffering to his rebellion against history. But if we reject Ivan Karamazov's approach, as Alyosha rejected it, we must act to make others suffer, in order to bring about a better society, better persons. Put differently, Dostoyevski shows that only a person who is willing to be guilty is also willing to dream and to work to realize those dreams.

I suspect that here is one of the areas where the Education for Peace Project failed. Persons were not willing to inflict suffering, or to undergo suffering, in order to change their situation. In other words, many relations within the Project and many relations between members of the Project and other persons were conditional; the relations would be good as long as someone did not "rock the boat" and make other persons suffer. But action research is bound to rock the boat; and when working, say, against hatred and bigotry I refused, and demanded that members of my staff refuse, to make any compromise. In short, I often deliberately rocked the boat.

Put differently, an educator for peace today cannot always be liberal; not all views, not all actions, are equally tolerable. This approach is partially accepted when I say that we must *fight* against Jews who believe that "the only good Arab is a dead Arab" and against Arabs who want "to throw all the Jews into the sea." By the word "fight," I mean refusing to listen to what they have to say and explain; I mean struggling against the holders of such views and inflicting suffering upon them. The minute I agree to listen to a Jew who firmly believes that "the only good Arab is a dead Arab," I have accepted his prejudiced bigotry as a legitimate viewpoint, and I have allowed his bigotry to be included as a possibility which the community of Jews will consider. In short, his prejudice has won recognition as a respectable human possibility, and he has retained his human image. But I taught that such views remove their adherents from the community of men, and each person who wishes to work for peace and dialogue must participate in making sure that this removing is forceful. One way is to immediately brand the holder of such a view as a prejudiced bigot, and to notify him that as long as he adheres to such an approach, he is your enemy.

Bigots, though, are often sly. When they gain power, they often hide their views behind abstract formulas which are ethically neutral. At times, the only way to counter such bigots is to reject such formulations and to find loopholes in the system that they control. For instance, at the end of the second year of the Education for Peace Project the Ford Foundation offered me a grant of $27,500 to help train Arab leaders for Buberian Learning Groups. After the grant was approved by the Project's Steering Committee, made up of professors of Ben-Gurion University, I was suddenly notified that the rector of the university refused to accept the grant. Political expediency and the problem of social tensions were mentioned as his reasons, but I received no explanation of what these words meant. After four months of waiting and of seeking ways to get the university to sign the grant contract, I let it be known that I had found an international organization which agreed to channel the Ford Foundation grant for us, and that the Ford Foundation, because of Ben-Gurion University's *de facto* refusal to accept the grant, had agreed to such a channeling. I also indicated that, once the grant was received by the organization, I would train the Arab leaders on campus, using my rights to hold classes on a volunteer basis. Within a week, the university signed the grant contract.

In much of the scholarly discussion about *The Brothers Karamazov*, Dimitri Karamazov has been overlooked. Scholars have preferred to argue about Ivan's presentation of the Grand Inquisitor, or to compare the *Weltanschauungen* of Zosima and Ivan, or to discuss the link between Ivan and Smerdyakov. Dimitri's lust for life has received very little attention. Ignoring this lust for life is unfortunate because, in a much more down-to-earth manner than Zosima, Dimitri lives his quest for love and for joy while rebelling against his social impotency. At times, as Dostoyevski shows, such a rebellion can be similar to the ravings of a drunkard or can be based on wild fantasies—but these are often the only manner to assert one's freedom to express passions and joy in life.

Dimitri Karamazov's responses have much to teach the educator for peace. He does not express his views abstractly; rather, he is talking about his own body, his own passions, his own love. His joy is bodily joy, his love is physical love, his love for life is a bodily love for life. Such love is often ignored or repressed. The result is that many persons relate to the horrors of war abstractly, and not because they love or find joy in life. Even in the Mideast, where war is an everyday reality, many educators and workers for peace prefer to remain on the abstract level of discussion. In a sense, they are thereby strengthening the warmongers.

Love is a teacher, Zosima says to his wards before his death. Dimitri learns that love is a teacher of the body (not only of the mind), and when the body learns to love, as Dimitri did, a person's love is richer and purer. Lust without love, as in Fyodor Karamazov's life, is bestial; but love without passion, as expressed by Madam Hohlakov, Katrina, and Ivan Karamazov, is impotent and borders on hysteria. The quest for love and joy in life is not a compromise between these two extremes, as many persons would suspect. Such a quest seeks to allow love and passion to be expressed fully and to blend naturally, authentically.

Persons who learn to compromise in their intimate life will tend to view compromise as a way of life. But dialogue is not a seeking for compromise; neither is education for peace. Dialogue, as Buber envisions it, is the meeting of two whole persons who bring their entire being to the meeting. But a person who lives his life as a compromise learns never to bring his entire being to any meeting. Living life as a compromise is accepting mistrust of the Other as the basis for one's ontological field of development; it is believing that one will be psychologically castrated by the Other if one dares to trust him or her. The need to reject compromise is probably one of the reasons why Nietzsche's Zarathustra emphasized the importance of dancing. When a person is dancing and fully giving himself to the music, in harmony with the movements of one's partner, he exists beyond the need for compromise.

But from early age, persons are taught that compromise *is* a way of life—nay, *the* way of life. Of course, compromise is important for the stability of any society or social group, but if love is to emerge, the role of compromise must be limited. For instance, in large segments of Arab society today, choosing a bride is basically an agreement between the groom, his father, and the bride's family—with the bride hardly being asked. In such marriages, compromise often becomes a way of existence for all involved and the possibility of conjugal dialogue is frequently extinguished. In Jewish society, compromise is demanded in less institutionalized ways; thus many couples will believe in the beauty of family life and compromise themselves to a frigid living, side by side with each other. In such milieus, persons like Dimitri, who refuse to compromise, are viewed as weird.

Thus educating for love and joy in life is often educating persons to break out of the general acceptance of compromise as a way of life. Here we encountered difficulties. Consider the following conversation I had with David, a Jewish group leader.

Haim: Your way of handling the workshops you lead is much too compromising, David.

David: What do you mean by that?

Haim: Put bluntly, you seem to be afraid to eat crap. You listen to what people say very carefully and always accept what they say as legitimate. You often try to correct a person by reflecting to him what he said. But frequently such reflecting gives support to the mistaken way of life the person has adopted.

David: I still don't see where I am compromising myself; and I *am* eating crap, or at least I feel I am.

Haim: Let me say it differently. Perhaps the only way to not be afraid to eat crap is to get people to agree with what you are doing while they disagree with you. It is more than confronting a person; it is telling him at times that he is obnoxious.

David: But what if I don't feel that a person is obnoxious?

Haim: You are right; obnoxious is a hard word to attach to a person, and it is too general. But in a workshop two months ago, I told Joseph in my group that he is masturbating his life away. He became very angry, but I think he is slowly beginning to see what I meant and how what I said can help him.

David: Be more specific about what I should do.

Haim: Perhaps I can explain what I want by comparing you to Alyosha Karamazov. As Dostoyevski portrays him, he is really a wonderful, charming person. You have charm, too, David. But Alyosha seems to lose much of his focus by being liked by everyone, by always being at their beck and call, by listening very carefully but being overcareful at taking a stand. He seems a bit less fluid at the end of the book, when he works with Kolya, Ilyusha, and the other kids. I believe that the reason Zosima tells him to leave the monastery and to go out and live in the world is so that he can learn to be less nice. He compromises himself too much.

David: But what should I do?

Haim: I believe that your mistake is that, like Alyosha, you rely too much on your strength and do not allow the areas where you feel you might be weak to emerge. There is thus a basic compromise in your being, in your way of life; probably this compromise emerges in your relations with friends and with women. But often our real power emerges when we go beyond the areas where we can rely on our strength. Thus your strength in leading a group is in encouraging people to trust you, but if you rely only on that strength it will slowly become a weakness.

David: I don't understand why, if participants in my group relate to me trustfully, you want me to approach them from a position where I am not too strong. Won't that limit my control and my ability to educate?

Haim: Perhaps, but now you are limited because if you don't work in areas where you are not strong you are not educating yourself; and then you cannot demand that others educate themselves too. But, in general, my feeling is that you are really afraid of not being in control; that is why you always work from a position of strength. Yet, often personal development begins when I agree not to be in control, when I open areas where I am weak and let whatever happens to happen so I can learn from it. In short, since you compromise your own life regularly, you lead the workshops in a compromising manner, and you don't educate persons to go beyond compromising. I'm talking about your existence, not about what you say to persons. You often say things that are true and pertinent.

David: Give me an example of how I mess things up by not exposing weaknesses.

Haim: Can I give you an example that might hurt?

David: Go ahead.

Haim: In the last workshop you led, when members of your group discussed the flowing of their life in relation to Kafka's parable of the river, you were showing people how they lack a direction of development; what you did not show is how weak you yourself are in this specific realm. Like a sparrow, you jump from branch to branch nibbling a bit here and a bit there. That may be O.K. for your life right now, but it is a weakness you should present, especially if you are demanding of persons that they seek a direction toward which their life should flow. You fear revealing this weakness, which is a sort of playing with your life, while you are demanding that other people work hard. And you hide it by your overconcern with the person you are working with; he is so happy that you can be trusted that he does not sense the lack of depth in your approach as an educator.

David: Why should all this hurt me?

Haim: Maybe because of one thing which I really learned myself

from Dimitri Karamazov. When you are compromising yourself, as you are doing, you really can't love. And I'm afraid,
David, that is where you are now.

One reason *The Brothers Karamazov* is helpful in education for peace is that it presents the complexity of multiple-
level relations in which each person exists. Dostoyevski
shows that becoming a subject is not the result of interaction
with one person, but of one's striving to be subjective in this
web of multiple-level relations. He shows that one must
attempt to be a subject on each level of relations. Consider
Ivan Karamazov. He has moments of striving to be a subject:
when he is confiding his rebellion against God to Alyosha and
telling him his poem, "The Grand Inquisitor." But such moments have no influence on a person's existence if he is
unwilling to continue to be a subject in less gratifying moments. After his cathartic, purifying meeting with Alyosha,
Ivan goes home, meets Smerdyakov, and immediately slips
back into his inauthentic self, which sanctions his father's
murder.

Many persons refuse to see how the interlocking web of
relations in which they exist limits their subjectivity. They
seek solace in the rare moments of being a subject that they
experience, while allowing the general trend of not living as a
subject to dominate their existence. For instance, they are
ready to strive to be subjects in areas which do not threaten
their status or acceptance by their peers. As Buber and
Kierkegaard indicated, such an approach is not a striving to
become subjective. Yet these thinkers did not show how
difficult it is to strive to become a subject in the interlocking
web of day-to-day relations, which are usually tainted by
problems of money, personal honor, love, passion, vengeance,
faith, hatred, deceit, etc. Dostoyevski did. Dimitri becomes
subjective while grappling with such a web.

One enemy of the person who wishes to act subjectively is
the political rhetorician. He attempts both to attract and
paralyze his listeners, by describing the objective reality as a

given which leaves no place for the individual to make ethical choices. According to these rhetoricians, a reasonable person can often view this frequently unfortunate reality from a comfortable perspective. But the person who strives to bring about a change is suffering from an illusion. The best one can do is to support a political party or faction that is trying to alter the historical situation minimally.

The rhetorician often succeeds because he embraces an important principle: One must endeavor to see historical reality in all its stark nakedness, as the interaction of forces upon which the individual has, at best, only minor influence. But he uses this truth to paralyze his listeners as ethical beings, to show them that their freedom is insignificant, and to indicate that since there is not much that they can personally do, they should support his political views. Once again, consider Ivan Karamazov. He was so successful in describing human suffering, and in depicting man's rejection of the freedom given by Jesus, that he convinced himself that there were no ethical choices to be made. At that moment, Dostoyevski shows, the political rhetorician becomes very dangerous.

During the second and third year of the Project we had weekly lectures on topics relevant to education for peace. Some of these lectures were by historians and social scientists; some were by political rhetoricians. One Jewish politician greatly peeved the participants. Here are some excerpts from his lecture and the ensuing discussion. (The lecture was given about a month and a half after President Sadat's assassination.)

Lecturer: When I try to evaluate the Israeli-Arab conflict today, I must say that I am very pessimistic. I see this conflict as being far from any solution, even in the remote future of say fifty years. The reason for this situation has nothing to do with the sides participating in the conflict, or with the Israeli-Arab disagreement. The reason for this situation is found in the objective givens of the world in which we exist, which do not allow us to reach a stable situation. The entire approach which says "let us sit down and talk about a peace treaty" is unrealistic. Perhaps the most important thing for us is to understand and to live with the knowledge that there is no solution. This is the political reality within which we are living. In 1945 the Nazi regime fell and Berlin was captured and divided between the Soviets and the Western powers. For a long period there was an argument: How does one solve the problem of Berlin? Today, everyone understands that there is no solution worth striving for, and that the problem of Berlin may or may not be solved in the near or far future. After the Second World War the country of Korea was divided. Later there was a long and cruel war between the North and the South, but Korea remained divided, and everyone accepts the subject as open. The same is true of Cyprus: people accept the idea that it is divided between two ethnic groups.

Only in our area do people around the world think that we have to find a solution; we, the Jews, must find a solution with the Palestinians and the Arabs. The same Germans who accept the lack of solution in Berlin demand it from us.

On the other hand, we should not go to extremes. War is a waste of time in our area because it will not lead to a solution. But then some people say that if war is untenable, let us sit down and solve our conflict of interests.

My response to that is: When I sat with Egyptians I found it difficult to be totally open with them. It would look different if the Mideast were stable as a political area, if I knew where each of the political players stood and what he wanted. But when I sign a peace treaty with a country like Egypt, with Sadat at its head, and I believe that President Sadat was a great leader, the greatest Egypt had in the past forty to fifty years. But with one burst of machine-gun fire Sadat is dead, and I ask who is Egypt and there is no answer.

In the Mideast we are dealing with unclear, unstable material. We must understand that, even without being linked to Israel, the culture and the regimes of the Mideast are undergoing a development and a revolution, and I don't know where this will lead them. They are not partners whom I can trust for an agreement.

So what can we do? Two things.

1. We must seek ways to live within an insolvable situation, with all the difficulties that such an existence brings. Look at it this way. It is as if we are disabled, both sides in the conflict, and we have to get used to the idea that we are disabled and that we should live with this disability with minimum pain. We should try and reach some general agreements that both sides accept, and I therefore accept the agreement with Egypt. We must bless every partial solution with an adversary.

Unfortunately, most people in Israel think there is nothing to be done. That is negative pessimism. Mine is positive pessimism because I believe that we can do something.

2. If we accept the idea that the conflict will be with us for the next half-century at least, we can nibble away at little parts of the conflict and reach agreement there. We can solve little parts of the general situation of conflict, even while the situation remains. Such a process has value and a dynamics of its own, and the political leaders must take the initiative.

Haim: Any questions to the lecturer?

Dana: You mentioned the peace with Egypt merely as an agreement. Why didn't you call it a peace? There is an Egyptian embassy in Tel Aviv and an Israeli embassy in Egypt. We don't have an Israeli embassy, say, in Russia; fewer Israeli tourists go to Russia than to Egypt, yet you wouldn't call what goes on between us and Russia merely an agreement.

Lecturer: Formally you may be right, but I am speaking realistically. We don't have the historical background of conflict with Russia that we have with Egypt. But what is more important is that Russia is not part of the developing Arab world which is undergoing a revolution and cannot be partners to an agreement. I more or less know what the Russian stand on an issue will be tomorrow; I do not know what the Egyptian stand will be. Of course, I am happy that we reached an agreement with the Egyptians, but believing that this is true peace is a bit unrealistic.

Mahmud: I am an Arab and an Israeli citizen, yet I feel close to the Palestinian aspirations of my Arab friends and relatives on the West Bank who live under Israeli military rule. What do you suggest that I should do to further peace?

Lecturer: I think that you should explain to them the main thrust of my lecture: That this situation is complex, that Israel is in the midst of a developing area which is unstable, that they are part of these developments.

Jeremiah: But Mahmud is asking what he should do, not what he should explain to the Palestinians.

Lecturer: Well, when the elections come around you should vote for the party that will try and stabilize the situation and not aggravate it. I'm sure you know that.

Jeremiah: Let me explain. Mahmud and I are in this Education for Peace Project a year and three months already. We are trying to do something about the relations between Jews and Arabs. But your lecture did not encourage us to do anything at all. You seem to be saying that besides going to the polls once every four years, I personally can do nothing.

Lecturer: I am sure that Dr. Gordon's work and research has favorable results, and I support it fully. But in politics we must realistically evaluate the situation and make decisions. Let me thank you for your attention.

After the lecture, quite a few second-year participants in the Project were very angry. We decided to discuss what angered them at the next meeting of their Buberian Learning Group. Here are some excerpts from the discussion that took place a week after the lecture.

Dana: I don't want to discuss the antipathy that the lecturer aroused in me; that is probably beside the point, even though it is worth mentioning that he had no personal rapport with us. I felt that he was trying to use language in a manner that would leave us with no power to respond.

Hussam (angrily): I don't like your evading the issues and trying to be a "pure soul," Dana. The man was obnoxious. First, because he lacked humility. Who the fuck does he think you Jewish Israelis are that no Arab country can be your partners. What does he mean by saying, and I'm quoting here: "I ask who is Egypt and there is no answer." Who the hell does he think he is—God? Wow, what a sick pride he has.

Second, he distorted facts like a third-rate politician, which perhaps is what he is after all. Everyone knows that comparisons in history are always distortions. Why did he choose North and South Korea as what to learn from and not France and Germany that fought for seventy years three bloody wars and now are together in a common market? And who says that persons or nations undergoing development cannot be partners to peace? Where did he find the assumption that nations undergoing revolutions cannot be realistic about peace? After the revolution in Russia in 1917 the Bolsheviks signed a peace treaty with Germany. Come on, the man is a third-rate, stuck-up politician who is really our enemy. Those are the guys this Project is trying to work against.

Haim: Easy, Hussam. I agree with your points. This is the kind of rhetoric we must work against, especially since the major thrust of his speaking was to render us impotent, to convince us not to do anything.

Ilana: I agree with that. Even though Hussam's temper often annoys me, I am ready to endorse everything he said. One major point that struck me was that the man could not and did not want to relate to our personal experiences. He was way out there in the field of objectivity, and all that we had undergone here or in Egypt was worthless for the objective picture he was painting. But, Haim, how do you change such politicians?

Haim: I'm not sure you can. They seem to have too much invested in the self-deceit that has characterized their life for years. You might try to surround them with people and facts that bear witness to a situation which is different than the one they are describing. Then there might be hope. But in a

regular argument such a politician will merely flip off anything you say, much as a person flips a bit of bird crap off his
coat after a walk in the woods.

But I should add two points. We are not only working
against such politicians, but for a future that will be better;
that is what education is all about and that is a strength the
politician does not have. Second, if each of us does not lie to
himself, he attains power to withstand the subtle—or in this
case not so subtle—insinuations of such persons as our
lecturer. And withstanding these insinuations, disagreeing
with his basic attitude, is somewhat making his milieu uncomfortable. We'll talk about more positive doing later.

Through his presentation of Zosima, Alyosha, and Dimitri
in *The Brothers Karamazov* and of Sonya in *Crime and
Punishment*, Dostoyevski shows that it is extremely difficult to
become a subject without a basic relationship to God and to a
religious heritage. In one's quest to become subjective, rejecting the political rhetorician is the simpler task. The more
difficult task is finding a direction of personal development
which allows one to love and to find joy in life while striving
to better the world that one encounters. Dostoyevski describes instances in which the linking of one's deep existential experience to one's spiritual heritage—in his case, to the
teachings of Jesus—will often open up such a direction. He
also indicates that a person's alienation from the living message of his heritage enhances the power of the objective
reality over his daily deeds. As in Ivan Karamazov's case, such
a person tends to reify abstract relations and to reduce
persons to objects.

Dostoyevski believes that a person who attempts to cope
with daily problems in accordance with the highest demands
of his spiritual heritage is seeking to live freely and subjectively. Unfortunately, as in the time of Dostoyevski, religious
establishments continue to water down authentic religious
teachings, to distort the spiritual message of their heritage, to
dogmatize the high demands of the spirit. This process

alienates many persons who cherish their freedom; they reject religion in general and, also, the spiritual message of their religious heritage. Thus today, much as in Dostoyevski's nineteenth-century Russia, or in Kierkegaard's Denmark, a person who is striving to become subjective, a person who seeks profound love and joy in life—such a person must often rebel against the religious establishment while seeking in his heritage the source that can sustain his quest. Ironically, Ivan Karamazov's rebellion against the religious establishment, as expressed in "The Grand Inquisitor," can help Alyosha, who wishes to express the love and joy in life that his mentor, Zosima, helped him find in the teachings of Christ. But this same rebellion cannot help Ivan, who merely wants to justify his lack of direction.

Alyosha Karamazov intuitively sensed that initiating change while remaining subjective requires having a direction of development. At times such a direction can be inspired by a very personal goal, such as Dimitri Karamazov's goal: attaining Grushenka's love by means as honest and as noble as possible and living an honest and noble life with her. But in education, Dostoyevski suggests that a person's direction of development will emerge when he learns to blend personal memories of good deeds with an authentic relation to his heritage and to express the knowledge acquired in daily deeds. Such was Zosima's educational approach.

The large majority of Jews and Arabs who joined the Education for Peace Project were alienated from their heritage. More often than not, such persons have no direction of personal development. Hence they feel much more comfortable reacting to social and personal developments than initiating change in their personal life and society. What is more, few had more than a superficial knowledge of their heritage or its basic source: the Bible or the Koran. In group meetings, I would often indicate that there is no way for a Jew or an Arab to bypass the hard task of learning about his heritage and endeavoring to relate this learning to one's memories and to one's strivings for a better world. Sahib, from Gaza, would support me wholeheartedly. Often we resembled two voices, calling to each other in an expanding desert. At the end of one of these meetings, Sahib approached me.

"You know, Haim, there is something basic about relating to one's heritage that the people here do not seem to understand. I don't know why."

"What?"

"That when you learn about your heritage, seriously I mean, it often opens new possibilities. I've talked to many Arabs here, even to members of the staff. It is not only dogmatic or fanatic Islam that turns them off. It is not only that they don't like to come to prayers. They seem to feel that intellectual development and Islam don't fit in together, that dialogue and Islam are incompatible, that personal freedom is lost if one believes in the Prophet. I tell them that in the history of Islam there were great periods of intellectual achievement, that Maimonides is an example of fruitful Islamic-Jewish relations. After all, he was doctor to the king of Egypt. I tell them that I feel that the Prophet brought freedom, that I am not enslaved by reading the Koran or by praying to Allah. But it seems to fall on deaf ears."

"I know exactly what you mean, Sahib; it is like with the Jews. Some are lazy; others seem deaf."

"You know, Haim, at times I feel as if such deafness or the fanaticism of other Moslems is like an illness."

"It is. At least, Buber and Dostoyevski also felt it was an illness."

"How do you heal it?"

"I don't know, Sahib. I wish I did. At times I believe, as Buber did, that inflicting pain might help. At other moments I just don't know."

We summarized the first two years of the Education for Peace Project during a weekend retreat at the historical seaport of Acre. I chose Acre because of the large percentage of Arab residents in the city (more than 20 percent) and also because Jews and Arabs have been living there together peacefully since the city was captured by the Israeli Defense Force during the War of Independence, more than three and a half decades ago. Participants were divided into groups of four or five, with Jews and Arabs in each group, and were given two assignments.

The first assignment was to roam around the city and find three Jews and three Arabs who would be willing to be interviewed. The group was cautioned to be honest with the interviewees and to advise them that the interview was part of a learning exercise. If possible, they were to conduct the interviews in the persons' homes. After some general information, they were supposed to discuss the problems of Jewish-Arab relations in the city, but to concentrate on concrete personal questions. Thus a Jew should be asked: Do you have a close friend who is an Arab? —If he answers No —Why not? —If he answers Yes —Describe the relation. Do you trust him with your personal problems? Give examples. Do you trust Arabs in general? Why not? Have they ever related mistrustfully to you? Etc. It was quite clear beforehand that the basic attitude we would encounter would be existential mistrust. Participants were coached not to draw out this specific attitude, mainly by asking the questions as innocently as possible. As it turned out, there was little need for such coaching since mistrust was immediately and spontaneously expressed by almost all Jewish and Arab interviewees. Some interviewees even said that they felt uncomfortable talking to a mixed group.

After the results of the interview were discussed with a group leader, the group was told to choose three or four of six persons they interviewed, go back to them, and ask them three or four additional, poignant questions, such as: How has your personal history contributed to the lack of trust between Jews and Arabs here in Acre? Looking back, in what way would you change that history if you were now able to do so? What do you plan to do in the future that can diminish the mistrust between Jews and Arabs here in Acre? After these meetings the participants formulated, in writing, what they had personally learned from the assignment, about Acre, and about diminishing existential mistrust in Israeli society.

The second assignment was shorter. On Friday afternoon, at about 5:30, persons were told to remove their watches and leave them with the secretary, find a spot on the seashore close to where the waves break, and sit there as a group, facing the sea and the sunset. Then they were to discuss the difference between the holy and the secular in their personal lives. After the sun set, they were to return to the hotel.

The weekend ended with a three-hour plenary meeting in which each of the fifty participants and staff explained what he and she had learned during the retreat and how this learning fits in with their summaries of the entire year. Here are some excerpts.

Mahmud (Arab man): **While we were interviewing an Arab man, I suddenly realized how far I had progressed during the year. Not only in establishing trustful relations with Jews, but in learning to live. Before joining the Project, I, like the Arabs here in Acre, was so concerned with trying to maintain peace and quiet that I forgot to love. Now I am beginning to live and am letting the peace and quiet take care of itself. Perhaps all this sounds like big words, so let me say that I feel much more comfortable expressing joy.**

Yafa (Jewish woman): **I have a problem with big words, like "soul" and "existentialism." So let me just say that if I would have been asked two years ago, if in my dreams or nightmares I could imagine myself doing the things I have done this weekend and this year with other Jews and Arabs, and feeling happy and comfortable about such doing, especially with Arabs—two years ago I would have sent whoever told me I would do something like this packing. And here I am, happy about walking around Acre seeking someone to interview, and elated about our talking about holiness, and now I am thinking about getting involved in some sort of political activity. I never liked philosophy in my B.A. studies, but I can** only say that Buber must have something going for him.

Jeremiah: In the interviewing exercise I learned how easier, in a sense, it is to be trustful. The Jews and Arabs whom we interviewed were all knotted up inside when we brought up the relations with persons from the other nation. The exercise on holiness and secular life was a waste of time—although the view was spectacular. I think this summarizes how I view the whole year, too.

David (group leader): Lately I have begun to see how tenderness and love on the one hand and strength and power on the other hand can go together. During the year I learned about the possibility of blending the two, and its importance emerged again in the interviews and the discussions about them. Most interviewees felt that if they want to be strong as Jews or as Arabs they cannot show any tenderness or love to members of the other nation. That was one reason why being interviewed by a group of Jews and Arabs made them feel uncomfortable.

According to my experience, the difference between the holy and the secular is that in the realm of the holy one has a direction and is seeking to follow that direction, while in the secular a person is often directionless. Here in Acre the relations between Jews and Arabs are directionless. That leads to my summary of the year. In Buber's chronicle *For the Sake of Heaven* two persons are discussing the bringing of the redemption. One of them says that redemption must be brought about in the city, in the house, in the heart. These are three significant circles, but I feel that most persons here are happy with what goes on in their heart. We have to start working in the two other circles too; that is also where the heart can be tested—like here in the streets of mistrustful Acre.

Sahib: Gaza, where I live, is as full of mistrust as Acre, so I learned little there. But I did learn something personal and general about the holy, yesterday in the exercise and during the entire year. We cannot take the realm of the holy for granted, as I often did; we must face it again and again with courage.

Like the setting sun yesterday, it beckons us, but we must be courageous to receive its sustenance. I don't know if I've made myself clear.

Haim: You have. I'm happy about the enthusiasm here. But enthusiasm is one thing and living with spirit is another. I'd like to summarize the entire year with a sudden insight that I had while sitting yesterday on the seashore. Suddenly the shore seemed to be the realm of the secular and the sea the realm of the holy. Most people sit on the shore, some venture to dip in the shallows for a few minutes, some even stand out there where the waves break. But most persons are afraid to abandon the safety of the shore and to swim beyond the waves where the water is fathoms deep. Immersing yourself in the realm of the holy means swimming beyond the waves; it means taking the risk of abandoning the safety of the shore. According to Buber that is also the risk of dialogue and of personal responsibility.

Let me add just one more thing. Swimming beyond where the waves break is wonderful. It gives you a feeling of personal freedom, of hovering above the depths, of tenderness and power, of courage and serenity. And if you give yourself to the sea and the sky, time seems to stop; there can be a moment of eternity.

Dina: But there was such a wonderful moment here last night, Haim.

Haim: Which moment do you mean?

Dina: At the end of the evening in the hotel disco. You were there. They announced that they were closing and then put on the last record: "Hevenu Shalom Aleichem" [We Bring Peace unto You]. And as if by a magnet all the Jews and Arabs in the Project got up and danced together; even those who never get on the dance floor were there, moving to the music. You looked at the faces, Haim, while you were dancing with us. You saw what I saw —Talk about Dostoyevski's quest for love and joy, talk about Zarathustra dancing—you had it all, at 1:00 A.M. in a small, out-of-the-way disco in Acre.

8. Naguib Mahfouz:
The Search for an Egyptian Thou

Knowledge without action is like a tree without fruit.
—ARABIC PROVERB

T H E Egyptian writer Naguib Mahfouz admitted that no one called him an existentialist before he met me. Yet he does describe many of the difficult existential problems that Egyptians and Arabs face today. Mahfouz spent long hours with me discussing these problems and their relation to our difficulties in education for peace. He is today recognized as the most celebrated writer in the Arab world, and his willingness to spend so much time discussing problems of education for peace bears witness to the fact, not mentioned frequently enough, that there are influential persons in the Arab world who are working for peace and understanding. Ironically, some of his fame is a result of his views on Israeli-Arab relations. For instance, when he wrote in 1975, in his weekly column in the newspaper *Al Ahram*, that the Arabs must seek for peaceful ways to live with Israel, his books were banned in many Arab-speaking countries. But that greatly increased their sales in Egypt and Lebanon. Arabs learned to smuggle, together with the hashish that passes from country to country, a few volumes of Mahfouz. For both commodities there would be many buyers.

151

Mahfouz was born in Cairo in 1911 and has lived in Egypt for his entire life. His books and stories depict the Egyptian landscape, be it the alleys or affluent suburbs of Cairo, or the boats on the Nile, or the Mediterranean Sea bathing the shores of Alexandria. Many of the characters he portrays wish to live a meaningful and just life. But, as he shows, the odds against an Egyptian living such a life are tremendous. In most cases, economic, interpersonal, social, and religious exigencies eradicate that wish. Persons learn to be cruel and hateful to each other, and to flee into the realm of fantasy, or excesses, or drugs. Attempting to live as a free, subjective person in Egypt is, in most cases, an exercise in futility. In short, Mahfouz describes the plight of most persons in Arab countries and, I suspect, in the Third World.

We started teaching Mahfouz' writings in the Buberian Learning Groups before I met him. I then believed that Arab students would find it easier to read Mahfouz' books and stories, and to respond existentially, than to read, say, Dostoyevski or Kafka. Mahfouz also gave his readers many insights into the workings of Egyptian society; so reading him was a good preparation for our upcoming trip to Egypt. Nevertheless, we were often unsuccessful in encouraging Arabs to respond existentially to Mahfouz' writings. Here is an example of one such partial failure, which occurred at the end of the first semester. The discussion is based on Mahfouz' short story "Zaabalawi."

Sheikh Zaabalawi is the name of a holy man for whom the narrator of the story is searching. He remembers his father describing Zaabalawi thus: "May his blessing descend upon you, he is a true saint of God, a remover of worries and troubles. Were it not for him I would have died miserably."[8] When the narrator reached a point in his life where he was afflicted with an illness for which no one possessed a remedy, he decided to search out Sheikh Zaabalawi. The story is a description of his relentless search through the richness and the back alleys of Cairo. Everywhere Zaabalawi is blessed by those who met him and were inspired by his holiness, but his whereabouts remain unknown. Finally the narrator is given a tip: a Mr. Wanas al Damanhouri, who frequents the Negma Bar, often meets with Zaabalawi. He finds the bar, but the intoxicated Mr. Wanas stubbornly refuses to talk to anyone who is not drunk. After some hesitation, the narrator begins drinking.

After drinking the second glass, the narrator loses his will power; with the third glass, he loses his memory; and with the fourth glass, the future disappears. His head sinks onto the table and he falls asleep. He has a beautiful dream of resting in a wonderful garden, with flourishing trees and the stars peeping from within their branches. Jasmine petals slowly fall around him, and his head and temples are sprinkled with the clear water of a fountain. He hears a faint music, perhaps the cooing of birds, and senses a great inner harmony and ecstasy. Suddenly he awakes and sees Wanas al Damanhouri regarding him with concern. Only a few sleepy drinkers remain in the bar. Wanas, finally, speaks to the narrator personally:

"You have slept deeply," said my companion; "you were obviously hungry for sleep."

I rested my heavy head in the palms of my hands. When I took them away in astonishment and looked down at them, I found that they glistened with drops of water.

"My head's wet," I protested.

"Yes, my friend tried to rouse you," he answered quietly.

"Somebody saw me in this state?"

"Don't worry, he is a good man. Have you not heard of Sheikh Zaabalawi?"

"Zaabalawi!" I exclaimed, jumping to my feet.

"Yes," he answered in surprise. "What is wrong?"

"Where is he?"

"I don't know where he is now. He was here and then he left."

I was about to run off in pursuit but found I was more exhausted than I had imagined. Collapsed over the table, I cried out in despair: "My sole reason for coming to you was to meet him. Help me catch up with him or send someone after him."[9]

The story ends without the narrator meeting Sheikh Zaabalawi, but he decided to continue his search.

In the exercise following the reading, participants are asked
to explain how the story, and especially the climactic meeting
with Zaabalawi, reflects Arab existence and society. Arabs are
encouraged to talk about themselves. Here are some excerpts.

Hassan (Arab man): There is something pushy about making us
relate the story solely to Arab society. Aren't there Jews who
search for Zaabalawi and become intoxicated and lose their
sense of direction in the process?

Dina (Jewish group leader): Who said there aren't Jews who
search for Zaabalawi? There are. But if Naguib Mahfouz is
today recognized as the greatest living Arab author, then he
has something very personal to say to you, Hassan. If you get
the message, you will have learned something significant
about yourself.

Hassan: I don't get any personal message from the story.

Dina: Come on. As usual, you are trying to make life easy for
yourself. Let us take a personal problem you brought up in a
recent workshop: the fact that your parents want to decide
whom you will marry, and that they even have chosen a wife
for you. You are not happy with the choice, yet you do not
confront your parents directly. Instead, you try to keep away
from home and stay here and study; you do get good grades
for your troubles, but you are also evading the issue and
hoping for a way out by some miracle. You told us all this
three weeks ago. Isn't that a sort of search for Zaabalawi?

Hassan: You know, you are right. In my fantasies, I often imagine
my great-grandfather, whom I knew as a child, appearing in
my father's dream and annulling their choice.

Mahmoud (Arab man): But what does the search for Zaabalawi
have to do with Arab society? I married a woman whom I
chose and did not submit to my parents' pressure. I am not
sure that the story relates to me.

Nira (Jewish woman): I think I know. Many Israeli Arabs here are
constantly talking of a Palestinian state as a way out of your

problems. It may be a way out, but your search is not constructive. The Palestinians seem to be waiting for the world to give them their state on a silver platter, and thus all their afflictions will be healed. Well, I got news for you—that is searching for Zaabalawi. Because building a society or a state is a constructive effort and not a search for a miracle panacea to an affliction.

Mahmoud: You don't know what you are talking about.

Dina: I think Nira is right. But we can phrase it more acceptably. The current structure of Arab society does not encourage grass-root efforts which could bring about change; moreover, many movements within Arab society seek to heal afflictions by a miraculous leap. Nasser's speeches appealed to this current of Arab life; Ayatollah Khomeini uses similar tactics in intoxicating his followers with fanatic Islam. I *know* he is not an Arab. But both leaders could never have succeeded if the search for Zaabalawi was not fundamental to Arab and much Moslem existence.

Mahmoud: There still is something very abstract in what you are saying, Dina. You seem to be approaching me from the outside and trying to make me conform to a story by Mahfouz. I don't think you are very dialogical.

Dina: I am not trying to make you conform to Mahfouz' story. I am trying to show you how to respond existentially to the plight of the narrator, who is seeking Zaabalawi. I may be imposing myself or my views at times, but as we pointed out in our discussion of Buber's essay "Elements of the Interhuman," education is also imposing one's views and oneself upon one's pupils. In short, I'm trying to educate you to respond existentially to what you read. [smiling] And I don't believe I am succeeding.

Mahfouz is not a lecturer. Crowds make him feel uncomfortable. He has declined invitations to lecture at the Sorbonne and other Western universities. He communicates best with no more than five persons. Since I first met him, in May of 1980 in Café Cleopatra on a bank of the Nile, he has always been happy to answer my questions. He rarely responded with his own questions. Yet the exchanges were in the spirit of dialogue. We were not intimate, but we gave what we felt was appropriate to the meetings, without trying to manipulate the other or the conversation. Since Mahfouz prefers to speak Arabic, I was often accompanied by an Arab staff member. At times, Mahfouz would add sentences in English. Later, I often invited other participants in the Project to my meetings with Mahfouz, but we were never more than five visitors. Here are some excerpts from the May 1980 meetings.

Haim: In your writings you seldom describe friendship. In the five books and many stories I have read, I did not encounter one relationship which I could describe as true friendship. A profound aloneness characterizes the persons you write about. Your book *Miramar* is a vivid example of this aloneness. How much does this description accord with your experience of Egyptian society?

Mahfouz: Egypt is undergoing a transformation of its basic social structure. This transformation has been going on throughout my lifetime. Previously, one was supposed to find one's friends in the hamula, the extended family. Now that structure is breaking down and persons are searching for friendship outside the hamula. But you are right; friendship is a relationship that I seldom describe.

Haim: Have you yourself experienced or seen true friendship?

Mahfouz: I think I have, but I have expressed it less in my books.

Haim: Let me explain what I mean by true friendship and then perhaps you can help me understand why you don't write about it. Consider two of your books that were translated into Hebrew: *Midaq Alley* and *A Beggar*. In both books you describe persons coping with a meaningless existence. In *Midaq Alley* it is the poor people in a back alley in Cairo, in *A Beggar* it is a rich, successful lawyer in Cairo. In these books, those persons who strive to change their meaningless existence do so by themselves. They have no one who is ready to confront them and to show them how their meaningless existence can perhaps be changed for the better—not through indulgence—but through worthy deeds. That is one of the things I believe a true friend should do: He can tell you when you are indulging and not doing the meaningful worthy deeds. I am asking all this because my impression is that in our Project there are very few true friendships among Arabs.

Mahfouz: We were always taught to respect the privacy of another person's problems. Perhaps this respect does not allow for what you call confrontation. You should help and respect a friend, so we were taught, not confront him.

Haim: But as your books reveal, because there is very little confrontation, there is very little dialogue, authentic dialogue, I mean.

Mahfouz: Probably [smiling, with a twinkle in his eye]. But are you confident that your Israeli manner of confronting has brought you closer to dialogue? [We all laugh.]

Haim: I very much enjoyed reading the story "Zaabalawi." I believe that you describe there an existential situation which constantly appears in Egyptian and Arab life. I mean the seeking for a person who has certain miracle powers that will heal the seeker. But often the seeker does not reach his goal because he allows someone to intoxicate him when he is on the verge of meeting Zaabalawi. Do you think the story describes the existential plight of Egyptians or Arabs?

Mahfouz: I am not sure that I understand what you mean by "existential" situation. If you mean that when social structures change, as they are changing in Egypt, as they are slowly changing in the Arab world, then people seek healers for their ailments outside their regular way of life, then you probably are right. If I recall well, I wrote this story in the period that I was very disillusioned with the deeds and the rhetoric of Gamal Abdul Nasser.

Haim: But if that is the situation, what should the Arabs do?

Mahfouz (laughing): Isn't that a question you educators should put to yourselves? I'm just a person who likes to tell stories.

Haim: But don't your stories have a message?

Mahfouz: I started writing when I was six years old. Most writers say they have a message to convey and therefore they write. But I started writing before I had a message to convey, and I enjoyed it, and it has been that way ever since. [We all laugh.]

I do not think that Mahfouz was evading my questions, as may appear from a first reading of these excerpts. He was responding as he writes, by describing the situation and not by confronting the issues. We soon learned that such a response was adopted by many Egyptians who wished to establish some sort of relation with us. They responded at the level of description, not at the level of confrontation. Our manner of confrontation often threatened them; it may also have suggested that we were not sensitive to all the nuances of their description. But at first these descriptive responses annoyed and aggravated us; they seemed to bar the way to any dialogical relation while encouraging an atmosphere of openness.

Our attempts to find counterparts in Egypt who would be willing to engage in dialogue with us can ironically be called "The Search for an Egyptian Thou." Ironically, because as Buber writes in *I and Thou*, "The Thou encounters me by grace—it cannot be found by seeking." We soon learned that our difficulties were not atypical of Egypt. Mahfouz' writings are crowded with persons who have no authentic relations with other persons, and like the narrator in the story "Zaaba-lawi" they are seeking a miraculous encounter. Other Egyptian and Arab writers—for instance, Tayeb Salih, Taha Hussein, Yusuf Idris, Sonallah Ibrihim—are no less vivid in their descriptions of the hatred, cruelty, and deceit that abound. The Egyptians and Arabs they describe have very few experiences of trust; hardly ever do they establish true friendship or find true love. Mahfouz does describe dialogical encounters; but these encounters seem to fade away immediately without influencing the participating Egyptians. Why does the dialogical encounter evade the Egyptian? More accurately one should ask, why does the Egyptian not recognize the Thou and respond to the Thou when he enters into this fundamental encounter?

As Mahfouz describes Egyptian society, especially in the novel based on his childhood, *A House in Cairo*, the Egyptian child is born into a web of interrelated, basic lies. By a "basic lie" I mean that a person lies to himself, embraces that lie as his way of life, and tries to convince his encompassing milieu that such a way of life is the normal way of existence. Fyodor Karamazov is one of Dostoyevski's vivid examples of a person who lives with basic lies. Such a person can no longer discern in his soul between truth and lies. As a result, he can no longer honor himself. Hence he demands honor from others, from all persons whom he meets. He may attempt to acquire this honor by acts of power or by a sharp wit; or he may encourage persons to insult or to offend him. When offended, a person knows that he can demand honor from the outside world. Basic lies have been described by many existentialists: Buber, Kierkegaard, Dostoyevski. Mahfouz' innovation is that he has shown the social outcomes of living in a web of basic lies. For instance, growing up in a web of basic lies brings even youngsters to fear dialogue.

Many of the Egyptians whom Mahfouz describes are faced with an ontological and ethical choice: Either one embraces one's basic lies and creates for oneself a distorted way of life, or one strives to live authentically. Most persons choose to live as basic lies. Moreover, the person who strives to be authentic suffers at the hands of the embracers of deceit; they also admonish him for not playing the game of social existence according to the rules of deceit which most persons accept. The acceptable manner is to help other persons live with their basic lies so that they will let me live with mine. Mahfouz also shows that one authentic person, such as Zohara in his novel *Miramar*, can wreak havoc on such a mutual complicity of self-deception. In Egypt, such authentic persons are often ostracized; the promoters of deceit do all in their power to eliminate them from the realm of social life.

As Faulkner, Hesse, and a host of other writers have shown,

the above paragraph could also describe Western society. Basic lies permeate much of contemporary life. Yet there are five problems which the contemporary Egyptian faces that make it much more difficult for him to reach dialogue than many of his Western counterparts. Two of these problems, life in a milieu of scarcity and the pyramidal structure of Egyptian society, will be discussed in the next chapter. Mahfouz does not address these problems; in his writings, they exist as the natural background of any Egyptian, governing one's life much as the flow and the ebb of the Nile once governed Egyptian agriculture. Three problems which he does address and which I shall briefly discuss are: the "nigger" status of women, the superficiality and meagerness of verbal intercourse—one must never discuss, or even verbalize, gut problems—and contemporary Islam's detachment from the daily problems of many Egyptians. Mahfouz shows how not coping with these problems imprisons the Egyptian in a superficial individuality and leads to personal corruption.

The intimate meeting between man and woman which culminates in love and sexual intercourse is probably one of the best opportunities for the partners to shed their reliance on basic lies. The physical nakedness of the encounter can help one reach a spiritual nakedness in which only truth exists, including one's loves and joys, and one's frustrations, fears, and hangups. Such intimacy is an ever renewed possibility for the rejuvenation of the partners in the relation, for new knowledge—the Bible calls such intimacy knowing one's spouse. Buber would have added that this is knowledge of the being of one's spouse, not of the impressions he or she strives to make.

As Mahfouz shows, most Egyptian men view a woman as an object to capture, despoil, exploit, and enslave. Hence the nakedness of sexual intercourse is merely physical nakedness; there is no intimacy, no rejuvenation of the partners, no personal or spiritual growth. When marriage becomes their lot, some women respond to their exploitation by seeking ways of psychologically castrating their spouses, but most women embrace the role of the exploited slave and flee into a world of fantasy. In short, Egyptian men and women confirm Hegel's insight that, in such a situation, both partners are enslaved by the master-slave dialectic in which they actively participate. Mahfouz also indicates that there is some minimal change lately in the way some men relate to women, but it has little influence on the prevailing view of her as "nigger." And interestingly, the few moments of dialogue that he describes in his books usually occur when a man can accept a woman as his equal partner.

On one of our trips to Egypt, a young, unmarried woman lectured to us about the research she had done for her Ph.D. thesis, on how the Egyptian husband perceives his wife. I do not remember the statistical details of her research, but the findings were much less encouraging than what Mahfouz describes. For instance, she did not find one Egyptian husband who felt comfortable confiding any of his deep personal problems—be they physical, psychological, spiritual, etc.—to his wife. She did not find one Egyptian husband who fully agreed that his wife should be his equal in every aspect of their life together. The lecture was attended by about ten Egyptian young men; some were married, the others were engaged or bachelors. They all agreed that her findings were appropriate to how they personally felt.

During the question period, one of our participants asked the young woman: "How will *you* choose your husband?" She answered: "I don't believe there is one man in Egypt who will be willing to marry me and to consider me his equal. Therefore, if I do get married it will be a compromise; and since my father is dead, the groom will have to be approved by the oldest male in our family, my younger brother, who is twenty-four years old, three years younger than me."

In Egypt, the richness of association which characterizes Arabic has become a screen which allows one to evade confrontation. The Arab child and young adult that Mahfouz describes learn that language exists in order to evade confronting the other. Hence one does not learn to confront oneself with a painful truth, or to allow others to confront oneself. Such a relation to language is also vividly portrayed in Taha Hussein's autobiographical books on his childhood. Both authors show how the child learns that one's deeper problems or feelings should never be verbalized. Language may be used to indicate the existence of something deeper, which perturbs or profoundly influences the speaker, but this "something deeper" must never reach verbal expression.

Mahfouz' book *A Beggar*, which describes Omar, a forty-five-year-old very successful lawyer who suddenly discovers that his life is meaningless, depicts such a poverty of verbalization. Omar cannot reach deep into himself and verbally express the source of his malaise; he simply calls it "my sickness." Mahfouz shows that Omar dares not verbalize the meaninglessness of his life and fears to confront its sources; hence neither indulging in sexual adventures with younger women, nor trying to resume his life along its old track, nor embracing Sufist mystical rites can heal this "sickness." He adheres to his superficial descriptions and sinks deeper and deeper into isolation. In *Chatter on the Nile*, Mahfouz shows how a group of thriving Egyptian intellectuals are addicted to superficial verbosity, much as they are addicted to the hashish they smoke together. In *Midaq Alley*, he shows how the superficiality of language adds a poverty of existence to the economic poverty of the inhabitants of the alley. Wherever one turns in Egyptian society, superficial language, rich with poetical associations, impoverishes existence and blocks dialogue.

But the Egyptian's playing with language cannot completely screen his wish to reach out to the person he encounters. If he senses that the other person is striving to be authentic, he may find nonverbal ways of reaching out. Mahfouz' warm and delightful reception every time I came to Egypt was his way of showing me that, despite answering my confronting questions with descriptions, he wished to continue the exchange. Something similar happened when I visited Enis Mansour on my second trip to Egypt. Still uncomfortable with the memory of our last meeting, I put off going to visit him until my last day in Cairo. Here are some excerpts from our meeting.

"So you have been in Egypt ten days already, Dr. Gordon. And you brought over a group of thirty-five Jewish and Arab students. Wonderful. How did they like it here?"

"It was a wonderful experience, after all these years of war; but as a group we did have our internal problems. Trust broke down between some Jews and Arabs. We also found, as in my first visit, that the Egyptians are not willing to engage in dialogue. So I decided to come to your office to see if the Nile is still flowing slowly."

(laughing heartily) "Wonderful, Dr. Gordon, wonderful. Yes, you can look out the window and see how beautiful it flows slowly. I believe you may have learned not to rush us. You Israelis want too much from us too fast. Just look at the pyramids and you will understand that we Egyptians have time."

"I've looked at them; at least in that sense they are impressive."

"So you're not crazy about the pyramids. All right, that is your prerogative."

(The phone rings. It is the Egyptian ambassador to the United States, calling from Washington. They talk in Arabic for a while and Mansour becomes serious as he puts down the phone.)

"Do you know, Dr. Gordon, when I first felt how slow the Nile flows? I was a young, successful journalist and was getting ahead in my newspaper. Then one day I wrote a piece which was a bit critical of Nasser's policy, at least it could be interpreted thus. And the order came down not to publish anything else I wrote."

"For how long?"

"It didn't say."

"Did they fire you?"

"No. I still got my salary. But nothing I would write would ever be published until a new order came down."

"What did you do?"

"I walked the streets of Cairo and took notes. I traveled abroad and wrote a travel book in Arabic, which was published. And mainly I watched the Nile flow slowly, and suffered."

"How did it all end?"

"Nasser died and all his decrees were abolished. That meant that it was permissible to publish me again."

"You were probably very lonely during that period."

"Yes, very lonely . . . You know, let me put you in touch with someone who will be willing to engage in dialogue with you. He is one of our top psychiatrists."

(He picks up the phone and asks his secretary to get in touch with Muhammed Shaalan.)

Mahfouz is a very religious Moslem. In his books, he hints that Islam could open the way for a fulfilling and meaningful existence. But he shows contemporary Islam in Egypt as a fusion of dogmatism and ecstatic Sufism which ignores the existential plights of many of its adherents. Many Moslems know that, even if they seek, they will not find a Zaabalawi who will relate to them—and if such a Zaabalawi exists, the police will be after him, as they are in the story. The Egyptians whom Mahfouz describes are deeply isolated; they sense that they are solitary wanderers in the society of man, and that they have been somewhat overlooked by God. They live in what Dostoyevski called the most terrible Hell—to be forgotten by God, and to know that He has forgotten you.

Isolation can be the beginning of an opening of oneself to the Other and to God. But the isolation which the Egyptian suffers does not allow him to relate his freedom to transcendence in a manner which will encourage him to develop as a person. Hence his freedom dissolves into caprice or into fatalism and fanaticism. Almost all the persons one meets in Mahfouz' books and in the works of other Egyptian authors are persons who have learned to live in this man-made, transcendent-less Hell. They understand freedom either as caprice or as the submerging of one's being in fatalism or fanaticism. Cruelty, hatred, ruthlessness, and despair are the staff of life. Few, very few, seek Zaabalawi.

After the first year, I understood that on our visits to Egypt we should expose our participants to a broad range of educational experiences which would reveal the difficulties the Egyptian has in relating as a free subject. I hoped that seeing these difficulties in many manifestations would indicate where one might begin to find ways to reach the Egyptian subject. But I was plodding in the dark and I knew it. On our first trip to Egypt, the Israeli Arabs had borne the full brunt of the Egyptians' disregarding a person's subjectivity. As already mentioned, many Egyptians refused to relate to the Israeli-Arabs as persons with an Israeli-Arab identity. But I wanted a broader vista of experiences. I therefore returned to Egypt with my staff in February 1981 and prepared a series of exercises in which our participants would learn, from many perspectives, the problems of living as a subject in Egypt. (It was on this trip that I finally met Muhammed Shaalan. When Enis Mansour called him on my previous visit, Shaalan had been out of the country.)

We prepared five day-long exercises entitled: Life in Cairo; Islam; Ancient Egypt; Comparison of Life in Cairo with Life in Alexandria; The Flow of the Nile. Participants were divided into mixed groups of four or five who did all the assigned exercises together, and at the end of each day discussed their findings with a group leader. In one group the exercise on Islam had interesting repercussions. Here is the assignment.

EXERCISE ON ISLAM

Part I. The Islamic Museum

1) In the Islamic museum each of you will find that there are three works of art which have a special message to convey to you. Find these works of art, show them to the members of your group, and explain their message. As a group, try and summarize the kind of messages Islamic art conveys.

2) As a group, find one Islamic work of art which appeals to all of you. Formulate why it appeals to you.

(If you have problems with these exercises, consult David or Dina, who will be in the museum.)

Part II. Mosques

Visit three mosques. Choose at least one small neighborhood mosque and one large city mosque among the three. Spend at least half an hour in each mosque. Summarize these visits by trying to formulate how the architecture of the mosques and the atmosphere in them helps one relate to Allah.

Part III. Reading Assignment and Summary

Read Naguib Mahfouz' short story "The Visit." Explain: How does faith in Allah help the Moslem in day-to-day life? Base your answer on Mahfouz' story and on your experience in the Islamic museum and in the mosques you visited.

("The Visit" describes an old, ailing, bedridden woman whose relatives have pretty much abandoned her, and who knows that her servant is cheating her when she goes out to buy food and is not giving her the assistance she needs. She is on the verge of despair. Suddenly the aged woman is visited by a blind sheikh, whom she has not met for more than two decades. In the conversation between them, the sheikh renews the woman's faith in Allah by relating simply and dialogically to her. When he leaves, the woman calls her servant and asks why she did not honor the sheikh while he was visiting. Her servant replies that no one visited her in the past hour. The old woman responds by confronting her servant and demanding to be served honestly and appropriately. The servant becomes frightened and complies.)

Here are some excerpts from the discussion.

Hussein (Arab man): I didn't like the Islamic museum; I didn't like the way things were cluttered together there, with very little appreciation for the person who comes to view the exhibit. Perhaps that is why I really didn't find anything that was supposed to convey a message to me.

Rina (Jewish woman): Yes, I also felt the lack of concern for aesthetic arrangement in the museum; but I found that it accords with the disregard for visual aesthetics here in Cairo and in Islam. People, houses, cars, streets, even the worshippers in the mosques clutter together. In such a physical situation, dialogue is stifled even as it begins to arise.

Hussein: Why? Dialogue did arise in the story by Mahfouz.

Rina: Because I believe that for dialogue to occur, man needs some space for himself. And if you want to be able to relate dialogically to a piece of art in the museum, it needs some space to itself. In Mahfouz' story the old woman was alone in her room. She had space.

Tarek (Arab man): Something here is bothering me. I am somewhat mixed up. I know I shouldn't ask, but what did you want to achieve in this exercise, Haim?

Haim: Why are you asking?

Tarek: Because, if anything, the exercise made me feel uncomfortable about being a Moslem.

Haim: Please explain.

Tarek: Look at the wording of your assignment. "Three works of art have a message to convey to me." Then a work of art should appeal to all of us. Then the architecture should help us relate to Allah. Well, what if nothing happens? What if the art in the museum is art, with no message to pass on to me? Even if I look at one piece of art for a half-hour, no message comes. What if the architecture of most mosques turns me off? What if in most mosques I find no place where I feel comfortable? No, don't tell me that the feeling of uncomfort will encourage me to turn to God—that could be true, but in my case it is a lot of bullshit. And then to top it off you give me this nice, but not too deep story by Mahfouz and want me to believe that if I have faith I will also attain courage. It might work for others, but for me this exercise was a waste of time.

Haim: What *do* you feel about Islam?

Tarek: Something similar to what you said you feel about Orthodox Jewish rabbis. You once argued that these rabbis in Israel are blocking the path to God by their fanaticism and by their passing decrees based on the Jewish *Halakah.* I feel that my way to Allah, if there exists such a way, is blocked by much of what I see of Islam. And your making me undergo an exercise of Islam won't help me.

Haim: In Mahfouz' story, the old woman's pain also helps her regain faith.

Tarek: Haim, pain is good for stories and discussions. But don't include me when you start distributing it.

Professor Muhammed Shaalan is head of the Department of Psychiatry at El Azhar University in Cairo. When we first met he was also president of the Egyptian Scientific Society for Group Training. He was succeeded in this role by Nabil Yunis, a professor of gynecology at El Azhar University. Our meetings with Egyptian students and professionals, members of that society, were very much a result of these two men's belief in the importance of Israeli-Egyptian dialogue, and of their dedication to realizing this belief. Thanks to this dedication, our meetings with Egyptians were interesting and exciting and often led to mutual understanding; but they were not dialogical. As one of our Arab participants put it: The Egyptian Thou was missing.

In the next chapter I will give a Sartrean perspective of what occurred at our meetings with the Egyptian Scientific Society for Group Training. Here I shall suggest that the outcome accords with Mahfouz' description of Egyptian society. But first I would like to partially contradict myself. Mahfouz is not an existentialist—not because he does not have the existential awareness which I quoted from Berdyaev in Chapter 2—he does. He is not an existentialist because there seems to be no place for existentialism in Egypt. Worse, I doubt if a person like Kierkegaard or Nietzsche, with a basic Socratic attitude toward life, could ever emerge in Egyptian society. In short, to feel the life throb of Egypt, one must begin by imagining a society without Socratic philosophers, without seekers for truth who are willing to spend their life in the marketplace of society pursuing that search. Much as the surrounding expanses of the Sahara Desert cannot sustain oak or pine, Egyptian society is barren of philosophical inquiry. Borrowing a phrase from Ludwig Wittgenstein, for the contemporary Egyptian "The riddle doesn't exist."

Bertrand Russell once noted that all great philosophy is a blending of certain elements of the mystic's vision with the logic underlying the scientific attitude. Such a blending is central to all the existentialists described in this book. In the case of Sartre, for instance, his vision is of the Hell that man creates for himself and his fellow man, and in his later years he based his inquiry on Marxist dialectics. The Egyptian lives in a world where vision and logical inquiry are incompatible. Hence his vision retains the unrealness of a dream, and his inquiry is sterile and ruthless. Like many of the characters whom Mahfouz describes, he oscillates between these two poles, never able to make the ends meet.

Nature abhors a vacuum, and the same may be true of human nature. Since philosophy is not allowed to find a space in Egyptian society, its place is taken up by psychology, political science, sociology, anthropology, and mainly, a rigid, apologetic theology. In short, seemingly there is a scientific answer; seemingly, the Egyptian has reached true repose; seemingly, there are no perturbing Socratic questions which will always remain unanswered to confront and to guide him. In the relations that Mahfouz describes, confronting is a psychological device, or an outpouring of one's feelings—it is not a way of life.

But without philosophy and without personal confronting, life often becomes insipid. In such a situation imagination only rarely leads to art or to wisdom; more often it leads to fantasy; perhaps it leads to faith in the healing powers of an unfound Zaabalawi or in the utterance of a blind sheikh. Furthermore in a life without philosophical questions and in which one's attempt to confront reality, even in its most tedious, lackadaisical manifestations is blocked—in such a life wisdom seems unattainable. Yet perhaps the worse outcome of a lack of confrontation is that fear, deep unexplained fear, is always with the Egyptian, wherever he goes, whatever he does. He is unaware of the simple truth which Plato repeatedly stressed: One often learns to become courageous by confronting the Other and oneself with questions which have no specific answers, and facing those questions daily with all one's being. In short, philosophers who live their quest for truth are also educators for courage.

In the democratic West philosophers are viewed as challengers of the system; in Egypt they are viewed with amusement. The Egyptian knows that philosophy is not the way to challenge the system in which he exists; hence these questioners must be some sort of entertainers. Elements of such an attitude were attributed to many of my efforts. Thus many Egyptians who met with us felt that meeting with members of the Education for Peace Project was good entertainment, even if the encounter included screaming at each other about one's hatred and mistrust. It was clear to them that existentialist philosophy could be played with, enjoyed, interpreted, or discarded. It had nothing to do with one's personal daily life.

It seems that the only attempt ever made to initiate Buberian dialogue between Egyptians and Israelis occurred during two meetings held in the spring of 1981 between forty members of the Education for Peace Project and a similar number of members of the Egyptian Scientific Society for Group Training. The participants in the meetings came from very different backgrounds. The Egyptian Scientific Society for Group Training encompasses students, therapists, and researchers who have at least reached the M.A. level. The contact between members is professional and at times personal, based on their meeting about once a month for seminars or group-dynamic workshops. I have already described our participants.

The meetings were held on two consecutive evenings in the large ballroom of the Continental Hotel in Cairo. The seventy-five to eighty participants were divided into three groups of twenty-five each with approximately an equal number of

Israelis (Jews and Arabs) and Egyptians in each group. The groups sat in circles in different corners of the ballroom. The language spoken was English, and at times participants asked for translation. On the first evening we were supposed to try to reach dialogue using methods which I had developed in accordance with Martin Buber's philosophy. On the second evening the Egyptians were supposed to help us reach dialogue using group-dynamic methods in which they specialized. But in fact both four-hour meetings were existential encounters in which much wrath, hatred, and mistrust spilled over from all directions.

No important insights emerged during these meetings. Perhaps such insights were stifled by the anger, the tension, and the mistrust that often prevailed. Here are some excerpts from how the Israeli group summarized the meetings on the evening following the two encounters.

Yaakov (Jewish man): At the first meeting with the Egyptians I thought we were getting somewhere in developing trust. But after the second meeting I feel that they were really playing with us. For the Egyptians we were a nice game. I was disappointed.

Gila (Jewish woman): I am not sure you are right, Yaakov. In our group Meliha, the Egyptian woman, was very vicious; she attacked many people. I'm not sure, though, that she was playing games, because her brother was killed in an Israeli-Arab war. Afterward I had a rare experience with her. She saw that her attacks had upset me and came up to me and asked me if I see her as a Jew-hater. I answered yes and burst into tears. She hugged me and invited me to visit her. I consulted Haim on this matter and he said that she might be a bit hysterical in her responses, and I should watch out for that; but I decided to try and meet her. Still, I would agree that the meetings were not very meaningful.

Rafik (Arab man): I had been wanting to reach dialogue with the Egyptians on this trip and I was looking forward to this meeting. But, as I look back on it, I feel that the Egyptians

were not really interested in any exchange with us Palestinians. We seemed to be interfering with their wanting to get to
know the Jews or to attack the Jews. At times, they even tried
to make me feel as if I was betraying the Arab cause.

Judah (Jewish man): I was surprised how ignorant the Egyptians
are about us. After all, there were many students and professors among them. And yet they lapped up stupid propaganda
and believed it. When we tried to explain the truth, they
responded with hatred or radical views. I think the encounter was a total failure.

Rifaa (Arab man): You talk about basic trust, Haim. What occurred
in the Continental Hotel was basic mistrust. They thought
that I was saying what the Jews wanted me to say. They
totally mistrusted me. And when I tried to refute them, they
refused to change their minds. Instead of trying to listen to
me, they were always trying to interpret me according to
their seemingly better understanding of my situation. I hated
it.

Sima (Jewish woman): I saw what other people here described;
but I also saw Egyptians and Israelis sitting after the meeting
and talking until the early morning hours; and when they
departed some Egyptians hugged some Israelis. So I am
mixed up. I accept that many of them were mistrustful, but
some of us were also mistrustful. There was good in the
encounter, too, and we shouldn't forget or overlook that
good.

Haim: If we take seriously everything that was said here, it seems
that although we were all in the same encounter, we participated in different encounters. I agree that there was much
hatred and mistrust, and also afterward many personal
conversations. But I think we have somewhere lost the
proportions in our evaluating of this event, because many of
us felt mistrusted, because many of us felt let down, because
many of us responded mistrustfully to mistrust—at least I
know that I did.

I ate crap from Meliha like others, I was screamed at like
others, I acted mistrustfully like others, I even told Meliha

that her rage was something of an act, and I hate her for that—and still I know that these two evenings were a great event. They were great because after thirty-two years of war, and in face of all the sick hatred that exists in this portion of the world, forty Israelis and forty Egyptians got together and sat for hours and tried, in their distorted and unsuccessful way, to reach some sort of dialogue. It was great because despite our pain, rage, and mistrust, we sat it out till the end, and after the first painful evening met again on the second evening.

It was great because it was a way of Israelis and Egyptians living with each other, even if it was a painful encounter. Expressing hatred and rage peacefully, without guns or bombs, is a way of living together.

In summary, I believe that thirty or forty years from now, when you sit with your grandchildren and they ask you if you ever participated in a historical event, I know you'll remember the meeting with the Egyptians and say: "I did. After thirty-two years of war, I participated in the first attempt of Israeli and Egyptian students to reach Buberian dialogue."

9. Sartre:
Rebellion in an Existential Hell

Franz: I shall renounce my illusions when . . .
Johanna: When?
Franz: When I love you more than my lies and when you love me
in spite of my truth.

FROM *Altona,* ACT IV, — BY JEAN-PAUL SARTRE

O N E can only benefit from Sartre's philosophy in education for
peace when one attempts to fulfill a demand analogous to
Franz' demand from himself and from Johanna: when one
likes the truth that Sartre reveals more than one's own lies,
and when one craves these truths despite their depicting a
vile, nauseating reality. While reading Buber, or Berdyaev, or
Marcel, or even Dostoyevski or Kierkegaard, one cannot but
receive the impression that these thinkers have somewhat
ignored the most brutal and sordid aspects of human existence. Sartre did not ignore these aspects. He vividly describes the bad faith, self-deception, and exploitation that
characterize most persons' everyday lives. He analyzes the
multiple ways by which man's social existence alienates him,
makes him into a killer, robber, and hater of his fellow
man—and he bases his analysis on the way man lives his
freedom.

In *Altona* and in other writings, Sartre shows that a person's reliance upon the lies he weaves allows him to evade
assuming responsibility for his actions. The lies vary from the
subtle to the profound and from the simple to the intricate;

these lies, like the filament that emerges from the spider's stomach, form a web which allows everything to stream through it except certain truths whose vitality must be sucked out so that the person who wove the web can continue to exist in his specific situation. Thus, the educator's problem is not to identify one specific lie which his pupil embraces and to tear it out of that person's web. Rather, he must shed a forceful light upon the entire web of lies, and carefully and slowly show his pupil how he relies upon that web in his everyday existence. In addition, the educator must help the person to find ways of diminishing his reliance upon his web of lies. Sartre would probably have noted that full success in such an endeavor is ontologically impossible—bad faith is a component of consciousness. But he also would have agreed that living authentically requires continually seeking ways of diminishing one's reliance upon one's web of lies.

In the Buberian Learning Groups, one of our first educational exercises which encouraged persons to be aware of their reliance upon a web of lies was the Death Game. Usually, it was an immediate success and a long-term failure. Here is the exercise.

THE DEATH GAME

An existentialist exercise for four persons with at least one Arab and one Jew in each quartet. Time: 12 hours.

Story of the Game. Two members of your quartet, one Arab and one Jew, were killed in a car accident. When their souls rose to heaven they were met by the angel Gabriel. He told them that during their sojourn on earth they had not done enough to bring peace in the Mideast, hence they would not be allowed to enjoy eternal life. He hands them a formal indictment. The two members read the indictment and each one formulates a rejoinder. Gabriel reads the rejoinder and says that he will allow these souls to return to their bodies and to resume their lives on earth, if each member of the quartet pledges to take upon himself specific responsibilities for peace in the coming months.

Rules of the Game

1) Choose two members of the quartet who will be the Arab and the Jew who were killed in the car accident.

2) Formulate with their help the formal indictment which Gabriel handed them. The indictment must be based on each person's own history. Submit the indictments for approval to your group leader. Time: 4 hours.

3) With the help of the indicted members formulate a rejoinder. The rejoinder must be based on each person's own history. Submit the rejoinders for approval to your group leader. Time: 4 hours.

4) Formulate the specific responsibilities to further peace and trust between Arabs and Jews that each member of the quartet pledges to take upon himself in the coming months. Each member will sign his page of commitments to indicate his approval of assuming these responsibilities. Submit the lists of each member to your group leader who will follow up on them in the future. Time: 4 hours.

For most participants, the Death Game was an exciting exercise in which, through concretely discussing their own lives, they learned four Sartrean insights. The first, depicted in *No Exit*, is that when I die, my life becomes a totality, a completed entity. By imagining my death I can see my life as a totality, which means that it cannot be changed, that it has no future, no open possibilities. Nothing can be amended, and the contradictions I have lived cannot be resolved by future choices. There is no exit from realizing how impotent and meaningless much of my life has been. But, on the other hand, imagining such a situation allows one to also imagine that the fears of a lived life no longer have power over oneself; hence one is often free to imagine new, previously unthinkable possibilities.

The second insight revealed in the game is that one can only change history by acting on the concrete level. Participants relate to the Arab-Jewish conflict, not as a detached, abstract problem to be solved, but as a concrete reality experienced through the quality of their daily lives and formed by the choices they make. The third insight is that my past experience and present condition are not determining— it is possible to choose a new way of life. The fourth insight is that a group that pledges to do something together can probably accomplish what isolated individuals cannot. Yet these insights faded quite rapidly; in most persons' lives their webs of lies quickly regained control.

Here are excerpts from a staff discussion on the long-term failure of the Death Game.

David: I believe that we are all prone to a certain sort of laziness, which we did not take into account when planning the game. I mean this laziness to get out there and to do something. It is much more simple to meet in a group and to discuss what needs to be done than to do it. It was part of the excitement of the Death Game to make commitments, but when the time for action came around people had lost the excitement.

Smadar: But laziness cannot account for everything; and what you are describing is evident in all education of character. I think that the Death Game and its unrealistic setting give the participants a basic feeling of unrealism, and they do not see how difficult small commitments can be. In this case the good aspects of the game do not encourage the person to actually assume responsibility. But there is something much more important that I believe we have not been seeing.

Tarek (Arab leader): What is that?

Smadar: Haim has a basic optimism that he passes on to us. But the real world is much more difficult, much more terrible, than what he often seems to convey. (Smiling) We have all heard him reiterate the importance of dancing through life; you know everything he tells us about Zarathustra. Well, at times, life is more like weeding an abandoned garden than like dancing. It is back-breaking toil just to get the land clear of weeds, before you even begin to plant flowers. And you *cannot* dance while weeding a garden.

Let me go further and say that our entire approach, including the Death Game, overlooks basic social and economic developments which daily influence our lives. I know Haim is aware of these shortcomings; he discussed his readings of Sartre's Marxist writings with me. As I see it we have not taken into account that we exist within a terrifying political process in which the right-wing parties in Israel are doing their best to discard many of the humanistic values upon which Israeli social and political life was based. At times I feel that I am living in a period somewhat analogous to the rise of fascism in Italy and in Germany in the 1920s.

Tarek: I agree. But what do you suggest should be done about this situation? And what should we do about the Death Game?

Smadar: I am not sure. The Death Game is a good educational experience. Arousing the passion to bring about change is important. The problem is that people don't follow up on their commitments.

I think it is a cop-out on our part to say that our participants are lazy, or that they don't try enough to fulfill their commitments. They are not lazy when it comes to participating in a Buberian Learning Group which takes up many hours and much energy. I agree, though, that they sink back quite quickly into their web of lies. But I find myself doing that too, at times, after a moment of passionate resolutions.

I believe that we must be much more radical. We must present the sick reality which encompasses us with enough force and understanding to show our participants that goody-goody doings are mere window dressing, and that anything short of an existential rebellion against fascism— yes, against the Jewish fascism which supports those Jews who beat and kill Arabs on the West Bank and in the Gaza Strip—anything short of an existential rebellion against this fascism is masturbation, or even worse it is helping persons live in their web of lies.

Tarek: I am still not clear about what you suggest that we do.

David: Smadar, at times your pessimism and social analysis are good, but now you seem to remain at the abstract level.

Smadar: I wish I knew what to do. It is quite clear to me that we have not done enough to encourage persons to assume responsibility for peace. Let me put it this way. Buberian dialogue and exercises like the Death Game are moments in which persons exist outside of history. But we must get them back into the flux of history with all its vile stinking situations. Only there can they assume responsibility for peace. We must all get our hands dirty.

Smadar was partially right, but she was also overlooking the fact that in the Death Game persons did see the existential Hell which they help sustain. Consider excerpts from the following two indictments which one of the groups wrote.

INDICTMENT AGAINST AMI (JEWISH MAN)
by the Angel Gabriel

You are accused of not doing enough to bring peace in the Mideast. Specifically this indictment will discuss your actions while being a soldier in the Israeli Defense Force and while you were on duty of keeping order in the refugee camps in Gaza. During this period you utilized the power you had and followed the general trend of terrorizing the Arab population, including women, children, and the elderly. You made no attempts to hinder actions in which the Arabs in these camps were brutally assaulted by Israeli soldiers in order to instill fear. You actively participated in some of these assaults. You did deeds which if done in other circumstances would have had you hauled before the law, but you never questioned these deeds yourself, nor did you ever bring up the legitimacy of these deeds in your discussions with fellow Israeli soldiers. Even in incidents where the Arabs tried to show some good will toward you, you ignored their behavior and stuck to your reign of power . . .

INDICTMENT AGAINST YUSUF (ARAB MAN)
by the Angel Gabriel

You are accused of not doing enough to bring peace in the Mideast. Specifically, this indictment will discuss two examples. You are an Arab and an Israeli citizen. After President Sadat's peace initiative about which you had mixed feelings, you did not express these feelings openly, but joined your friends in the radical camp who rejected the Israeli-Egyptian peace because it may hurt Yasser Arafat's PLO. You still felt that Israel was your country and that peace was good, but you refused to voice these views in front of your radical friends, because you feared the truth as you saw it and lied to those persons whom you called your friends, in addition to not calling their attention to the good that can arise from peace between Israel and Egypt.

The second example has to do with the sports event which you, as a teacher, organized between your school and a Jewish school. Instead of using this event to promote understanding, you insinuated to your pupils

that if they win this would be a good opportunity to get back at those
Jews . . .

The problem is not that persons do not see the existential
Hell which one helps to sustain. They see it. The problem is
that they do not know how to rebel against it. Existentialist
philosophers saw and described this existential Hell from
different perspectives; by teaching these perspectives, we
helped our participants become more sensitive to their milieu. Thus many participants could probably explain that
Buber's Hell was a world in which all interpersonal relations
were I-It; that Zarathustra rebelled against the insipid, bland
Hell of the mediocre, cowardly man; that Kafka described the
rationalizing Hell of alienation which exists in each person's
mind and which mirrors the bureaucratic rationalizations
which encompass us. The participants also perceived that
these and other perspectives of our existential Hell, like
vampires, were always around us, sucking out the vitality of
our endeavors. In the Buberian Learning Groups, we had
taught them quite a few antidotes, which momentarily rob
these vampires of their power. They sensed that these antidotes were effective only if coupled with dialogue and the
search for truth. And here was where we were stuck.

We were stuck partially because of a central characteristic
of existentialist philosophy. Most existentialists profoundly
criticize their society, but they do not suggest how one can
act within history so as to change the social trends they
dislike. They have no social philosophy that takes into account contemporary developments; they give no indications
which concepts one could use to describe the social processes against which they are rebelling. A prominent excep-
tion is Jean-Paul Sartre. Blending Marxist philosophy and an
existentialist approach to history, he developed a powerful
conceptual framework and a broad perspective of social
developments.

Put differently, at the end of the second year it was very
clear to me that I had run out of Buber's philosophy before I

ran out of problems in educating for peace. Social, economical, and political realities were pretty much beyond the scope of Buber's vision. He did give guidance as to how a person should attempt to attain social and political goals without sacrificing one's conscience; he demanded a daily repulsion of the wish, which many persons experience, to become fanatic or apathetic. But he had no social writings from which one could weave a guiding thread to help one find one's way in the maze of social, economic, and political exploitation which characterizes contemporary society. An anecdote about Buber, which I heard in Heidelberg, helps to clarify the limits of his vision.

In 1937 a Gestapo squad conducted a sudden search of Buber's house in Heppenheim. It notified Buber that the reason for the search was to find works that he had written against the Nazi regime. After hours of futile seeking in Buber's library and study, the officer in charge approached Buber and asked him. "Haven't you published anything which attacks the Führer and disparages his work?" "Of course I have," Buber answered, and handed him a copy of his translation of the Bible.

Whether true or false, the anecdote does express Buber's response to the Nazi regime. Later he probably learned that the power of the Bible was not enough to endanger the Nazis. Brute force was needed. German fascism had to be fought, not compromised with as Chamberlain suggested, or taught to live with, as emerges from Buber's activities in Germany in the years 1933–38. But Buber never admitted his mistake. The brutal man-made Hell of exploitation, degradation, and murder, of death squads, gas chambers, and starving children never appears in his writings.

As time passed, it became clear to me that one cannot educate for peace without addressing the dialectical developments of one's society. Thus, since 1967, Israel has become very much a colonialist power on the West Bank and in Gaza, exploiting the Arab workers there who do most of the menial work in Israel, often for less than the minimum wage. Israel also has taken land from Arabs and given it to Jews who wish to settle there. Perhaps I should add that many of these settlers call themselves pioneers, but they refuse to settle on land in other sections of Israel where Arabs would not need to be expelled—i.e., the Galilee. Furthermore, all the developments that Sartre describes in his discussion of colonial exploitation by Frenchmen of Arabs in Algeria are occurring between Israelis and Arabs. The Israeli army is, *de facto*, the governing force on the West Bank and in Gaza. The Arabs in these areas relate to Israel through the many aspects of exploitation and oppression which they encounter daily. Israelis attempt to justify the mistreatment and persecution of Arabs by citing the difficulties of Israeli security. To underline the importance of such security, they agree to devote greater and greater resources to the military and the military-industrial complex. But the need for security is partially a result of the exploitation and oppression of Arabs. Meanwhile, the growing military-industrial complex is continually seeking ways to justify growing military expenses and a militaristic political stance.

The above is, of course, a superficial overview of economic and social processes in which we exist, but it does indicate that the educator for peace in Israel cannot and should not ignore dialectics. But what should he do? Here are some excerpts from a personal discussion with Smadar.

Smadar: Don't misunderstand me, Haim, what we are doing in dialogue is good. But somehow the situation in Israel is running away from us, getting worse while all we are doing is learning to relate dialogically.

Haim: What do you suggest?

Smadar: I know that going to political rallies has limited influence. It is like a sauna; you get rid of some excessive frustrations, but you hardly make any impact on the political process. At times I feel greater political impotence after participating in a rally than I did before it.

Haim: Let me tell you some of my recent deliberations; I'm not sure they will help, but they do show where I am. My problem is that I dislike superficialities, but I cannot attack all the problems that I see on as profound a level as I would prefer. Let me start from something seemingly remote from economical and political processes: Judaism. What Defense Minister Sharon and Chief of Staff Eitan are doing in the name of Jewish survival is a caricature of the heritage and values of Judaism.

Smadar: Just like Hitler was a caricature of German values.

Haim: I wouldn't sanction that comparison, even though you may be right if we confine it to what is being done with values. But such a confining would be wrong, dead wrong. It is the actions that count.

But let us stay in the realm of Judaism. Sharon and Eitan are like the Biblical kings and their ministers who sinned and brought the people to sin by encouraging them to worship earthly idols instead of the true God. In the time of the Israelite or Judaic kingdoms this was one of the worst sins possible. Today one of our earthly idols is the Israeli Defense Force; and Sharon and Eitan are utilizing many Israelis' tendency to worship this idol in order to further their own political ends and to justify cruelty, oppression, and murder in the occupied areas. So grasping Judaism profoundly, as a way of everyday life means hating what these two are doing in Gaza and on the West Bank. But I just don't have the strength or the time to further these thoughts, to develop them and to write them up, or to teach them. I am over- whelmed by the daily chores in the Education for Peace Project.

Smadar (smiling): Stop pitying yourself, Haim. You know that one of the reasons I work here voluntarily is that I love you and I admire what we are doing together. Go on with your deliber- ations.

Haim (smiling): O.K. But it's good to hear your encouragement ever so often. Now to economic realities or historical Marxist developments. We Jews are all partially living off the exploitation of Arabs. Here, this apartment in which we are now sitting and in which I live was built by Arabs who do most of the hard construction jobs. But even if I can educate that we must change this system of exploitation which is very much defining my daily existence, I really do not know what such education means in daily terms, except making people aware of what is happening. Sartre gives us very good concepts to describe and to define situations; he strips us bare of all illusions about ourselves and the system which governs our existence. He shows us our quiet compliance with our society which defines its superfluous human beings and gets rid of them. In the West, the superfluous are the poor; in the Soviet Union, it seems that much of the population is at the level of being superfluous, but especially those who criticize the regime. But Sartre does not tell us what to do next. Let me give you an example.

Smadar: Go ahead.

Haim: Consider the problem of terrorism. Sartre points out that terrorism doesn't start when, say, a person from Al Fatah infiltrates into Israel and kills some Jewish children. He agrees that such is terrible. But he asks if terrorism didn't start when, say, by Israeli law, land was taken from that terrorist and he was given minimum compensation —Isn't that an act of terrorism? Isn't that an act of making an Arab feel totally superfluous? Can't that start a dialectic which is terroristical? Can't the apartheid laws in South Africa—and they are laws—don't these laws support and encourage terrorism?

Smadar: Wonderful. You are beginning to see the light, Haim.

Haim: Yes and no, if the light is an extreme Marxism. Yes, I am beginning to see how our system is creating its antithesis in its making the Arabs our proletariat, and in the way it robs them of the fruit of their labor and tries to make them superfluous. But no, if I return to existentialist terms, or even to the same Marxist analysis of the other side. The Arab countries surrounding us are much more ruthless in their relation to their own citizens than we are to the Arabs working for us. You have seen how superfluous human life is in Cairo. You have read Mahfouz and Idris about how terribly Egyptians exploit Egyptians. And Syrian Prime Minister Hafez Assad is a killer; in the past ten years he has probably killed more Arabs, most of them Syrians, than we Jews killed since the Crusades. You see, as Dostoyevski said, everything can be made to cut both ways: psychology, Marxism, even religion.

Smadar: So what are your conclusions?

Haim: I have no conclusions, yet. I'm here in this Mideast maze trying to educate persons to relate differently, and I'm stuck. I've succeeded on a very minimal level in the area of Buberian dialogue, but now I must learn more if I want to know where to go.

Smadar: Since I'm giving you compliments today, Haim, let me give you another one.

Haim (laughing): Please, don't hesitate.

Smadar: That is another thing I love about you. You are willing to be stuck, to admit it, and to go back and start relearning something from the beginning.

Haim: Isn't that what action research is all about?

Smadar: Yes, and life too.

The *Critique of Dialectical Reason* is Sartre's main contribution to social philosophy. Perhaps the most striking aspect of this book is that it is plebeian through and through. In abstract dialectical language, Sartre is dealing with the common man, not so much as he thinks or feels, but as he attempts to make himself in the world of scarcity. Furthermore, he is dealing with these people not in their finest moments, but in the everyday dragging moment of toil, of *praxis.* The Chinese peasant, chopping up scrub and thus contributing to the deforestation of his own land, to erosion, and to clogging floods in the rivers, or the Spanish merchant in the seventeenth century, hoarding gold and thus contributing to its loss of value, or the woman working at a machine in a cosmetics factory and dreaming of her sexual adventures—these and others are the commoners who populate

Sartre's *Critique*. In short, Sartre has written a description of the common man and the way he lives his relation to scarcity in our common material world.

Yet let there be no misunderstandings: Sartre's vision is of the Hell that man creates for himself in this world of freedom and scarcity. We, the petty bourgeois, often sense this social Hell when we learn about genocide in Cambodia or in Nigeria, or famine in Central Africa or Sri Lanka, or the Gulag in the Soviet Union. But our response is often a response of compassion and not of comprehension. Here lies the *Critique*'s significance: it is neither an attempt to show a way out of this social Hell nor an attempt to show how it may be made less intolerable. It is a clarification of the interplay between forces which man initiates and which, through him, work to create this terrifying world in which man lives, works, and kills, reifies and alienates himself and his fellow man. Hence the *Critique* ends where the educator's challenge begins.

As an example of the assistance I gained from the *Critique*, I shall briefly analyze the Egyptian-Israeli encounter that I described in the last chapter, using three Sartrean concepts: the "third person" or the "third party," the "superfluousness of man," and the "fused group." I am drawing these concepts out of Sartre's lengthy dialectical discussion of man's social ensembles (in a sense, I am misrepresenting him: I am presenting as partially rigid certain social concepts which describe a constant flux. But as Sartre once remarked, we often distort the truth in order to seek the truth.) I shall first describe these concepts at some length.

Sartre holds that the third person is the creator of the objective reality of any other two persons whom he sees engaging in their praxis. This objective reality is created *through* the third person and his praxis. When three persons meet, they create three objective realities, since each person gazes at the other two and establishes a relation between them and between each Other and himself. Of course, any two persons can act as accomplices against the objective reality created by the third party, but their mutual reality will usually break down under the gaze of the third party, as Sartre has shown in his plays from *No Exit* to *Altona*. In a totalitarian or dictatorial-police state, the third person as possible informer establishes an ontology which drains the vitality of any possible meeting between two persons, an ontology which stifles dialogue before it is born. Thus if I wish to reach dialogue with another person in Egypt, or in Roumania, or in Vietnam, where any third person can be an informer, my partner in dialogue and I must construct a new ontology of relations. As accomplices, we must negate the ontology created by every person whom we encounter. Such is almost an impossible task. Hence, most persons in a totalitarian or dictatorial-police state have given up on dialogue: they exist in a wasteland of objective relations created by the third party as possible informer.

In Egypt, where personal privacy is rare due to mass poverty, much of a person's life evolves under a gaze of the Other—the role of the third party is prominent. Furthermore, from my readings and from my encounters with Israeli Arabs, Palestinians, Lebanese, and Egyptians, I have learned that in Arab society there are very few possibilities for two persons to shut themselves away from the world and to ignore the third party as a diminisher of the vitality of their encounter. Persons in Arab society grow up in the group—even the interior setup of the Arab home is group oriented, not person oriented; hence the ontology underlying their relations is constantly created by the third party, and only rarely by the arising of dialogue.

The superfluousness of man, Sartre argues, is a result of our existing in a milieu of scarcity, where there is not enough for everybody, where each person is aware that, due to economic or political developments, he may become superfluous. Perhaps in Western Europe, North America, Japan, and Australia, persons can overcome or ignore the threat of superfluousness, but in most of the world it is a very real threat which may suddenly be fulfilled. Consider the Mideast. The Palestinians and the Israelis have at least one common aim: to eradicate the possibility that their nation will become superfluous. Consider the expulsion of two million migrant workers from Nigeria, or the killing of the tribes in the Brazilian rain forests by thugs hired by multinational corporations, or the Soviet Union's murderous rampage through civilian villages in Afghanistan. All these are examples of man making his fellow man superfluous in a milieu of scarcity.

As I briefly mentioned in Chapter 2, if a person fears to become superfluous he will be reluctant to let himself go in developing relations with other persons. He will always seek ways of holding on to what he has or to what he is. Put otherwise, only when a person knows that his life is of value, that his uniqueness is appreciated, that he is worthy of being loved as a specific person, in short, that he is not superfluous—only then will he be willing to engage in dialogue. Thus many Jews resist dialogue with Arabs because they fear to become superfluous in the Mideast. They do not believe that our Arab neighbors will view our existence in this area as valuable.

According to Sartre a fused group arises when three conditions are fulfilled: first, a group of persons finds itself threatened by some external enemy or situation; second, members of the group respond to the threat by breaking down their usual relations of exteriority and mutual alienation and accepting the solidarity of a threatened group; and third, each member of the group, as a third person, participates, through his praxis, in creating a new objective reality which counters the threat and its legitimacy. Sartre articulately describes the forming of a fused group from the population of Paris before and during the storming of the Bastille. Another example could be the Warsaw Ghetto uprising against the Nazis in 1943, or perhaps even the PLO stand in Beirut in 1982. After a fused group has played its role, it does not disappear; it remains potent in the memory of its participants, and often a "pledged group" is established, in which members pledge allegiance to the new reality created by the fused group.

Due to almost four decades of external threat, Israel is very much a pledged group. Attitudes of the fused group tend to emerge when an immediate external threat reappears. If a person projects himself as a member of a fused group, he will find it extremely difficult to reach dialogue with members of other groups which threaten him now or have threatened him in the past. Such dialogue must break through a hard-won objective reality.

We can now review the encounters in Cairo and analyze them using Sartre's concepts. I shall discuss an Egyptian response, a Jewish-Israeli response, and an Arab-Israeli response which emerged in all three encounter groups during the two evenings. A prominent Egyptian response was to demand that we Israelis, and especially the Jewish Israelis, identify with their pain and suffering. It could be pain as a result of the Mideast wars or as a result of living in Egypt, say as a woman seeking freedom in Islamic society. When an Egyptian expressed pain, he felt that he was reaching a deep level of sharing with his partner. The more positive-minded Egyptians seemed to be saying: We must share our pain; that will lead to understanding, to identification. A more negative response was: Either you Israelis identify with our pain or we will have nothing to do with you. Of course, I am simplifying these responses, and in the flow of a group encounter they were rarely said outright. But one need only listen to the tapes of the meetings to hear the clear and strong Egyptian demand for identification.

As I have repeatedly stressed in this book, identification with pain is not Buberian dialogue. The person who seeks identification is not relating to the otherness of the Other. Neither is the person who identifies himself with the pain. But why was such a response dominant in our meetings? As I briefly indicated in Chapter 2, I believe such a response developed on the background of two fears which are prominent in the Egyptian mind: the fear of becoming superfluous and the fear of the third person as informer.

The Egyptians who took the time to come to encounter

with Israelis sincerely wanted to reach some level of dialogue with us. Yet from early life they had learned that speaking straightforwardly is very dangerous. The secret police can always call one for a series of interviews, which totally disrupts one's life and peace of mind. If they are not careful, there will always be persons who are willing to replace them, to thrust them down from the level of the social pyramid which they attained with difficulty. Worse, one can be silenced, as Enis Mansour was silenced, or even jailed for views which anger the regime. The Egyptian has also learned that speaking about one's pain is not too dangerous—everyone in Egypt undergoes periods of suffering. As long as one talks of events that occurred in the past—under a different president, or during a period characterized by a different approach from that of the current president—one is not treading on thin ice. In short, they learned that the only secure way of being open with the Other is through the expression of pain.

This pseudodialogue serves the needs of the regime. Buberian dialogue can become a positive social force because it opens up a new aspect of reality and it assures each person that he or she, as a specific person, is irreplaceable. Both attitudes—that the reality confronting a person is not the only one possible and that as a specific person one is irreplaceable—are the antitheses of the manner by which dictatorial regimes assert themselves. Hence a pseudodialogue in which suffering is expressed is a manner of allowing persons to relate to each other without threatening the regime.

As I have repeatedly stressed in the previous pages, the participant in Buberian dialogue must also confront the Other. But such confrontation, by persons as whole beings, persons not plagued by fears, can weaken the hierarchical structure of any society, be it the structure of a university or of the pyramidal society of Egypt. Once again, pseudodialogue ensures the present social structure. In short, the Egyptians chose the only way they had learned to be open with the Other: the expression of pain and the demand of identification.

Slowly, we began to understand that the Egyptian response at the meetings was an expression of deep malaise, which had many manifestations. Here are excerpts from a discussion a few Israelis had on one of the most evident manifestations. It took place many months later, on another visit to Egypt.

Dina: Every time I come here, the Egyptian men turn me off, and each time it is worse. I hate the way they continually try to touch me when I am walking in the streets of Cairo. But worst of all, I hate their gaze, the way they look at me.

Haim: What is so bad about their gaze?

Chava (Jewish woman): Let me explain. These Egyptians do not look at us the way an Israeli would look at us, and I am including the Arabs I have met in the Project as typical Israelis—I haven't met too many Arabs outside the Project. Anyhow, the Israeli man will look me over and, say, wonder if I am wearing a bra today.

Suliman (Arab man): Are you wearing a bra today, Chava? (Everybody laughs.)

Chava (smiling): It's none of your damn business—but I am . . . What I mean is that the Egyptian gives me a feeling that he is trying to rape me with his eyes. His eyes express more than a wish to strip me; they are a sort of penetrating into my body, into my existence.

Dina: Right, and after you've been repeatedly touched or pinched by an Egyptian, as most of us women have, the gaze is even more repulsive. It is a disgusting, defiling penetration that makes me shudder.

Haim: I think the gaze has to do with the entire existential situation in which the Egyptian finds himself. It is not only, as we discussed while reading Mahfouz, that the Egyptian man relates to the woman not as an equal, but as an object to be captured, despoiled, and enjoyed. It is that your freedom as women threatens his entire being and makes him feel superfluous.

Chava: I don't understand.

Haim: Then let me try again. The Egyptian man is constantly
afraid that he may suddenly become superfluous, that he will
find himself without a job, without status, honor, and all the
things that make his life meaningful. Then, suddenly, his
small area of existence is invaded by you young women, who
are happy-go-lucky, casually dressed, seemingly without any
worries in the world. You are not the women he is accustomed to deal with, and your freedom threatens his dominant sex role, one of the few areas where he is absolute ruler.
So he responds the only way he feels himself potent to
respond, by sexually assaulting you with his eyes. And when
he can, he follows up this assault with a touch or a pinch. He
thus invades your area of dominance and regains some of the
power he has lost.

Chava: But doesn't he understand that this action is a sort of rape
and that it also degrades him?

Haim: No, I don't think he understands. And I believe he gets some
sort of satisfaction from defending his being with his sexual
intents. I know that all this sounds weird, but if you recall
Tayeb Salah's book *Season of Migration to the North,* where
he describes the degraded Arab sexual response to the invasion of Western culture, you'll know what I mean. Fighting
against becoming superfluous has many sick manifestations.
And it is perhaps only natural that it appears in one's sexual
responses.

A prominent Jewish response at the Cairo meetings was to
stress the intergroup relations among the Jews and, at times,
among the Jews and the Arabs in the Education for Peace
Project. It took the form that if one Jew was attacked others
stood up for him, or if one got mixed up, other Jews attacked
him for not answering to the point. Jews often felt the need to
explain each other to the Egyptians. (Often there was a need
for such explanation. Very few Egyptians who participated in
the meetings knew much about life in Israel. Not one of them
ever visited Israel. I also suspect that it is difficult for a person
growing up in a dictatorial regime to understand what it

means to live in a democracy. Also, the Egyptian mass media give very few insights into life in Israel.) But the Jews often explained beyond clarification of the facts or misunderstanding. At times they were aggressive in their explanation; they frequently explained in order to justify. They were acting as members of a fused group.

Many Jews grasped their being misunderstood, and perhaps slandered, as a threat to one's otherness. They responded by fusing together. But by such a fusing, they were not letting each individual Jew give himself to the encounter. Each Jew, as Other, blocked each other Jew's quest for dialogue by projecting the reality of the fused group and indicating that it was the sole interpretation of the Egyptian response. Thus, as a member of a fused group, each Jew viewed each Egyptian as the Other who is unwilling to be a partner in dialogue and who, on the basis of his self-imposed distortion of facts, might become a threat. But by creating such an objective reality, the Jews as subjects, as persons, vanished. Like the Cheshire cat, only their smile of understanding haunted the encounter.

Merging into a fused group has become very much a natural response of many Jews in Israel. They interpret the saying of the Jewish Fathers that all Jews are responsible for each other, as requiring that each Jew fulfill the demands of the Jewish fused group. In short, they advocate a responsibility which is antidialogical and which Buber vehemently degraded. Thus in Cairo, the Jew who wanted to reach dialogue with Egyptians was in a dilemma: he felt that for dialogue to occur, he must abandon his fused group—seemingly, he must betray his fellow Jews and give up a component of his Jewish identification. Few—if any—had the courage to do so, especially since the Egyptians demanded that the Israelis identify with *their* pain.

The Israeli Arabs were caught in a crossfire between Jews and Egyptians. Some of them followed the Egyptian lead and tried to demand identification with their suffering as Palestinians; others tried to show that, despite their suffering, they were part of the fused group created by the Jews. Both responses aroused anger. When they demanded identification, they angered the Jews, who saw in this behavior a betrayal of all they had learned together in the Education for Peace Project. When they joined the fused group created by the Jews, they angered the Egyptians, who took them to task for disregarding true Arab suffering. In short, the dialectic that developed led the Israeli Arabs to see themselves as superfluous to the encounter, as hindering the attempts of Jews and Egyptians to reach dialogue, and, at times, as scapegoats of the Jewish-Egyptian alienation. Some of them responded to this development vehemently; others retreated into passivity.

The feeling of superfluousness of the Israeli Arabs in the encounter reinforced what every Arab who participated in the Education for Peace Project learned about his political situation during the trip to Egypt. As already mentioned, many Israeli Arabs call themselves Palestinians and would like to see themselves affiliated with a Palestinian state which would emerge on the West Bank of the Jordan River and in the Gaza Strip. But the large majority of Egyptians whom members of our Project encountered all over Egypt, whether intellectuals, white-collar workers, students, or laborers, viewed the Palestinian problem as a downright nuisance. Unfortunately, the dialectical development of the encounter in the Continental Hotel only made this sad existential situation more acute. Both the Jews and the Egyptians tried to use the Israeli Arabs to forward their own needs. The Israeli Arabs wavered. Instead of attempting to become a third party and thus to create a different objective reality, they allowed the discussion to reveal to themselves their social and political impotence.

"Good morning, Haim. This is Meir. How are you?"

"Tired. We just got back from Egypt yesterday afternoon, and it was hot and exhausting riding through the Sinai desert. That was my third trip to Egypt with a group of students and

I am sick of being in charge; it was taxing. Too much erupted, and taking care of eighty people was difficult."

"I heard that you erupted too, Haim. Why can't you be more elegant in your responses?"

"What are you talking about?"

"What you said about Defense Minister Ariel Sharon. I have a note here on my desk to the effect that you wished him a fatal heart attack one of these nights, and that you expressed this wish at a meeting in which Egyptians were present."

"Wait a minute. We all got back from Egypt yesterday at 5:00 P.M. It is now 8:15 in the morning. How did you get that note so quickly?"

"That's none of your business, but you know that I have friends."

"You mean that the moles in my Project were that quick to report on me, that even before they took a shower and had a good night's sleep they rushed to the phone to call security."

(Chuckling) "You were supposed to teach them the true value of dialogue and trust, weren't you? You've been working on your Buber stuff since the fall of 1979, and today is late April 1982; so you can evaluate the measure of your success, my friend. But aren't you evading the issue, Haim?"

"What issue?"

"Did you or didn't you express the wish that the defense minister of the Israeli government, Ariel Sharon, get a fatal heart attack at a meeting in which Egyptians were present?"

"I sure did. And it is none of your business."

"As long as you are a faculty member of Ben-Gurion University on a trip which the university sanctions, it is my business. But let us leave the details of this discussion for your meeting with the president of the university. I'm sure he won't be delighted to hear this."

"You are the epitome of the faithful bureaucrat, Meir."

"Don't worry, he won't get it from me, but he will get it. Since I am a bit curious, could you tell me why you said that wonderful remark about Sharon?"

"Two reasons. First, I believe that Sharon is leading us into a mess from which there will be no getting out on the West Bank, especially in the manner he encourages our soldiers to kill Arab children. That is despicable and a minister of a Jewish government who does it—whatever his political exigencies—is working against everything that is valuable in Judaism."

"After three years of eating crap in the Education for Peace Project, you are still naive, Haim. And what is your second reason?"

"We were in a specific situation in which the Arabs of our Project felt totally superfluous. At that meeting the Egyptians and the Jews were in the process of reaching some sort of understanding from which the Arabs were left out. They rebelled and needed some sort of support, and naturally they looked to me for that support. So I said what I felt about Sharon. But, believe me, I would not have said it if I did not firmly believe that it would be better for the Jewish people and the Mideast if Sharon would disappear, immediately."

"I can only say, Haim, that you really are unpredictable. Oh yeah, and you are lucky that you already have tenure."

(Three weeks later I was called to the president's office to discuss the "wish for Sharon's death" incident. I pleaded academic freedom. The incident was turned over to the rector to take the necessary measures. He was slow. In the meantime Sharon sent us into the quagmire of Lebanon, where my son fought and I served a reserve stint of forty-five days. Thanks to that swamp where hundreds of Israelis were killed, thousands wounded, and much devastation and death brought upon all parties involved, the investigation of my wish was dropped.)

On June 6, 1982, Israel launched the Peace for Galilee Operation, which later became the Lebanese war. Immediately, much of the mistrust that had diminished between Jews and Arabs who had participated in Buberian Learning

Groups emerged, as if from nowhere. Vicious arguments erupted, relations became strained, a lack of dialogue prevailed. Political adherence seemed to have vanquished any attempt to relate dialogically. Some of the Jewish participants in the Project were immediately called up for reserve duty; some Arabs responded by shunning our meetings; others used them to screamingly condemn the invasion of Lebanon. The school year ended two weeks later.

Despite the situation, Jews and Arabs continued to meet sporadically for many months; there seemed to be a need to give vent to one's frustrations together. In the meantime, my contracts with the funding agencies terminated and I formally closed the Education for Peace Project. Some participants attempted to establish an Education for Peace Society, but without success. A group of Project graduates did initiate a peace curriculum program in some Israeli high schools; the program was partially successful and is still in its initial stages of development.

In the fall of that year, Smadar visited me. Here are some excerpts from our discussion.

Smadar: What have you learned from this breakdown of trust in our groups after the invasion of Lebanon? Perhaps, in your overemphasizing of Buber, you were barking up the wrong tree?

Haim: Perhaps. But I don't think we can adequately evaluate what happened now, five months after we terminated formal activities. Good educational accomplishments have ways of turning up in deeds done many years later. I can tell you that this entire experience did teach me much about the limitations of dialogue and the importance of a dialectical comprehension of society as developed by Sartre.

Smadar: Please explain.

Haim: Well, I'm not sure I can. My thoughts are only half baked. You see, dialogue seems to have very little to do with what Sartre calls *praxis.* And if the main creator of our objective

reality is our praxis, is our everyday doing, then whenever
the objective reality is in turmoil, dialogue is bound to break
down. Dialogue does not create an objective reality which
can counter the objective reality created by praxis. Buber
knew this; therefore he stressed that the influence of dialogue must appear in one's everyday life. He was right, but
also wrong.

Smadar: You have me all mixed up. Give me some examples.

Haim: Take the Jew from our Project who is called up to his
reserve unit to fight in the Lebanese war. Say he does not
know yet what we know now, that the war was stupid and
meaningless. His praxis is to load the tank with ammunition,
to make sure everything functions correctly, to travel along a
specific road where the enemy will not perceive him immediately, to open fire when approaching the Palestinian
stronghold. In short, he is creating an objective reality which
will be his past and which has nothing to do with dialogue.

Smadar: All that is simple; we've gone through that before.

Haim: Yes, but what is not simple is that in order not to do that, he
must create a different objective reality which also has nothing to do with dialogue. In other words, when we enter the
historical process and try to change it for the better, we are
not dialogical, or only very rarely. My mistake in the entire
conception of the Education for Peace Project was that I did
not grasp that dialogue can emerge in the historical doing; it
cannot come instead of that doing.

Smadar: I understand. But where do we go now in education for
peace?

Haim: We might be going in a parallel direction, but at least, with
Sartre's concepts, we know better what we are up against.

Smadar: You mean that you can now define the Arab and Jewish
situation much more clearly. And this clarification can help
us see where to go in this maze.

Haim: Exactly. You're on my wavelength. Take quite a few of the
Arabs who participated in the Education for Peace Project.
We often told them that they persist in refusing to assume
personal responsibility for change. They are always con-

cerned with what some of their friends think, not with what is the right thing to do.

Smadar: They bask in their impotency until it becomes a source of power. And whoever doesn't join them, they reject. I often felt that the dialogue we achieved with them was a way of helping them to continue to be politically impotent and to justify it. That is one of the reasons I have been criticizing you.

Haim: Keep it up. I'm ready to learn. But now I can analyze their response. It is a serial response, whereby the person is concerned in being a member of a series, that is, of a group which has no intent to change any objective reality but is grouped together for some specific external reason. Persons who grow up and always live as serial beings, without dialogue, without any attempts to change objective reality— these persons have learned that social impotency is a way of life. They can emerge from such impotency to scream and yell, to kill or murder, to join a fanatical group, but they do not believe in slow meaningful doing. Worse, the slow work of changing an objective reality by praxis, by daily doing, is beyond the scope of a serial person's existence. And you are right; in such cases, dialogue can become a support of one's impotency—Dostoyevski shows all this beautifully in *The Possessed,* but I wasn't wise enough to see it.

Smadar: I don't see our Jews running out and slowly changing objective reality either. But you are right about the Arabs. One of them who is doing, who is trying to change some things in his village school, told me recently: "With some of us, discussing is like quicksand; it submerges us and chokes out our vitality."

Haim: I don't think the Jews are better or worse. Perhaps they bear greater responsibility because they have more political freedom. They live in a different dialectic, that of a pledged group. In this dialectic, doing is worthy as long as it will forward the interests of the pledged group called Israel. Thus the army has become the model for the true Israeli; serving in the army means you are worthy of being Jewish. But that is exactly where Buber was right. If that is what being Jewish is all about, then we all are no longer Jews. We have betrayed our heritage.

This war showed me the dialectics of all this. Some Jews felt comfortable relating dialogically to Arabs as long as it did not threaten their existence as a member of a pledged group. And the Arab in our Project, once the war broke out, was viewing the Jewish person not as a Jew whom he had met yesterday. He was viewing us, correctly, as a member of a fused group that was trying to annihilate the PLO. In this specific Jew, he was encountering the Other Jew, who was killing him as the Other Palestinian.

Smadar: Interesting. But where does all this lead us?

Haim: Well, we've learned much—more than I ever expected, even though it was probably the most painful learning I ever went through. We'll rest a bit, gain perspective, and plod along.

Smadar: And what about you personally; how do you feel about all this?

Haim: I don't know. No, . . . maybe I do. I feel a bit like Santiago, you know, the old man in Hemingway's *The Old Man and the Sea.* I went out and caught a great, beautiful fish that was too big to put in my meager boat. I struggled with the sharks and got back to shore with only the bones intact. But I still love fishing, and after I rest a bit, I'll try it again.

INITIAL RESEARCH PROBLEMS

In developing the research component of the Education for Peace Project, four immediate problems arose. The first was that what I was doing was theory development. No one had ever sought educational methods in order to bring Buberian dialogue into the daily lives of Jews and Arabs. The few writings on the relation of existentialism or of Buberian dialogue to educational practice were theoretical. No one had tried to teach persons in a conflict situation to establish Buberian dialogue between them. There were no writings on how a person could use existentialist philosophy to educate for peace. In short, I had an ambitious idea, but was confronted with unexplored territory. I had to rely on my insights, on my imagination, on my educational intuitions, on my faith in existentialist philosophy and in Buberian dialogue. Only after a theory was developed could I hope to do basic research on its multiple aspects. But, as this book shows, developing the theory took three years. Hence the results that I present in the Appendix are only a beginning of what can be learned about coping with existential mistrust, about educational approaches to realizing Buberian dialogue, about building trust between Jews and Arabs, and, in general, about existentialist philosophy and education for peace.

Developing the theory took three years, but that does not mean that the theory is developed. My work showed that existentialist philosophy and Buberian dialogue can be the basis of new approaches to peace education. It also rejected two basic assumptions that underlie almost all current approaches to conflict resolution and to peace education. The first assumption is that conflict resolution and peace education must be based on analytical reasoning, which includes pragmatic thinking, sociological analysis, game theories, etc. In basing my approach on existentialist philosophy, I viewed education for peace as a dialectical process which is beyond the comprehension of analytical reasoners. The second assumption which I rejected was that one must work from the ontological assumptions which prevail where one started and accept those assumptions as facts of life. But Buber, and also Marcel and Berdyaev, held that through the establishing of dialogue a new ontology emerges. In showing that such can occur in a conflict situation, I was disparaging what conflict-resolution methodologists are talking about. I was also showing that one need not confine education for peace to the realm of the I-It.

Thus, I have shown much, but everything still needs to be done. For instance, many formal aspects of the theory need to be developed: dialectical processes need to be described; hindrances to dialogue need to be identified, understood, coped with, and surpassed; additional insights and concepts of existentialist philosophers need to be examined; the dialectics of the historical processes in the Mideast must be made intelligible and related to existentialist philosophy. All these endeavors must be tempered by data supplied by persons who undergo the educational process. In short, the problem of developing a theory that links existentialist philosophy to education for peace is still very prominent.

While developing a theory, much of the data that one gathers is preparatory and not theory confirming. This brings up the second problem: How should the data be collected, so as not to diminish the force of the educational approach based on dialogue? Put differently, we demanded from our participants that they relate as whole beings, while all research is concerned with one aspect of a person's existence. We demanded that they relate as subjects, while in research we were forced to view them as objects. After much deliberation, I decided to use a host of methods of research, which included questionnaires, interviews, observation, etc. I assumed that spreading out the data collection to different perspectives would better accord with relating to the whole person.

The third problem was the need to develop research tools and methods that would accord with existentialist philosophy and Buberian dialogue. My response, which was partial, included the following. I tried to use dialogue as a means for research; for instance, many personal meetings were directed and recorded. Since "using dialogue" is a contradiction in terms, this approach was, at best, problematic. Second, I used many of the educational exercises, such as the Death Game, as sources of data. Thus we know that about 90 percent of the personal commitments to work for peace at the end of the Death Game were never fulfilled. And third, I formulated the following scale of development.

Scale of Development from the Impression-Making Person to the Dialogical Educator

The ensuing five models of existence and manners of relating to the world are based on concepts coined by Martin Buber. The steps in the scale describe stages in the development of a person from the impression-making stage, which is quite common in Western society, up to the dialogical educator.

It should be kept in mind that according to Buber, Nietzsche, Dostoyevski, and other existentialists, a person develops and realizes his or her personality through relations to the Other, to the It, to the Thou. One must therefore not confuse the following stages with the approach developed by various psychologists (Freud, Maslow) who begin with a description of the structure of a person's psyche and find in that structure, and not in the manner in which a person relates, the source for personality development.

In a person's life the stages often blend. For reasons of clarity they have been presented separately. It is highly improbable that persons in higher stages can fully free themselves from some remnants of lower stages.

First Stage: The Impression-Making Person. The person is primarily concerned with the impressions he or she makes on other people and generally relates to the Other as an object and to nature as an It. The person imposes on the Other, often uses stereotypes, does not speak straightforwardly, and evades personal responsibility. The person is very much affected by public opinion and often lives in bad faith.

Second Stage: The Conscious Person. The person distinguishes between seeming (impression making) and being, and between relation to the Other as an object and as a subject; he or she is conscious of the possibility of relating personally to nature. The person is aware of the faults of imposing oneself on the Other, is aware of his or her moments of bad faith, is willing to describe personal failings to another person and begins to doubt stereotypes. The person expresses interest in self-education, wonders if his or her potential is being fulfilled, and begins to be aware of the importance of personal responsibility.

Third Stage: The Person Who Educates Himself or Herself to Relate Dialogically. The person learns to listen to the Other, attempts to relate to the Other subjectively, to trust him or her, and to be aware of his or her otherness. The person makes first attempts to live in accordance with one's being, allows oneself to be spontaneous, rebels against stereotypes, and refrains from imposing oneself on the Other. The person speaks straightforwardly and begins to establish a relationship of communion with nature. The person is aware of one's freedom and destructive tendencies and is constantly seeking new ways to realize his or her being.

Fourth Stage: The Dialogical Person. The person can develop a genuine dialogue and make oneself present to the Other; he or she is open to the Thou, and allows moments of I-Thou relationships to guide one's life. The person responds trustfully to the Other, accepts responsibility, and knows how to support the Other lovingly. The person seeks ways of directing one's destructive tendencies to constructive channels and expresses one's freedom creatively. The person seeks a vision of just, human relationships.

Fifth Stage: The Dialogical Educator. The person has a definite direction for personal development and is responsible for the fulfillment of a vision of humanity. The person sees the Other, that is, his or her strengths and existential situation, and is willing to teach the Other to realize one's personality in light of the vision of humanity. The dialogical educator is willing to bring suffering to the Other, knowing that at times there is no other way to help the Other develop one's creative powers; yet he or she remains sensitive to the suffering and to the pain that the Other undergoes. The dialogical educator trusts other persons and the world, listens to the demands of the world, and relates as a whole being to his or her pupils.

Another problem was to train the research staff to do its work in a manner that would not hinder our educational goals. By requiring each member of the research staff to participate in a Buberian Learning Group and personally to undergo the educational process that he was studying, this problem was partially solved.

10. Buber: The Struggle for the Realization of Spirit

We make peace, we help bring about world peace, if we make peace wherever we are destined and summoned to do so: in the active life of our own community and in that aspect of it which can actively help determine its relationship to another community.

—MARTIN BUBER

I OPENED this book with the proposition that existentialist philosophy can help one educate for peace. I there held that the search for peace must begin with our trying to live what existentialist writers told us to do in order to be creative, dialogical, and courageous. Furthermore, I indicated that if a person does so, he will be weaving an Ariadne thread that will help him through the maze of interlocking conflicts in which he finds himself. But, in a sense, I have been misleading the reader. Because instead of presenting the suggestions of existentialist writers systematically, or telling the story of the Education for Peace Project, I have been partially doing both and not fully doing either one. Actually, I have been telling a completely different story, which may be called: Stations in an Attempt to Realize the Spirit of Dialogue and Peace. Like all attempts to realize Spirit in everyday life, it is a personal story; whether I like it or not it is primarily my story—the ways I succeeded and failed to learn and to live the existentialist writings that I read.

This story has one component which I would like to address once more, this time a bit more systematically: the component can be formulated, a bit clumsily and naively, into a question: Why was Buber's philosophy so central to the Education for Peace Project? The answer is both simple and complex.

The simple answer is: Buber's philosophy was central to the Education for Peace Project because dialogue helps persons cut through their webs of lies. In genuine dialogue one attains the power to confront these lies and to face truths whose vitality one has been repressing, truths which a person alone often fears to face. As mentioned, such dialogue may lose its power if it does not attain recognition in an objective reality, albeit a limited one. In hindsight, this was an important role of the Buberian Learning Groups: they provided an objective reality which allowed persons to benefit from dialogue and to cut through webs of lies.

Why should a person cut through and attempt to eradicate one's web of lies? Often, as Marcel, Sartre, Ibsen, and Gide have pointed out, such webs help persons overcome difficult situations. The answer is simple to formulate and difficult to achieve. Man cannot develop as a spiritual being if he is constantly encompassed by a web of lies which he participates in weaving. Only by attempting to realize spiritual goals in one's everyday existence, an attempt which must begin with the eradicating of lies, can one hope to become somewhat of a spiritual person. Hence the complex answer: Buberian dialogue is a first step in becoming a spiritual person.

That is the trap into which I was led by existentialist philosophy. I began educating for dialogue and peace, and I ended by failing to assist most participants to attain a more spiritual existence. Somewhere along the road the goal of the Project changed—existentialist philosophy and daily realities merged to bring about this change. I became aware of the shift in my perceptions much later, after the invasion of Lebanon, when relations were tense. I then saw that my goals had been high, which made participants very uncomfortable; but if they had been low, I would have been merely weaving a new web of lies. Here is where the paradoxical and the tragic will always accompany the teaching of existentialist philosophy as a way of life. We educators cannot personally attain the goals of Zarathustra or of Father Zosima. We can only partially teach our pupils what need be done to attain such goals. But the paradoxical attempt to do so, the faith in the possibility of the Spirit emerging in everyday life, coupled with the minor tragedy of totally failing to achieve this goal—such an attempt is the first step toward our own living spiritually and our teaching pupils to live thus.

A few participants did develop spiritually beyond dialogue. Their development often evolved in three stages, the last two of which somewhat parallel Zarathustra's three metamorphoses. Let us follow the development of one such participant, Adina, a Jewish woman.

In the first stage, a person recognizes the importance of dialogue in helping one change one's life. Here are excerpts from a long meeting in which Adina and her Arab dyad partner were questioned by one of our research staff. (They had been partners for about five months when this meeting took place. Usually, we change dyad partners three times during the year. But that year, for purposes of research, four dyads, among them Adina and Yusuf, remained permanent.)

Researcher: Describe your first meetings.

Adina: At first, we met only to write up the assignment.

Yusuf: Even though we met to do the assignment, I knew that I was the first Arab she ever spoke to personally. I told her about my work, about life in the Bedouin tribe. As time went on, we spent less time on the assignment and more time on other topics. I remember being deeply influenced by Buber's writings and trying to relate in such a manner to Adina. The meetings were always in her home.

Researcher: How did you feel, coming to her house?

Yusuf: I didn't feel uncomfortable coming into a Jewish house, but the entire area of Jewish suburbia did scare me. The first time I came, as I approached Adina's gate a big dog arose in the yard and started coming toward me. I got scared, got back into my car, and drove away. I was even scared to yell to Adina or to honk my horn.

Researcher: Were you uncomfortable with Adina's husband around?

Yusuf: No, I felt that he accepted me.

Adina: At first, Yusuf scared me most among the Arabs in our group. His wild hair and coal-black eyes frightened me. Maybe this was a result of the word "Arab" being a cussword where I grew up. I still feel uncomfortable when I hear the word "Arab."

Yusuf: I repeatedly told her what it is like to be an Arab, but she counters by saying that I am not the typical Arab.

Adina: In my relationship with Yusuf, I neutralize his being an Arab, maybe because I never saw him in his home environment, his tribe, his family. I'd like to meet his wife and children.

Researcher: Why haven't you visited his home, after all these meetings?

Yusuf: She never expressed the wish to see my family.

Researcher: Didn't her interest in your family lead you to understand that she'd like to meet them?

Yusuf (excited): No. No. I never felt that she wanted to visit my village. We only talked about her visiting the school where I teach.

Adina: He grasps me in a manner that is not friendship. I sense that he feels inferior to me when we speak, and that is perhaps the reason he didn't invite me to visit his tribe. He wants to invite me to some festival, when things are special. Maybe if I had pressed more he would have invited me. Perhaps he feels uncomfortable living in the village, in a lower quality of life.

Yusuf: Adina's impressions are wrong. Perhaps she reached these conclusions because of these last few weeks. I had many problems. I told her that I had problems in the tribe.

Researcher: Did you describe the problems?

Yusuf: No, I just told her that I had problems, especially when she told me that I am evading our meetings.

Adina: You see, Yusuf helped me neutralize his being an Arab by not sharing his problems with me. Yusuf, did you feel the need to share the problems with me?

Yusuf: These past few weeks I've gone through the most difficult period in my life.

Adina: He doesn't answer me. Like in the Death Game, when I asked for support, he didn't turn to me.

Yusuf: I thought you already had an image of me, so I was afraid to share my problems with you.

Adina: Would you have shared the problems with me while the things were happening? You know that sharing is different after everything has been resolved. Perhaps you evaded me because I am a woman?

Yusuf: No.

Adina: From the beginning of our relationship I felt that he lacks spontaneity, and that I am much more open. I lead the discussions and try to not let him evade me. I ask, inquire, listen. He does not give me the feeling that he wants to know about me. Yusuf, tell me if this is true.

Yusuf: In most of my relations with friends I am clear to the other person. Here it doesn't happen, and I am at times appalled at the conclusions that Adina reaches.

Researcher: What was the most significant event in the development of your relationship?

Yusuf: For me, it occurred when Adina arrived late for the Death Game retreat. She joined our quartet after things were moving. During the game there was a clash between Adina and Yafa, and I felt that I must intervene in support of Adina. I saw that she was tired; we all were tired; I had not spoken much to Yafa before the game, and I didn't intervene. I knew that if I would support Adina something would explode, but I felt uncomfortable not giving support. Afterwards we talked about it and I was surprised that Adina blamed herself.

Adina: I seem to generate very little support for my views, and that includes Yusuf. I support him much more than he supports me.

The most significant event, in my view, happened when

my husband was in the reserves. Yusuf arrived at about 5:00 P.M. It was the first time he saw my children. We spoke a bit and were supposed to do an assignment. I became very tense, due to the fact that I was alone in the house with Yusuf. Yusuf was also tense; his hands were shaking when he lifted the coffee cup to drink. We didn't finish the assignment. I put the kids to bed. Yusuf asked me why I was so tense. I answered that, personally, I try and not get into close relations with men, because I don't believe that friendship between a man and a woman can be divorced from sex. But Yusuf answered something that I will always remember. He said: "In my tribe they make us undergo the engagement ceremony to our future wife at the age of thirteen. I never met the woman who is now my wife before that. Since then I have lived in a marriage relationship framework and I can develop Platonic relations with other women, and such relationships can be significant for me."

I don't know how what Yusuf said works, or if it works, but at that moment it restored my peace of mind. Once again I seemed to be grasping Yusuf's words, but not his being . . . I mean his Arab being.

Some months later, Yusuf and Adina stopped meeting. I suspect that Yusuf could not deal with Adina's passionate appeals for dialogue. Toward the end of the first year, Adina receded into herself. She was less active in the Buberian Learning Group. At the beginning of the second year, she seemed to be living with some of the burdens of Zarathustra's camel. Here are some excerpts from a meeting I had with her.

Adina: My whole situation makes me sick. At last I seem to have freed myself from my inhibitions so as to be able to relate dialogically to an Arab, so as to try and be concerned about peace—and the response of the group to my efforts, the response of the outside world is totally unsupportive. I seem to be learning a lot of pretty good things which I will never be able to do.

Haim: I think that you are making a mistake that I frequently make. You think that if you have slightly changed personally, then the world should change with you. Well, it doesn't work that way. You often have to create the responses of the outer world to your personal changes together with those changes.

Adina: That isn't new to me, Haim. You are not listening to me attentively.

Haim: Go ahead.

Adina: Why should I go on burdening myself with this Education for Peace Project and all the learning that goes along with it? It is not that I don't get some personal satisfaction; I do. It is that the burdening does not seem to lead anywhere beyond that limited personal satisfaction. I often feel all this learning is like a weight which gives me nothing.

Haim: It will eventually give you some personal and social freedom.

Adina: I don't see that coming.

Haim: Anything that I say now will sound a bit stupid. You know, like that freedom is beyond the next bend in the road, or that you are now in the cocoon stage and soon things will open up and you will be able to fly like a butterfly. All this sounds stupid and presumptuous, so I'll shut up. But I can ask you to do me a favor. Trust me. You are in a stage of development. Don't give up. Because suddenly, like a champagne bottle, a cork will pop, and you'll see where all this fermentation and waiting led.

Adina: I hope it tastes like champagne then.

Toward the end of the second year, Adina seemed to be emerging from her period of fermentation and waiting. She took it upon herself to open a series of class meetings in which students tried to relate personally to a religious text in the manner suggested by Buber in his essay "The Man of Today and the Jewish Bible": that one open the religious text to a passage one finds significant and let its message illuminate one's being. In these meetings Jews related to the Bible and Arabs to the Koran. Here are some excerpts from the meeting Adina led.

Adina: I do not want to sound presumptuous, but I chose the sections from Exodus where Moses stands before Pharaoh and tries to get him to free the tribes of Israel.

Haim: What personal message did these passages pass on to you?

Adina: What impressed me was that in this whole situation, of ups and downs, of plagues and broken promises, of the people rebelling and Pharaoh rejecting God, Moses stood firm—even though he stuttered. I read the entire section a few times and kept thinking what it means to struggle against such difficulties, especially for a person who stutters. The stuttering attracted me and I began to wonder why. And it seemed to me that I had been so afraid to stutter that I had never gotten into situations even partially analogous to Moses' situation. More important, I seemed to understand that perhaps something like spirit is expressed through stuttering.

Hamida (Arab woman): I think I understand the first part of what you said, about being afraid to be in situations where you might stutter or mess up. But what do you mean when you say that the spirit is expressed through stuttering?

Adina: Well, one part of it is pretty evident, that at times we are so concerned with presenting an idea, or a thought, or ourselves, perfectly, that we lose the spirit in our concern for perfect form. This has to do with Buber's rejection of always making an impression. The other part has to do with the spontaneous expression of spirit, which is often stuttered.

Hamida: You still are not clear. Maybe give us a personal example.

Adina: Let me think for a moment.

Haim: Maybe you should try and give an example from your relations with some of the members of this group.

Adina: O.K. I suddenly felt, while reading about Moses, that there are periods when we are trying to undergo a change and to change things around us, and these are periods of stuttering. In this group and in life in general, we often try to cover up our situation by appeals for support. I did not accept myself as a stutterer who is seeking for something spiritual; I also demanded support.

What is more, my relations with most of you sitting here are similar to what I described. None of us, including Haim most of the time, allowed stuttering. We wanted clear, concise, explanatory responses. We wanted clear responses to a story by Kafka or to an Egyptian mosque. We criticized each other when we were unclear, when we gave a stuttered reply. We did not understand that the search to express spirit must often be unclear. We did not know how to help each other. We overlooked the fact that the stutterer often needs a brother who will be his spokesman, like Moses had Aaron. I have nothing more to say, except that now I am a little more willing to stutter, and a little more willing to let my partners in dialogue do so. I don't know if we'll reach anything spiritual, but if we are afraid to stutter, we surely won't.

Perhaps the most important insight I gained while trying to teach Jews and Arabs to relate dialogically to each other is that such teaching is a struggle against the mediocrity which pervades society. All teaching of existentialist philosophy, in the manner existentialists believe it should be taught, is a struggle in which personal freedom is pitted against this mediocrity. Hence existentialist philosophy can arise and influence education only where such a struggle is tolerated. It cannot arise in Egypt, or in the Soviet Union, or in China or Jordan or Syria, or even within the Palestinian Liberation Organization. In these societies, any outward defiance of the mediocrity in power is not tolerated. Furthermore, as a bastard child of dialectical thought and human freedom, existentialist philosophy will only flourish where both its parents are tolerated. Thus most English or American philosophers and educators, who abhor dialectics, have not been able to develop any relationship to existentialism.

The blending of dialectics and human freedom can be clearly seen in the dialogical encounter, in which both participants give of themselves freely and wholly. When such occurs, as Buber pointed out, something new emerges which exists in "the between" that the participants in dialogue created. This new dimension of the interpersonal has arisen dialectically, and it can only be understood dialectically. In analytical reason, the whole is the sum of its parts, and nothing new can emerge when two parts meet. But the new dimension of the interpersonal which emerges in the dialogical encounter cannot be reduced to its participating parts. It cannot be reduced at all.

All this is not new. What is new is that we methodically attempted to use the dialogical encounter as the first step in changing history. We soon found ourselves immersed in many new dialectical processes. One process resembled what occurs in Kafka's novels: at each new level, one will encounter persons who reject dialogue and whose sole goal is to entrench the mediocrity deeper in its position. As Kafka repeatedly showed, the archetype of such a person is the bureaucrat, who despises dialectical developments and personal freedom. His goal is to maximize analytic efficiency that reduces man to an object which can be manipulated. Dialogue and the dialectical development it arouses threaten the bureaucrat; often he will seek ways of smothering such threats, either by getting the problem removed from his desk or by keeping it there indefinitely. Hence educating for peace means educating persons who have reached dialogue to be able to initiate and create new dialectical processes in face of such external hindrances.

The external hindrances are not merely bureaucrats; often they are dialectical processes which lead to enmity and to war. I have already mentioned the military-industrial complex in Israel which directly employs close to 20 percent of the Jewish work force and thus creates a practico-inert force which pulls the entire society in the direction of war. Or consider the reemergence of Islamic fundamentalism. It has created a dialectic which has de-alienated the contemporary Moslem while having him pay for this de-alienation with the giving up of his personal freedom. Many have paid willingly—for such persons the dialogical encounter is meaningless. They do not even sense that their group affiliation has swallowed up their personality.

Put otherwise, as all existentialists have held, living as a free person means defying those dialectical processes which reduce persons to objects. It means creating new dialectical processes by struggling against the various manifestations of the practico-inert; it means being alienated but free, joyful but often rejected, lonely in the crowd but able to grow in solitude, authentic but misunderstood. It also means being able to relate personally to a vision of human existence, and pulling one's weight in trying to realize that vision. Such a pulling is the infusing of Spirit into everyday life.

In summary, I envision the existentialist educator as a person who daily struggles to realize a vision of human freedom. I can only compensate him for his efforts with two lines from Schiller's "Wallenstein":

For if your own life you're not willing to stake,
That life will never be yours to make.

As I have shown, Buber's philosophy was central to our endeavors because it provided both a means and a goal. The goal was to reach dialogue, and the means of reaching dialogue was to confront the Other with one's wish to relate dialogically. The dialogue between participants had specific content, such as Jewish-Arab relations in Israel and in the Mideast, existentialist philosophy, ways of assuming responsibility for change, personal feelings and thoughts, and problems of self-education. Such dialogue can only become a force for peace when it is coupled with self-education; the opposite is also true—only when self-education is coupled with dialogue can it lead to peaceful relations and to the assuming of responsibility.

I do not have much to add concerning dialogue and self-education, except that the merging of the two with the assuming of responsibility for peace is a beginning in the struggle to realize Spirit. This entire book describes these processes, and the educational methods I used to further such a realization. I have not hidden my regret that we did not do more, but perhaps such is inevitable in all struggles.

My regret was slightly tempered some months after the Project closed when Sausan, an Arab woman participant, visited me. Here are some excerpts from our discussion.

Sausan: It took me a long time to come here, but I have been wanting to tell you how I feel for some time.

Haim: I'm happy you came.

Sausan: You see, when the Lebanese war broke out many of the Arabs were angry at the Jews in the Project, including you. You were surprised. I must say that I was not too surprised.

Haim: Why?

Sausan: Because of something that Buber said and that you as a man seemed to overlook in your relations with the Arab men in our Project. If I understood Buber correctly, relating dialogically must influence a person's entire being. I was quite sensitive to the fact that even those Arab men who did relate openly and trustfully to you Jews, did not relate dialogically to us Arab women. In many instances we were degraded. In short, there was a distortion all along which you, which we, did not notice.

Haim: Thanks, Sausan, you've added one more failure, and one more explanation to our other failures.

Sausan: No, Haim, I've added a success.

Haim: Please explain.

Sausan: You see, it is a problem of weakness and strength. You wanted to give the Arab men strength through trusting them. You gave it to them, but they became stronger where they already were often too strong, in their identity as Arab men, as fighters. Now when the war broke out, these men felt totally impotent; they were both Israeli citizens and Palestinians, and they sided with the Palestinian cause but were afraid to do so openly as Israeli citizens. They became frustrated. Add to this that the Jewish men, some of whom

218 BUBER: THE STRUGGLE FOR REALIZATION OF SPIRIT

were fellow participants in the Project, were called up for
reserve duty in the Israel Defense Force. This also hurt their
Arab fighter identity. So the Arab men took out all their anger
upon you Jews.

Haim: I still don't see where all this is leading.

Sausan (smiling): It would seem very simple to you if you were an
Arab. Anyway, this feeling of impotence suddenly revealed to
me how little we had done to work on dialogue between Arab
men and women, and how this lack of dialogue isolated these
men from a source of power which could enhance them as
persons. This source of power could help them cope with
their political existence. Let me put it a bit poetically: you
know that we Arabs love poetry.

Haim: Please do.

Sausan: Well, these Arab men are like a ship without an anchor;
any political wind can blow them off course, or even into the
rocks off some God-forsaken shore. But now I know that this
situation exists because we overlooked the anchor, which is
our own relations between men and women.

Haim: But where is the success?

Sausan (smiling): How blind can you be, Haim? Just look at me
and you'll see your success!

11. New Research Problems

For us man is characterized above all by his going beyond a situation, and by what he succeeds in making of what he has been made—even if he never recognizes himself in his objectification.

—JEAN-PAUL SARTRE

T H E initial research problems, described above, remained with us, but that did not preclude new problems. In the day-to-day work of education for peace, it was almost impossible to do much more than to list the problems or to cope with them intuitively; one hoped to return to them at some distant date, in order to deal with them systematically. I have not yet had the opportunity to reexamine these problems; hence I shall merely identify eight problem areas, explain the little that has been done to cope with them, and suggest research possibilities where such ideas exist.

1. Most of the Jews and Arabs who participated in the Education for Peace Project were alienated from their heritage and from their religion. Even those few who were religious understood "being religious" as a feeling or as a way of identifying with a dogma or doctrine. Thus most participants identified living religiously or relating to one's heritage as a separate compartment of existence which has nothing to do with one's everyday life. Such an approach was vehemently attacked by Kierkegaard and regarded as antidialogical by Buber. Dialogue, as Buber described it, must be based on

219

one's otherness, which is also one's relation to one's heritage and to God. Hence, after achieving an initial level of dialogue, I had to work on showing participants how that dialogue can be broadened and deepened, how it can enhance one's existence if a person will seek to develop a more authentic relation to one's heritage and to one's religion.

I soon learned that pointing out, as Buber does, that a person should not confuse his alienation from a confining religious dogma, or from an insidious religious establishment, with the possibility of establishing a personal relationship with one's heritage and with God—such a pointing out presents the problem on the abstract level and does not usually help persons overcome their deeply entrenched alienation. Showing how to relate to a religious text existentially, as Buber suggested, may help, but only partially. Explaining to Jews and Arabs, as I often did, that by developing an authentic relationship to their own heritage they will help establish a better future, because they will have attained a positive direction of development—such explaining is very close to preaching, and attains similar results. I now believe that the way to respond to such alienation is by leading persons to those moments of their life in which dread, despair, anxiety, love, compassion take hold of their entire being, and showing them how these moments attain a new depth and meaning when coupled with a meaningful relationship to one's heritage and, possibly, to God. Of course, there is a vicious circle here with which the educator must cope. A person will be willing to undergo such an experience only if he trusts the educator and can relate dialogically to him. But such trust is often hindered by one's alienation.

2. It was extremely difficult to educate persons to assume personal responsibility for peace outside the Buberian Learning Group. The relations between Jews and Arabs in Israel have gone from worse to terrible in the past five years, and few persons have the courage to swim against the tide. But dialogue without responsible action that stems from the

dialogue, as Buber and other existentialists indicated, loses its vitality.

The social structure of Jewish and Arab society in Israel does not encourage such an assuming of personal responsibility. Democracy was pretty much imposed from above in Jewish society when Israel became independent. There is no tradition of grass-roots work to establish a better society or to attain greater freedom. In much of Arab society, the elder of the family or the sheikh rules, and there is no encouragement to assume responsibility in areas which he does not sanction. Thus in demanding that our first-year graduates assume responsibility for peace, we were making a demand of the kind that persons were not acquainted with and, also, not giving them the tools or the knowledge on how to fulfill such a demand.

In addition to conveying the knowledge of how to work for change in a democratic society, we might, perhaps, have assisted our participants by identifying institutions and areas in which they could work actively for peace. One such institution is the Israeli high school system, within which a few of our graduates are currently developing a curriculum for peace.

And yet, I do not believe that everything can and should be explained by historical, sociological, or anthropological reasoning. I do not believe that showing how to assume responsibility will bring a great many persons to do so. Many Jews and Arabs, graduates of the Education for Peace Project, did not have the courage or the readiness to work actively for peace. I suspect that whatever the educational program would have included, quite a few persons would have chosen to take it easy.

3. There were more than a few hindrances to dialogue in the specific milieu in which the Project arose. I shall give only two examples; others have been partially described above. Quite early in the process of educating for dialogue, the Israeli Secret Service let me know that it had planted moles in

the Buberian Learning Groups and that I better watch what I and others said. I complained to the university that such spying limited my academic freedom, but my complaints were ignored. This spying continued throughout the duration of the Project. The second example has to do with our main funding agency, the Hans Seidel Foundation. It seemed to be encouraging our work, but mainly to show it to visitors. Two years later, the Israeli press broke the story that the Hans Seidel Foundation had been channeling funds (often illegally) to right-wing politicians in Israel. In the 1981 elections, Mr. Ariel Sharon and his anti-Arab cohorts received three times as much money as we received in the three years of our existence. We were a facade for these activities. I did my best to ignore such examples of pervading deceit while educating for trust.

But do the last two problem areas have anything to do with research into education for peace? —Of course. Even the pessimistic statement with which I finished problem area 2—that many persons would have chosen to take it easy— brings many questions to mind. For instance, does the wish to take it easy have anything to do with age? We limited participation in the Buberian Learning Groups to persons under 45. We noticed that participants in the 35 to 45 age group seemed less inclined to change, and often, after undergoing a limited change preferred to take it easy. Is this observation valid? And if so, is learning to relate dialogically and to act responsibly easier for certain age groups? Or is such a learning mainly an outcome for the personal history of the participants? Many such questions arise when we look more closely at what I described in problem area 2.

The same is true for problem area 3. Research into education for peace in a conflict situation must ask about the effectiveness of betrayers, and must take into account the atmosphere of deceit which often encompasses such an endeavor. (I remember being calmed after I read a few books on how inefficient the CIA has been and on the limitations of its influence on persons.) One may also ask if and how one may use such an atmosphere to encourage trust. This question is neither academic nor stupid, if one takes into account many a person's wish to live trustfully, especially when mistrust pervades one's life, and also that moles often bring opposite results—dialectically, they may encourage trust.

4. The Jews and the Arabs who met in the Education for Peace Project were not only from different cultural and religious heritages, they also came from different social structures. The Arab who grows up in the hamula (the extended family) will find it much harder to confront a person and to establish dialogue through such a confronting. He is used to living in the public eye of his hamula where confronting is regarded as disrespectful. Furthermore, many have often learned that the only way to survive in Israeli society is through eloquence which hides their true thoughts. Thus an Arab will often find it much more difficult to reach dialogue, because of background influences which molded and continue to mold his being.

As I have indicated, the relationship between dialogue and social structure was pretty much ignored by Buber. Hence, in examining the manner in which social structure and dialogue are interrelated one must go beyond Buber. The little I have done in this area, mainly by using a Sartrean perspective, indicates that one can gain fascinating insights by exploring this realm. For instance, in the discussion with Sausan at the end of Chapter 10 she outlines an interesting research problem. Does the limited freedom of women in Arab society hinder the emerging of the dialogical encounter? Does it make these Arab men less free? If so—and my gut intuition says it is so—how does such occur? What is the dialectic of such a development? And where and how, in such a situation does the educator begin to educate for dialogue?

5. The path to dialogue begins with the confronting of the Other with my otherness and asking him to confront me with his otherness. But confronting can become a hindrance to the

development of the dialogical relationship after initial dialogue has been achieved. Riffat Hassan, who visited our
Project as a member of our international advisory committee,
perceived this problem, and described it thus.

Authentic dialogue makes possible the facing of "the real guilt" and "the
painful truth" because it is rooted in that relatedness which I call love. As I
mentioned in my report, during my visit to the project I felt that some staff
members were emotionally sterile and did not understand how important
the "heart" is in any kind of meaningful dialogue. They had learned about
confrontation but not about compassion and thought that they could carry
on a dialogue with the other with the detachment of a surgeon performing
an operation under clinical conditions. By learning the technique of
dialogue one can confront the other with the hurt within. But mere
confronting of the hurt will not lead to healing. In fact, it can sometimes be
very dangerous, for it can cause a person to fall apart totally under the
pressure of the internal pain. Rabindra Nath Tagore said, "He only may
chastise who loves." I believe that it is also correct to say that only that
person may dialogue (or confront) who loves. Jesus' golden words "Love
thy neighbor as thyself" are, in fact, the foundation principle of authentic
dialogue, for if I could love the other as myself then I would be willing to
confront the other with the "painful truth" but also to share in the pain.[10]

Although I do not fully agree with the above passage, I must
concur with Riffat that in the Education for Peace Project
there was often an undue emphasis on confronting the Other.
Of course it would be better if much more love were expressed—but educating a person to love is not that simple.
Riffat is right in pointing out that for dialogue to continue
beyond confrontation, each partner in dialogue must learn to
give of himself to the Other. Educating persons for such giving
was extremely difficult. It must begin with educating persons
to assume responsibility for even the smallest deed. But what
the educator can and should do is still not very clear to me.

6. It soon became clear that one important test of our
approach to developing Jewish-Arab dialogue was: Could I
train Jewish and Arab persons to become leaders in Buberian
Learning Groups? Of course, there was a well-known problem
here. One can teach prospective leaders certain methods, but

one can only partially show a person how to convey the spirit of dialogue—one can give him the Ariadne thread. Without the spirit, methods are merely techniques.

It seems as if I had much more success training Jewish leaders. I have no idea whether this result is due to my personal limitations, or to the fact that I had luck in finding good Jewish leaders, or to the problem that I discussed above concerning confrontation and dialogue in the Arab milieu. I believe that the secret of becoming a good leader is rooted in one's willingness to strive for authenticity, to educate oneself, and to try and reach the fourth stage in the scale of development presented above. But much more research needs to be done in this area.

7. The methods developed in the Buberian Learning Group to diminish existential mistrust can be used as a starting point for other research problems. For instance, one could check whether the relation of Jews and Arabs to the causes and consequences of aggression and violence between them changes after one has participated in a Buberian Learning Group. In other words, does the enhancing of trust spill over into other areas of human existence, and if so, how?

Put differently, it seems that our methods can be used both in education for peace and in conflict resolution; they probably influence participants in a host of areas relating to one's existential situation. But much needs to be done to examine these influences.

8. One area of research to which I have been particularly drawn has to do with Sartre's fused group. As pointed out above, Sartre holds that a fused group arises when three conditions are fulfilled. First, a group of persons finds itself threatened by some external enemy or situation; second, members of the group respond to the threat by breaking down their usual relations of exteriority and mutual alienation and accepting the solidarity of a threatened group; and third, each member of the group, as a third person, participates, through his praxis, in the creating of a new, objective

reality which counters the threat and its legitimacy.

Could the Buberian Learning Group become a fused group that would work together for peace and against the external threat of war? What would need to be done to initiate such a process? Do the relations of dialogue between some of the participants in a Buberian Learning Group facilitate such a process, or do these relations, perhaps, hinder its development, by somewhat diminishing the force of the external threat? One wonders.

These few research problems suggest many educational and philosophical challenges. Thus, the relationship between existentialist philosophy and education for peace opens new vistas of research for philosophers, educators, and social scientists.

12. Summary: Vision and Blindness

What makes one heroic? Going out to meet at the same time one's highest suffering and one's highest hope.
　　　　　　　　　　　　　　—FRIEDRICH NIETZSCHE

W O R K I N G on education for peace in Israel and in the Mideast resembles the plight of the great Egyptian author and academic Taha Hussein. Born with vision, he was blinded as a baby by the village barber in the course of a treatment for an eye infection. Still, he became one of the foremost men of letters in contemporary Egypt. His autobiography describes his blind determination to project himself into the world of knowledge, despite his initial handicap. Such blind determination is the stuff which helps fulfill visions. Including the vision of peace.

But blind determination is not enough. One must learn, as Taha Hussein learned, that failures are the *viaticum* of personal progress, that one will always be accompanied by misunderstandings of one's intentions, that the search for truth is a powerful force, even if many persons whom one encounters sustain themselves by weaving a web of lies. The Education for Peace Project was a search for truth, for dialogue, and for trust in which blind determination to work for peace on the basis of existentialist philosophy changed or touched the lives of a few score Jews and Arabs. It was an attempt made by these Jews and Arabs to be blind to political and social forces while striving to establish a relationship of dialogue and trust between them. Such blindness helped. It helped reveal, among other things, the possibilities and approaches for bettering human existence which can emerge from existentialist philosophy.

In summarizing the Project I am repeatedly struck by the blending of blindness and vision which characterized our endeavors and impact. The following two vignettes are examples of such a blending.

Dear Haim,

I found it pleasantly surprising that you remembered my presentation on the Bible in our Buberian Learning Group and wanted to include it in your book. But I am not sure that I have too much to add to what is simply written in the text, and to what I said then, two years ago.

My Bible is open to chapter 14 of Samuel I, the chapter I then chose to discuss. Yet in order to relate fully to this chapter I feel that my immersement in Buber is lacking, or maybe that same atmosphere which prevailed in the group, the smells, the words, the concepts . . . What struck me then was that Jonathan, Saul's son, was standing before a fateful deed and a moment that demanded a decision. Should he scale the cliff alone and attack the Philistines? . . . To do this he must betray his traditional way of responding and relating to God. He must emerge from the well trodden paths and dare. He decides to betray, to leave these paths because of his faith in God and in his own power. I felt that something of such a betrayal, a being blind to our unconscious ways of coping with the reality in Israel, was essential in the Buberian Learning Group; I also felt that I had trouble daring to scale the cliffs you urged us to scale, even if I believed you, that like Jonathan, I would be victorious.

Yes, for a long time I had trouble taking the blind leap into a new way of coping with our sick reality in Israel, even though I agreed with your vision. I doubt that this letter is clear, but you will probably understand, if you ultimately decide to include me in your book . . .

Yaacov and I served in the same reserve unit until I was transferred after the Lebanese war. He is a business executive whose job takes him abroad frequently, and whose unflagging interest in what is happening in the world attracted me. We would talk frequently during reserve stints, but hardly ever meet between stints of duty.

When I received the initial grant for the Education for Peace Project he asked to read the proposal which I had submitted. After studying it carefully, he had only one comment: "Either you are totally naive, Haim, or you are one of the most sophisticated crooks I ever met." Yet, he continued to inquire as to the Project's development whenever we met. He inquired, but hardly commented.

In Lebanon, we disagreed. I insisted that our army had no business invading Lebanon, and that the Palestinian problem should be solved by negotiations with Arabs on the West Bank. He was not against negotiations, but he also thought that the invasion of Lebanon might better our cards at the bargaining table with King Hussein of Jordan and the Palestinians. We argued.

Two days after the Sabra and Shatila massacre the phone rang.

"Hello."

"Haim, this is Yaacov. I have to talk to you."

"What happened?"

"You see, I have not been sleeping these past two nights. I cannot get the idea out of my mind that our soldiers sat back and watched the Christian Phalangists massacre Palestinians in Sabra and Shatila; or that our commanders knew that this was happening and let it happen. God, what is happening to us?"

"You're right; it is terrible."

"You see, Haim, my parents were in the Holocaust, and I know how terrible that was. How could we Jews agree to participate even passively in such a massacre? I can't get it out of my mind . . . And that is why I called you, so maybe I can sleep tonight."

"What does this have to do with me?"

"Nothing, except that I felt that perhaps if I told you that you were right, that we had nothing to do in Lebanon and had no business going into that country, I would feel better. I would know that at least I had admitted to the truth and to my mistake."

"I understand, Yaakov, thanks for trusting me."

"Sure. And one more thing, Haim, don't give up on your education for dialogue thing. Even though I kidded you about it, keep up the work."

Appendix: Some Research Results

I do not need to emphasize, what the reader has probably already sensed, that it is extremely difficult to pin down research results in an educational project as complex and ambitious as the Education for Peace Project. Still, we succeeded in obtaining some results which tell quite a bit about the impact of our educational endeavors on participants. Here, beginning with Table 1, are parts of the collected data and our analyses of data which I believe the reader will find significant.

Table 1 Applicants and Persons Accepted to Education for Peace Project in 1979–1981

	Applicants	Persons Accepted	Persons Not Accepted
Total	372	204	168
Men	219	121	98
Women	153	83	70
Jews	175	98	77
Arabs	197	106	91
Arab men	161	92	69
Arab women	36	14	22
Jewish men	58	29	29
Jewish women	117	69	48

Among those "not accepted" were 22 who *were* accepted but did not show up to join the Buberian Learning Group.

From these numbers, one can learn quite a few facts about the background of the Education for Peace Project. First, we did not lack applicants. Quite a few Jews and Arabs were interested in building some sort of deeper personal relations between them. Second, very few Arab women applied, and those who did were often not qualified. Third, twice as many Jewish women as Jewish men applied. When we became aware of these trends, we tried to counter them by seeking out more Jewish men and more Arab women and encouraging them to apply. As the numbers show, we did not succeed. I believe that the numbers reflect the fact that very few Arab women are independent and well educated and that many Jewish men are not attracted to unique educational projects. The numbers also present the factual background for the badmouthing leveled at the Project by Jewish bigots: that our major concern was to help Arab men get to know (and to sleep with) Jewish women.

Persons who applied were interviewed twice before being accepted. In the first interview, usually a Jew and an Arab interviewer explained what would happen, gathered some general information, and partially confronted the person and demanded that he respond dialogically. Those who passed the first interview were invited to a second interview, with their designated group leader, who tried to lead the interviewees into a dialogical encounter. In short, we attempted to choose persons with whom some success was possible.

During the interviews we questioned as to the motives for joining the Project. The answers (in Table 2) were given before the persons knew what education for peace, as I conceived it, was all about. But once again we were confronted with evidence that many Jews and Arabs in Israel are seeking opportunities to meet each other. When such a meeting occurs in a university setting, it is often more appealing to participants because it is not charged with the political or emotional overtones that often characterize other Jewish-Arab meetings. It also assumes an air of legitimacy. These may be some of the reasons for the Project's broad appeal.

Table 2 Major Reasons for Joining Education for Peace Project

Major Reason	Percentage
Seeking an Opportunity for Arab-Jewish meeting	59
Academic interest	15
Interest in self-education	8
Curiosity	13
Other	5

Table 3 describes participation in the two-year educational process. Since, after the Lebanese war, the Project was formally closed, one first-year class of about 60 graduates was not given the opportunity to continue a second year. These figures describe, therefore, the 101 persons who joined the Project during its first two years and had the opportunity to continue a second year—that is, to participate two years in a Buberian Learning Group.

Table 3 Participation in Buberian Learning Groups

	Arabs	Jews	Total
Began 1st year group	55	46	101
Dropped out during 1st year	18	7	25
Dropped out after end of 1st year	23	12	35
Began 2nd year	14	27	41
Completed 2nd year	13	20	33

The first-year dropout rate for Arabs is somewhat large because it includes an attempt to set up a group with ten participants from the Gaza Strip, and eight of these Arabs dropped out during the first year. The dropout numbers also include instances where persons were asked to leave because they were not fulfilling academic requirements. Among those who dropped out at the end of the first year were at least ten who had a valid reason, such as moving out of the country for a year, or moving out of town, or taking a new job, which did not allow them to continue participating in the Project.

Based on these figures, I would hold that at least one third of the participants in the Buberian Learning Groups were influenced significantly. Academic credit was given only for the first year of participation; hence learning to relate dialogically and active participation in an attempt to work for peace were primary motives in continuing to participate. Put otherwise, these figures serve as an adequate background for our research results.

This book describes many instances of dialogue and education for peace. These instances could not have been presented if persons were not undergoing a significant educational process, if mistrust between Jews and Arabs had not diminished significantly. In presenting research results, I will be relying on the above-described instances as illustrations. For instance, a rather persistent outcome at the end of the first year was that 65 percent of the participants held that their existential mistrust toward participants from the other nation had diminished during the educational process. Such a diminishing can be found in many of the discussions (cited throughout the book).

Table 4 shows the major changes we examined with first-year participants. The results are based on participants' testimonies, on questionnaires, and on staff observations. The table helps explain what occurred in the Education for Peace Project. If we consider the difference between the results in rows 2 and 3, we find that 26 percent of the Jews and 15 percent of the Arabs did not transfer the diminishing of existential mistrust within the Buberian Learning Group to persons outside the group. These numbers partially explain the large dropout rate at the end of the first year (see Table 3). Persons who decided not to transfer what was occurring to them in the Buberian Learning Group to their everyday life probably had little incentive to continue their participation in the Project.

Row 3 can and should be viewed from two perspectives. First, despite our carefully choosing participants and despite the intense educational process, only 47 percent testified, at

Table 4. Results at End of First Year ($N = 204$)

	Jews	Arabs	Total
1. Dropped out	16%	25%	22%
2. Existential mistrust diminished toward participants in Education for Peace Project	78	55	65
3. Existential mistrust diminished toward all members of other nation in Israel (Jews who now trust all Arabs more and vice versa)	52	40	47
4. Reached dialogue with member of other nation in Buberian Learning Group	60	51	56
5. Believe they advanced one stage in scale of development*	55	49	52
6. Advanced one stage in scale of development, according to questionnaire and staff observation	41	30	36
7. See importance of striving for self-education and dialogue in their daily life	55	43	50
8. Daily strive to live dialogically and to educate themselves accordingly	18	10	14

*In the middle of the third year we reached the conclusion that it would be wise to add an additional stage to the scale of development. That stage would come between the second and third stages in the original scale of development and would be called "The Conscious Person Who Begins to Educate Himself." The percentages in this table that relate to the scale of development take this change into account. I chose to leave the original scale in the text because that was the scale we used with the participants. Ninety-five percent of the participants entering the project were in one of the first three stages in the new six-stage scale, or in one of the first two stages in the original scale.

the end of one year, that they now mistrusted members of the other nation less than previously. (These 47 percent were out of the 100 percent who began the Project. Of the 78 percent who completed the first year, 60 percent had diminished their mistrust of members of the other nation.) In short, much still needs to be developed in order to educate for trust. The second perspective is that despite the conflict situation in the Mideast, despite the great lack of dialogue and trust in contemporary life, despite the grave political differences of Jews and Arabs who were chosen to participate, and despite the different milieus in which Jews and Arabs grow up—despite all these hindrances 47 percent of the participants testified that their existential mistrust toward all members of the other nation had diminished. The results are rather astounding. I believe that they bear witness to what can be achieved by attempting to persistently teach persons to relate dialogically.

The percentage of persons who reached dialogue with a member of the other nation is based on testimonies. Usually, the person testifying would mention the occasion or the person with whom he had reached dialogue. Once again it is important to remember that the numbers do not include those who dropped out, so that 72 percent of those who participated in a Buberian Learning Group for an entire year testified that they had an experience of genuine dialogue with a member of the other nation. The percentage is high. I attribute it largely to the atmosphere of dialogue that prevailed. The fact that quite a few persons noted at the end of the year that they had not reached any sort of dialogue with a member of the other nation is an indication that persons did not fear to admit this point.

The most important rows in the table are 5 through 8. The difference between row 5 and row 6 shows how easy it is for persons to believe that they have changed significantly when they think that such a change is important. But our way of life, our mode of existence, changes very slowly, even when we are working strenuously for a specific change. Row 8 shows how difficult it is to try to realize in one's daily life what persons accept as correct in row 7. Only one third of the Jews and one quarter of the Arabs, who saw the importance of striving for self-education and dialogue in their daily life, strove daily to educate themselves and to relate dialogically.

From the data presented I can roughly conclude that we did not influence, or influenced only marginally, around 50 percent of the persons accepted into the Education for Peace Project. Included in this number are 22 percent who dropped out. I believe that around 25 percent were deeply influenced. This general trend is also revealed in our observations of four Jewish-Arab dyads chosen randomly in the 1980–81 school year for observation by a researcher. (I have cited some of the data which were gathered in Chapter 10, in the meeting between Adina and Yusuf.) Here are the results.

SUMMARY OF REVIEW AND OBSERVATION OF FOUR JEWISH-ARAB DYADS IN 1980–81

Two dyads met regularly during the year for a weekly meeting. Two dyads met very irregularly and no meaningful relationship was established between them.

First dyad: Met once or twice a week during the entire year and continued to meet after the end of the academic year. A genuine friendship developed between them, which is characterized by mutual support, straightforwardness, openness, and the ability to demand changes from each other.

Second dyad: Met irregularly, usually in order to submit an assignment. No personal relationship developed.

Third dyad: Met regularly during the entire year, but the relationship was unstable. They did not solve the difficulties of relating personally to each other. [This is the dyad of Adina and Yusuf.]

Fourth dyad: Hardly ever met. After four months one member of the dyad left the Project. The other member did not make attempts to find another partner. Toward the end of the year a new partner was assigned but they met only once.

The observation of Jewish-Arab dyads was repeated in 1981–82, with similar results.

Like the above summary, most of the data collected did not lead us much beyond the obvious, or beyond what can be seen in the discussions which I cited at length. For instance, every three months we asked each person to write a personal summary of how he had developed in the Buberian Learning Group. Most of the summaries are drab, not giving too many details, and present in high-flown language what we tried to make concrete in the educational process. Here and there, though, there were better summaries which helped us understand that we were moving in the right direction. Here are excerpts from one such summary, written by a young rabbi after participating three months in a Buberian Learning Group.

SUMMARY AFTER THREE MONTHS

Because I joined the Education for Peace Project there were some changes in my mode of existence. This was my first opportunity to get to know an Arab on a deeper level. I was surprised how difficult it was for the Arabs I met to identify with the State of Israel in which they are citizens. I found myself able to understand their alienation, but unable to suggest any solution to this problem.

This revelation led me to understand that it is important that I reach a position on Zionism which will support Israel as a spiritual center of the Jewish people, but also as a home for some Arabs. When I visited the home of one of my Arab friends in the project, I realized how difficult his life must be, even though he lives not far from me.

I also learned how deeply I am influenced by external behavior. At first I was very angry at the style of Haim Gordon. But in one of our workshops, in which he participated together with our group leader, he emphasized the difference between outward actions and content—I suddenly grasped the distinction.

I learned from that how much I can help another person if I have the courage to say true things about his mode of existence. I also learned that when things get emotional I tend to turn off and look at them from the side—I am outside the circle. I find it hard to oppose behavior which I dislike. I hold back too much.

At times it was very hard to understand Buber. When I did understand him, I found that my behavior belongs on the negative side of what he is describing, . . . and I didn't know how to get to the positive side. For instance, I find it very hard not to live in the world of seeming and not to continue to act out certain roles which I have adopted . . .

Notes

1. Martin Buber, "Guilt and Guilt Feelings," in *The Knowledge of Man* (New York: Harper, 1965), p. 135.

2. Nicolas Berdyaev, *Dream and Reality* (New York: Collier Books, 1962), p. 84.

3. Martin Heidegger, "Who Is Nietzsche's Zarathustra?" Trans. Bernd Magnus, *Review of Metaphysics* 20 (1967): 415.

4. Friedrich Nietzsche, *Thus Spoke Zarathustra*, Trans. R. J. Hollingdale (Harmondsworth: Penguin, 1961), p. 54.

5. Ibid., p. 55.

6. Ibid., p. 70.

7. Franz Kafka, "The Great Wall of China," in *The Complete Stories* (New York: Schocken Books, 1946), p. 240.

8. Naguib Mahfouz, "Zaabalawi," in *Modern Arabic Short Stories*, selected and translated by Denys Johnson-Davies (London: Heinemann, 1976), p. 135.

9. Ibid., p. 144.

10. Riffat Hassan, "Response to 'Buberian Learning Groups: The Quest for Responsibility in Education for Peace,' by Haim Gordon and Jan Demarest," *Teachers College Record* 84, no. 1 (Fall 1982): 229.

Bibliographical Essay

The reader of this book will perceive that the inspiration for many of my deeds came from Martin Buber's philosophy. Such is also true of my approach to reading. Buber was concerned that persons did not read many primary texts, which he believed could change one's life. In confronting and battling such books, Buber held, a person becomes more courageous and can learn and do more. I believe that he was right, and the major influence on my work in education for peace was primary texts.

Raphael Buber and Margot Cohen published *Martin Buber, A Bibliography of his Works* (Jerusalem: Magnes, 1980), in which one finds all of Buber's publications. From the more than 1,400 items listed there, I will mention only those which I believe directly influenced our work.

The works with which students had direct contact were *I and Thou* (New York: Scribner, 1965); the essays "Elements of the Inter-human" and "Guilt and Guilt Feelings," in *The Knowledge of Man* (New York: Harper, 1966); the essay "On Education," in *Between Man and Man* (London: Fontana, 1947); the essay "The Prejudices of Youth," in *Israel and the World* (New York: Schocken, 1948). They also read Buber's chronicle *For the Sake of Heaven* (New York: Atheneum, 1969).

Other books by Buber, which influenced me, were *The Legend of* the *Baal Shem* (New York: Schocken, 1969); *The Tales of Rabbi Nachman* (New York: Avon, 1956); *Hasidism and Modern Man* (New York: Harper, 1958); *The Origin and Meaning of Hasidism* (New York: Harper, 1960); *Tales of the Hasidim, Early Masters* (New York: Schocken, 1947); *Tales of the Hasidim, Later Masters* (New York: Schocken, 1947); *Pointing the Way* (New York: Harper, 1957); *On the Bible* (New York: Schocken, 1968); *Moses* (New York: Harper, 1958); *Good and Evil* (New York: Scribner, 1952); *Eclipse of God* (New York: Harper, 1952); *Two Types of Faith* (New York: Harper, 1951); *Paths in Utopia* (Boston: Beacon, 1958); *On Zion* (New York: Schocken, 1973); *On Judaism* (New York: Schocken, 1967); *The Prophetic Faith* (New York: Harper, 1960).

There exists, of course, a wealth of secondary writings on various aspects of Buber's work. I mentioned some of these in my bibliographical essay on this topic, "Studies on Martin Buber's Life and Thought: A Review of Recent Trends," in *Religious Studies Review* 4 (Mar./Apr. 1979): 198–209. The two major books of essays on Martin Buber's work are P. A. Schilpp and Maurice Friedman (editors), *The Philosophy of Martin Buber* (LaSalle, Ill.: Open Court, 1967), and Haim Gordon and Jochanan Bloch (editors), *Martin Buber, A Centenary Volume* (New York: Ktav, 1984). Many writers in the latter volume criticized Buber quite severely—hence its importance.

In learning how to withstand attacks of the mediocres, Friedrich Nietzsche's writings were most helpful. I also learned much from his vision of the educator in *Thus Spoke Zarathustra* (Harmondsworth, Middlesex: Penguin, 1961). Other books by Nietzsche which guided me were *Daybreak* (Cambridge: Cambridge University Press, 1982), *The Gay Science* (New York: Vintage, 1974), *Beyond Good and Evil* (New York: Vintage, 1966), *The Birth of Tragedy and the Case of Wagner* (New York: Vintage, 1967), *On the Genealogy of Morals* (New York: Vintage, 1969), *Twilight of the Idols* (Harmondsworth, Middlesex: Penguin, 1968). The only secondary source I would like to mention is Walter Kaufmann, *Nietzsche: Philosopher, Psychologist, Antichrist* (New York: Meridian, 1956).

Søren Kierkegaard's writings brought many insights, such as understanding the ways we seduce ourselves and each other, perceiving the insipidity and vapidity of an ethical life without passion or of a religious life without risks, pinpointing the superficiality of most academics. *Either/Or* (Princeton: Princeton University Press, 1949) was read by a few staff members; they were deeply influenced. Other books which I suspect influenced our work are *For Self Examination and Judge for Yourselves* (Princeton: Princeton University Press, 1944), *Training in Christianity* (Princeton: Princeton University Press, 1944), *Concluding Unscientific Postscript* (Princeton: Princeton University Press, 1968), *Works of Love* (Princeton: Princeton University Press, 1962), *Philosophical Fragments* (Princeton: Princeton University Press, 1962), and *Fear and Trembling* (Princeton: Princeton University Press, 1941).

Much has been written about the profundity of Fyodor Dostoyevski's writings in portraying all areas of human existence. Most of our participants were acquainted with *Crime and Punishment* (New York: Signet, 1957), since this text is required reading for matriculation exams in Israel. Second-year participants in the Education for Peace Project were required to read *The Brothers Karamazov* (New York: Signet, 1957). The staff read and discussed *The Possessed* (New York: Signet, 1956). Other books which I found important for my work were *The Idiot* (New York: Bantam, 1981) and *Memoirs from the House of the Dead* (Oxford: Oxford University Press, 1983).

There is no doubt that the writings of Franz Kafka helped me understand and fathom important aspects of the reality within which we worked. Most of the participants were acquainted with some of his works. Here are the main texts I relied upon: *The Castle* (New York: Knopf, 1952); *The Complete Stories* (New York: Schocken, 1976); *The Trial* (New York: Schocken, 1968); *Amerika* (New York: Schocken, 1962); *Letter to His Father* (New York: Schocken, 1962).

Only three of Naguib Mahfouz' books have been translated into English: *Children of Gebelawi* (London: Heinemann, 1981), *Midaq Alley* (London: Heinemann, 1976), and *Miramar* (London: Heinemann, 1974). Mahfouz told me that his book *The Thief and the Dogs* should soon appear in English. Another superb Egyptian storyteller is Yusuf Idris, whose short stories we often used. His only book in English is *The Cheapest Nights* (London: Heinemann, 1978). The stories in this book reek with the sweat, ignorance, and lack of sensitivity that abound in country and city life in Egypt. Other important books in English by Egyptian writers are Tewfik El Hakim, *Fate of a Cockroach and Other Plays of Freedom* (London: Heinemann, 1978), Sonallah Ibrahim, *The Smell of It* (London: Heinemann, 1978), Taha Hussein, *Egyptian Childhood* (London:

Heinemann, 1981), Denys Johnson-Davies (editor), *Modern Arabic Short Stories* (London: Heinemann, 1976). In learning about Arabs, I was also influenced by T. E. Lawrence's *Seven Pillars of Wisdom* (Middlesex: Penguin Books, 1962).

Jean-Paul Sartre's work greatly influenced the development of the Education for Peace Project, primarily because his writings deal with social problems. *Being and Nothingness* (New York: Washington Square Press, 1956), *Search for a Method* (New York: Vintage, 1968), and *Critique of Dialectical Reason* (London: NLB, 1976) are Sartre's three major philosophical works. Other important writings are *Essays in Aesthetics* (New York: Washington Square Press, 1966), *The Psychology of Imagination* (New York: Washington Square Press, 1966), *Antisemite and Jew* (New York: Black Cat, 1962), *What Is Literature?* (New York: Washington Square Press, 1966), *Situations* (Greenwich, Conn.: Fawcett, 1965), *Sketch for a Theory of the Emotions* (London: Methuen, 1971), *Between Existentialism and Marxism* (New York: Morrow Quill, 1979), *Nausea* (Harmondsworth, Middlesex: Penguin, 1965), *The Words* (Greenwich, Conn.: Fawcett, 1964), *Saint Genet* (New York: Mentor, 1963), *The Devil and the Good Lord and Other Plays* (New York: Vintage, 1960), *Altona, Men without Shadows, The Flies* (Harmondsworth, Middlesex: Penguin, 1962), *No Exit and Three Other Plays* (New York: Vintage, 1949), *Literary and Philosophical Essays* (New York: Collier, 1962), and *Existentialism and Humanism* (London, Methuen, 1973).

Two additional existentialists who influenced me are Gabriel Marcel and Nicolas Berdyaev. I prefer Marcel's *The Philosophy of Existentialism* (Secaucus, N.J.: Citadel, 1956) and *The Mystery of Being* (2 vols.; Chicago: Gateway, 1960). The works by Berdyaev whose influence I felt were *Dream and Reality* (New York: Collier, 1962) and *Slavery and Freedom* (New York: Scribner, 1944).

In my understanding of contemporary social developments, I have also been influenced by Hannah Arendt, especially her major work: *The Origins of Totalitarianism* (New York: Harcourt Brace Jovanovich), 1951.

Finally, there is a wealth of literature on the civil rights movement in the United States from which one can glean how the approach I developed was different from the workings of that movement. I shall mention only four books which support my assertion: Martin Luther King Jr., *Strength to Love* (Philadelphia: Fortress, 1963),

Stokely Carmichael and Charles V. Hamilton, *Black Power* (New York: Vintage, 1967), Ann Moody, *Coming of Age in Mississippi* (New York: Dell, 1968), and Herbert J. Storing (editor), *What Country Have I? Political Writings by Black Americans* (New York: St. Martin's, 1970).

Index

ABOUT THE AUTHOR

Haim Gordon is Senior Lecturer at
Ben-Gurion University of
the Negev, Beer Sheva, Israel.